ROUTLEDGE LIBRARY EDITIONS:
HISTORY OF EDUCATION

EDUCATION FOR LEADERSHIP

EDUCATION FOR LEADERSHIP

The International Administrative Staff Colleges
1948-84

By

A. T. CORNWALL-JONES

Volume 2

 Routledge
Taylor & Francis Group

LONDON AND NEW YORK

First published in 1985

This edition first published in 2007 by
Routledge
2 Park Square, Milton Park, Abingdon, Oxfordshire, OX14 4RN

Simultaneously published in the USA and Canada
by Routledge
270 Madison Ave, New York NY 10016

Routledge is an imprint of the Taylor & Francis Group, an informa business

First issued in paperback 2010

British Library Cataloguing in Publication Data
A catalogue record for this book is available from the British
Library

Library of Congress Cataloging in Publication Data
A catalog record for this book has been requested

ISBN13: 978-0-415-41978-9 (Set)
ISBN13: 978-0-415-43211-5 (Volume 2)(hbk)
ISBN 13: 978-0-415-61169-5(Volume 2)(pbk)

Publisher's Note
The publisher has gone to great lengths to ensure the quality
of this reprint but points out that some imperfections in the
original copies may be apparent.

EDUCATION
FOR
LEADERSHIP

THE INTERNATIONAL ADMINISTRATIVE STAFF COLLEGES 1948-84

A.T. CORNWALL-JONES

ROUTLEDGE & KEGAN PAUL
London, Boston, Melbourne and Henley

First published in 1985
by Routledge & Kegan Paul plc

14 Leicester Square, London WC2H 7PH, England

9 Park Street, Boston, Mass. 02108, USA

464 St Kilda Road, Melbourne
Victoria 3004, Australia and

Broadway House, Newton Road,
Henley on Thames, Oxon RG9 1EN, England

Set in Sabon, 10 on 11pt
by Columns of Reading
and printed in Great Britain by
St Edmundsbury Press,
Bury St Edmunds, Suffolk

Library of Congress Cataloging in Publication Data

Cornwall-Jones, A.T., d. 1980.
Education for leadership.
Includes index.
1. Cornwall-Jones, A.T., d. 1980. 2. Business
teachers—Great Britain—Biography. 3. Management—
Study and teaching—Great Britain—History. I. Title.
HD30.42.G7C67 1985   658'.007'11 [B]   84-26711

British Library CIP data also available

ISBN 0-7102-0464-7

For Joan
Giving thanks always for all things.
St Paul to the Ephesians

CONTENTS

Contents

FOREWORD

C-J, as the writer of this book was universally known among those connected with the higher direction of the war in both London and Washington, was a captain in a Gurkha regiment, seconded in early 1939 to the Committee of Imperial Defence for a brief period. He was never to return to his beloved Gurkhas again. When he retired in 1950, he had been for a number of years in the military secretariat of the Cabinet. After May 1940 he had been fully, and with increasing responsibility, at work in the Churchill war-making machinery. After the war he continued to be fully involved in serving those who were coping with the great problems of reorganising our defence services in Britain's markedly changed circumstances.

His job had been for more than ten years to remain one of the clear-headed generalists amidst a wealth of exceptional talent in many specialised fields and amidst a weight of service and professional experience also. His constant concern was to set down promptly and succinctly on paper the fruit of the interplay of these many and diverse minds whilst retaining the whole time the confidence (in many cases the confidences) of those amongst whom he worked.

I had seen him at work during much of the war. When I learned in 1950, not from him, that he was retiring, I believed that his almost unique experience could be of great value to the Administrative Staff College at Henley, which was just emerging from the formative period of testing the market for what it had to offer and was going on to consolidation and planning for future developments.

The basic idea upon which the college was founded emerged slowly from a series of discussions of a small group who invited, over a period of three years, more than a hundred people – leading politicians, industrialists, bankers, civil servants, trade-union officials and academics – to discuss with them their concern that after the war, when great changes were to be expected, very heavy burdens would be imposed on those moving from middle- to higher-management responsibilities in many different sectors of national life. The discussions had ranged over the whole of management development. In early 1945 it was necessary to narrow the range. Under the leadership of Geoffrey Heyworth, their chairman, the group decided to concentrate upon the needs of those moving from 'departmental' to higher management. On behalf of the group (now the Court of Governors of the Administrative Staff College, recently incorporated) Sir Hector Hetherington, Vice-Chancellor of Glasgow University, wrote an article for *The Times* in November 1945 setting out the main objective of the College:

> A time comes in eight or ten or fifteen years when, having learned and practised his calling, a man does well to cease for a little from action and to think about what he is doing, and why and how he is doing it. That is apt to be the most fruitful educational phase of all. The best thinking springs from practice; but a man who, by thinking, has more thoroughly possessed himself of what he is and does is ripe for greater responsibility.

A few months after the publication of this article I was given the responsibility of translating the ideas of the group into practice: to design a course of studies suited to the special needs of those for whom it was designed and to build up a staff to prepare the detail of the course and to put it into operation.

The project was particularly hazardous because to an unusual degree the success of each course would depend upon the qualities of the individuals sent to it and the relevance of their different experiences in industry, commerce, finance and in different areas of public life. (It should be noted that the college was a private-enterprise organisation with no government grant, relying for its finances upon the support which it could command.) It was a cliff-hanging experience in facing which we could do little to help ourselves. After the first three or four sessions (as each of the separate courses was called) we began to get nominations from firms and public departments who had sent people to the earliest sessions and were renominating. It was clear that the basic idea had got across correctly. The right kind of people were being sent and the qualities and experience of new nominees were settling down at higher rather than lower levels of ability and experience. By the beginning of 1950 we regarded the evidence as conclusive. We increased the directing staff and planned much needed changes and improvements on the buildings, which were then held on short leasehold but were shortly to be purchased.

There had from the first announcement of the setting up of the college been considerable overseas interest in what it proposed to do, but until we had tried out the methods we intended to use, there was little that we could show or tell to visitors. By 1950 that phase was over. By that time we had had several hundred visitors, including many from different countries who had come to see what we were doing and how we had set about it. It was in the late spring of that year that C.-J. retired from the Cabinet Office and joined the directing staff of the Henley College.

The basic method, which the college was developing, was designed to demonstrate the processes by which different specialisations and diverse practical experiences contribute to the formation of policies and to the introduction of changes in organisation and structure necessary to bring them into effect. In these circumstances C-J's transition to the directing staff at Henley was not very difficult: it involved him in demonstrating, in much less tense circumstances, an art acquired under the pressures of grave responsibility. In addition it required accepting responsibility for all those with whom he worked and an interest in their needs. This had been the basic training of regimental officers in the inter-war period.

C-J joined Henley at the beginning of the eighth session, May 1950. By that time we had learnt a good deal about the demands made by the Henley method upon the directing staff. Each took charge of one of the six syndicates, session by session. This involved him in having contact with ten diverse, mature and experienced men or women for virtually seven days a week throughout their 11-week course with three 4-day weekends off. It involved, too, taking a significant part in arranging and introducing material of many different kinds needed for the work on each part of the course. The Henley course was short in comparison with the typical 8-9 month courses provided at that time in, for example, America, for 'managers' with comparable practical experience to those who came to Henley. The shorter the course the more thorough and comprehensive must be the preparation. Fortunately, as it now seems with hindsight, the long delays, due to the economic circumstances of 1947-8, in securing stationery, telephones, adaptation of buildings and all the paraphernalia needed for a residential course, gave the small group of five, which prepared the first course, 12-15 months to do so instead of the planned 3 or 4 months. The relevance and the importance of adequate and relevant preparation will be apparent in each of the main sections of this book. With the completion of more than a hundred courses at Henley this is still the case. The current prospectus for the General Management Course reads: 'The Henley method involves unique care and attention to the learning needs of individual course members.' It also requires the materials provided course by course to be updated, modified and rearranged to meet changing economic and political circumstances. This has proved to be equally necessary in the overseas colleges with which C-J was concerned.

To meet the considerable overseas interest in the college the first thing we were able to do was to include session by session, as we greatly wished to do, five individuals whose educational and practical experience had been outside the United Kingdom. One of the consequences of this was that by 1950 we began to receive an increasing number of requests for assistance in setting up comparable colleges in other countries. In response we were able to provide opportunities for senior people to visit Henley as observers, to see the work in progress, but the number of Henley staff with adequate experience was still too small to enable us to spare one of them for the substantial period of time necessary to assist in planning a Henley-type course appropriate to local circumstances and to see it through at least a first session. However, by 1953 and the completion of eighteen courses at Henley, it began to appear that there might be substantial advantages to the college as a whole, as well as to individual members of the staff, in accepting invitations to help in setting up new colleges by lending a member of the staff for the development period. There was a double advantage in doing so.

As has already been shown, the demands made upon the directing staff by the Henley method of work were unusually heavy. Relief from having to take three syndicates a year was essential to maintain vitality and widen the experience and interests of the staff, not to mention some relief to wives for the disturbance to home life made by the demands of each session. It was not at that time easy to find an appropriate solution to this problem. The individual needs of the staff differed widely. Some with specialised interests in one or other part of the course could fruitfully spend a period of six months (i.e. one session preceding or following the long summer recess) in pursuing their major interests. Others with continuous sessions off had a period long enough for observing, and in one or two cases participating in, advanced management courses in other countries, where quite different methods from our own were used. But for some perhaps the best stimulus of all could be to help plan, in a new college abroad, a course suited to local conditions and to see it through at least a first session. This would require at least eighteen months absence from Henley.

With these considerations in mind, we began as early as 1951 to develop a new policy. Each member of the directing staff was expected to take a syndicate at Henley for eight out of each successive series of twelve sessions; that is to say, an average of one session 'out-of-syndicate' in each calendar year. Each member of the staff was encouraged to make his own plan for periods when he would be out of syndicate, the college undertaking to assist him in making suitable arrangements. We increased the permanent directing staff to make possible the new arrangements. Instead of a permanent director of studies, each member of the directing staff took his turn for a year as director of studies. By this means an increasing number of the staff improved their knowledge of the course as a whole.

This policy was introduced gradually. About two years after its introduction it became clear that well-grounded requests for help in setting up colleges in other countries could no longer be declined. In the autumn of 1953, at the invitation of four such countries, I spent twelve weeks in visiting Australia, New Zealand, India and Pakistan. Two of these were already intent upon setting up their own colleges. Australia was making preliminary enquiries while New Zealand had been running successfully, without much formal organisation, periodical comparable courses. As was to be expected, the sources and strength of local support for setting up a college differed widely as did proposed financial arrangements. But there was no doubt that some substantial institution would emerge in each case. Australia was the first off the mark closely followed by India, which is only briefly mentioned in this book as another member of the Henley staff, J.W.L. Adams, went to Hyderabad to help Principal Shrinagesh to set up the Adminstrative Staff College of India. In Australia a group of enterprising members of the business community acted with promptness and decision. I was told the night before I left Sydney, in October 1953, that they had already taken the first steps to bring into legal existence the Australian Administrative Staff College. Subsequent steps, including finding the right principal, took longer. It was not until the spring of 1956 that Sir Douglas Copland, the first Australian principal, was free to pay a lengthy visit to Henley to see the college at work. At the end of his visit he asked for the loan of a member of staff to work with him in preparing a suitable Australian course and to see at least one session through. I left him to make his own selection. He told me before he left that it was to be C-J, whom he later invited to join him. C-J takes up the story in the first overseas part of this book.

There were longer delays in setting up a college in Pakistan, but by 1959 it was decided to go ahead. The first principal, Mr A.K. Malik, visited Henley and asked for assistance. Given a free choice he invited C-J to join him in Lahore. The reputation he acquired in coping with the distinctly different circumstances in these two assignments resulted in a personal invitation to him to give like assistance in the Philippines. Later, after he had passed the Henley retiring age, he undertook to give brief service to Ghana.

The pages which follow speak for themselves. They tell of the enthusiasm of C-J and his wife for the work he had been doing at Henley and the relationships established there with his colleagues and with members coming from overseas countries who had worked with him in syndicate. He had a keen desire to share these experiences with others. His loyalty to, and co-operation with, the principals setting up colleges in their own countries was the basis of his success. Each of the overseas colleges has, in its different way, contributed to the understanding of and to improvements in the original experiment and to each other's growth. There is an increasing number of them, only some of which can be included in this book. It is greatly to be hoped that they will all continue to benefit mutually by the exchange of experience and that each in the changing circumstances of today will feel able to extend help to any interested newcomers.

> Sir Noel Hall,
> First Principal,
> Henley Administrative
> Staff College

PREFACE

This book is concerned with the years 1950-70, which I spent at home in the United Kingdom and abroad in the service of The Administrative Staff College at Henley-on-Thames. Its main purpose is to discuss the issues I encountered in helping others who, in Australia, Pakistan, the Philippines and Ghana, wished to make some use of the ideas for which the Henley College then stood, and in the process to contribute a little to an understanding of these Staff Colleges and their original aims.

Of these twenty years, I spent in all nine in the Henley College itself and eleven in these other countries and in the coming and going over the miles between them.

I was fifty years old in 1950 and had just retired from the Army. I had had a wonderful twelve years with a battalion of Gurkhas in India, a couple of years at the staff college at Quetta, half a dozen years on the staff in district and brigade. By 1939, when the war came, I had already begun what turned out to be a series of appointments which took me from the Chiefs of Staff Organisation in London to the Defence Committee in the Middle East, to the Anglo-American Combined Chiefs of Staff in Washington and, ultimately, in 1946 to the Inter-Service rump of the Chiefs of Staff Organisation, which remained in the Cabinet Office when the Ministry of Defence first appeared. For these last eleven years, I found myself working with people who were making history in and just after the Second World War. It was intensely interesting and stimulating but the lack of field service and command experience in it was not going to open up for me the prospect to which I aspired.

This meant, then, that I had to set about seeking a new and enduring career and I count myself fortunate to have found it with a private enterprise – The Administrative Staff College at Henley. I was not certain in my own mind how far I would be able to meet what was required of me in this new life; but when in March 1950 I went down to Henley with my wife Joan, to talk it over with Mr (later Sir) Noel Hall, whom I knew well in the war, I was impressed with the task he had taken on. I saw some affinity between the work I had already done and that which would be required of me in his college. It would be a big step to take and I did not want to make a mistake, but it held some fascination for me at once. I was to be concerned with the development of middle managers drawn almost entirely from civilian life – from private enterprise with its immense variety, from the Civil Service, diverse enough in itself, from the nationalised industries and their surrounding controversies; in fact from all three sectors of the economy, each with its own purposes, conventions, traditions, practices and prejudices. I felt this was 'It'. Noel Hall seemed to want me. So at the end of that day I threw caution to the winds, went home and three months later retired from the army and joined him at Henley. Neither my wife nor I had any idea of the interest the college was to evoke or the opportunities it was to open up for us; least of all did we imagine that it would claim our involvement for the rest of my working life.

The college had started in 1948 and had hardly settled down when applications to send men on its sessions began to arrive from other countries, mostly but not all from the Commonwealth. These were welcomed, not least for the diversity they added to the basically British composition of each session. They seemed, too, to have been satisfied by their experience. As the number of applications increased, their nominators came to visit Henley to see for themselves; and then some of them showed interest in having a similar type of Staff College of their own. Noel Hall gave enormously of his mind and of his time to all such inquiries and interests, and in due course made substantial visits overseas to any so-minded to help them think it through. When at the next stage most of the overseas principals asked for a man from Henley to help them get started, I frequently had the luck to be invited. My wife and I left our growing family behind at school in England and shared in the whole experience.

By the time my first chance came, in 1957, I had been at the college for seven years and was on the way to discovering what it was trying to do and how it was doing it. I had got to know well a great many people in the three sectors which the college sought to serve – private enterprise, nationalised industry and government. I had been inside the plants and premises of goodness knows how many enterprises, both public and private, and visited some Government departments I had never seen before. I had been instructed briefly in the mysteries of cost accounting, in the complexity of the wages structure in the engineering industry, encountered some, but all too few, trade unionists, and sweated through the best part of a sabbatical year preparing some case studies for the Institution of Works Managers. I felt I was learning. There was a fund of knowledge and talent in the membership of a syndicate of eleven and in a session of sixty-six, which could be tapped on the site, and outside the college a community from which talents of almost any kind could be marshalled with a little foresight, so that many of the gaps in the skills and knowledge available in a small team of staff could be filled from other sources. I suppose we on the staff had particular difficulties of our own in so wide a course of studies. I certainly had, as the reader will see in due course. But we had much in common with members because we all had some experience in management, albeit in different fields. This, I discovered gradually, was an asset. It seemed to make us sensitive to members' needs. It certainly made us, and members, more aware of our strengths and weaknesses.

The course of studies was structured, unfolding gradually in a way which sought to help members build on what they knew already and go on to more complex matters later in the course. The subjects, carefully delineated in their boundaries, were fitted together to make sense in members' minds, contributing to each other as they went along. Pressure on the individual fluctuated as his responsibilities varied in the course. Days were long, but there was some time, every now and again, for more than just work.

Most of the small directing staff were a bit older than the members of each session but there was no master/pupil relationship. This did not mean that there was no teaching. What it meant was that teaching was two-way traffic. It took some time to find this out and see in perspective the discretion each member of the staff had in deciding whether, when and how to try and help, or whether to 'let 'em find out for themselves'. I enjoyed the exercise of this discretion, but it was responsible business, more in it than was often imagined. As members of the staff, we were free to develop our own style. Within the boundaries of each subject and inside the general concept of the staff role there was a lot of room for manoeuvre if one was interested in the idea of helping maturing men and women develop. Yes, I had been lucky. I had found another career which was full of interest as I had sensed that day in March 1950 with Noel Hall.

As we came to the end of the assignments, and much later to the end of this book, I was perplexed as to the manner in which Joan and I, who had shared so much of the whole experience, could give thanks to all those who helped and encouraged us on our way. We had met and made friends among those who had put their faith and belief into their new college and their energy, determination and enthusiasm into getting it established. I worked intensively with the principals and their staffs, helping them to organise and run their early courses. I worked during session with the scores of members who came and went on these courses and many of the streams of local men and women who were invited to contribute to college discussions. In the developing world we met many of the host of foreign consultants who were offering their varied skills and who were usually ready to stimulate us in one way or another. We had witnessed the wisdom and the generosity of the Ford Foundation and the men and women who had made it work. We had also lived and worked among the people of the lands in which we found ourselves, sharing in their lives where circumstances and language permitted, motoring where we could, walking the fields, climbing the hills, bathing in the rivers and seas, and so often thrilling to the grandeur of what we saw. Everywhere we were made welcome. Everywhere help was needed and we so often received what we sought. Thus was our task made possible and rewarding.

Finally, so many personal friends encouraged me to press on with the completion of these accounts. From all these sources of strength and support a few names appear naturally in the text as part of the stories I have told. I pray that all those who do not so appear will forgive me for not mentioning them by name – that they will absolve me from the charge of ingratitude. Their faces, their personalities, lie embedded in the rich memories they gave us as we enjoyed the privilege of living in Henley and, for a while, in Australia, Pakistan, the Philippines, India and Ghana.

C-J
Snowball Hill
Russell's Water
Henley-on-Thames
July 1980

ACKNOWLEDGEMENTS

After my husband died in August 1980, I spent the next four years preparing his book for publication. I should not have been able to do this but for the support and friendship of many people in the countries he writes about, and especially Mr J.P. Martin-Bates, principal of Henley 1961-72, and Mrs Barbara Margerrison, principal's secretary 1966-70, registrar 1970-80. To them all, thank you. I am also deeply indebted to the present principal of Henley, Professor Tom Kempner, for his support and financial assistance in making publication possible.

In the spring of 1983 I was saddened by the death of Sir Noel Hall, the founder and first principal of Henley, without whose vision the philosophy common to all these colleges would never have been established.

C-J and Noel met in the War Cabinet Office in 1940. Their paths crossed many times during the war and they worked together from 1950 when C-J joined Henley. I would like to offer the work I have put into this book in memory of them both.

Joan Cornwall-Jones
1984

GLOSSARY OF TERMS USED

Administrative Staff College is the title used in Britain, Australia, Pakistan and India. In the Philippines the parallel term used is Executive Academy; in Ghana, the College of Advanced Management. Sometimes it is convenient to refer to the different colleges by the name of the place in which they are located, and sometimes the name of the house in which they are accommodated. Thus I refer to:

The British college as Henley, which is the town nearby, or Greenlands, which is the name of the house in which it is accommodated.

The Australian college as Mount Eliza, which is the town nearby, or Moondah, which is the name of the house.

The Pakistan college as Lahore, which is the city in which it is situated.

The Philippine Executive Academy as the academy in Manila or in Baguio, the former being its headquarters, the latter the place in which its sessions were actually in operation.

The Indian college as Hyderabad, which is the city in which it is located, or as Bella Vista, which is the house.

The Ghana Institute of Management and Public Administration had two wings – The College of Advanced Management and the School of Public Administration – both of which live in the Achimota area and operate under the same director. Together they tended at the beginning to be referred to as GIMPA, the college being referred to as the Ghanaian College.

The Title of Principal

Except in the Philippines, where the title was that of administrator, and Ghana where it was director, the chief executive was referred to as principal.

Session

This word was used in all the colleges except Ghana to describe the body of members who attended the 'senior' courses, which were then their sole preoccupation. It was used to distinguish them from the more common word 'term', which seemed to imply some connection with previous terms, e.g., in schools or universities, whereas, in the Staff College concept, nobody on arrival had any connection with any previous session, each of which started from its own beginning.

Syndicate

The term used to describe the small group of ten or eleven carefully mixed people to whom much of the work in these colleges was assigned. In the Philippines the term 'panel' was adopted in its place.

Modified Syndicates

These were based on the same criteria as ordinary syndicates but the membership was different. The object was to enlarge each individual's experience of working with others.

Specialist Syndicates

The specialist members of the session – e.g., accountants or marketing men – were brought together to discuss special problems in their own fields and subsequently to make their conclusions available to the rest of the session.

Members

Various terms were used to describe the individual who attended these 'senior' courses at the different colleges – participant, student, member. I use the word 'member' because it was in more common use and perhaps best conveys the idea that a man or woman who joined any session was more than a student: was a member of the college, participating with the staff, who were also members of the college, in the struggle to grapple with the managerial issues of the day.

Manager/Administrator

There seemed to be little point in trying to distinguish between the terms manager and administrator. Both, we thought, were concerned to provide the conditions under which the work of a team could come to good effect in the achievement of some common purpose.

PART I

1

EARLY HENLEY – THE ADMINISTRATIVE STAFF COLLEGE, 1948-57

====

The Concept

Before inviting the reader to accompany me overseas I must try and describe the ideals for which The Administrative Staff College at Henley stood in its early years, beginning in this first chapter with the thinking on which the college had been built as I understood it when I went on my first assignment to Australia in 1957.

I had discovered by then that the men and women who had launched it had identified a great opportunity in the field of management education. Some years before the end of the Second World War, they had seen that the task of the manager of the future was going to be much more exacting as the growth and complexity of all kinds of enterprise and the intermingling of government and business activity increased. More should therefore be done, they thought, to help managers get themselves ready for the responsibility they would carry if they reached the higher ranges in whatever field of administrative activity they might be engaged: government, local government, nationalised industry, private industry and commerce, trade unions, etc. If we were to avoid slipping back into the tragedies of the inter-war years, they ought not to be left to acquire knowledge laboriously and inadequately on the job as they had been in the past. There surely must be principles of administration and organisation which could be explored and taught; surely the level and vigour of management thinking could be raised; surely the co-operative effort of the war could be projected into the peace. Where to make a start was a critical question to which Sir Hector Hetherington, the then vice-chancellor of Glasgow University and a member of the first Court of Governors, supplied an answer in now well-known words:

A time comes, in eight or ten or fifteen years when, having learned and practised his calling, a man does well to cease for a little from action and to think about what he is doing, and why and how he is doing it. That is apt to be the most fruitful educational phase of all. The best thinking springs from practice; but a man who, by thinking, has more thoroughly possessed himself of what he is and does is ripe for greater responsibility.

It was to the service of men and women at this stage in their working lives that the Henley College was created. Their ideas were likely to be firming up but would not be fixed. If they could be carefully selected for the college, it should be possible to help them accelerate their own growth and development. From their ranks many would later be selected for greater responsibility and placed in positions where others as well as they themselves would profit from their experience. And so the college might make a contribution to the national well-being.

Our founders were impressed by the idea that such people would profit from exposure to one another at close quarters, as well as from exposure to the many others who could be marshalled from the community to challenge and stimulate their thinking. The college would become a residential forum for managers from all forms of activity. The strength of the group assembled would spring not only from its maturity but also its variety, which would invite, if not compel, the individual to compare his knowledge, his experience, his outlook, his style, and his capacity with those of his contemporaries. He would have the opportunity to discover the roles played by those in other walks of life, to find out that many of their problems would not be so different from, and indeed would often be similar or at least related to, his own. Thus the barriers of mutual ignorance and consequent mistrust between people, which too often prevailed, might begin to fall and people might be helped to find a greater unity of purpose in our national life. Discoveries like these, as they unfolded in the individual member's mind, would broaden his sympathy and quicken his perception, surely leading to a better understanding of other people's way of life and point of view. In all this, special emphasis was laid upon there being continually represented in the college men and women from central government, local government, nationalised industry and private industry, whose capacity to work together would improve as they each discovered the different work situations and responsibilities of the others. The cross-fertilisation of thinking and practice between these four vital sectors in our economy might indeed make a major contribution to the college purpose – 'not theory but better practice directed to the fuller service of the public interest'.

If the college was to attract people of this standing and in this variety it was doubtful if their employers would spare them, from the responsible jobs they held, for courses that lasted for more than three months. As they would inevitably come from widely different educational backgrounds, traditional academic methods would be quite unsuitable to them. Members would need to participate in the process of learning and take a large share in the responsibility for the work they did. This would be done largely in small groups of ten or eleven members. The subjects laid before them would be of a new character; the staff would be of a different kind – a small group at the centre of a web where the needs of individual members and groups could be observed at very close quarters and their development encouraged; and the need for help from outside the college could be recognised and built into a developing course of studies.

The college would be pioneering in almost all it did. To get it started it would have to be made clear that the whole idea had the support of a substantial number of influential people who believed in what they were doing; who could persuade others to support it; who would find the right man to be the first principal, see that he got what he needed to start, and back him when the idea was put to the test. Later on in this book the reader will become aware of the blood, sweat and tears that attend upon principals as they approach the opening date of their college. I will not drag you through the agony that must have attended the first principal of all in his struggle in the aftermath of the Second World War to set up the first. I shall assume that his difficulties were overcome, as they were, and turn now to draw my picture of Henley as I saw it when I joined in 1950.

Translating Broad Intentions into Practice: Admissions

There is in existence, as far as I know, only one really authoritative account of the way the college at Henley was put together. This comes from the mind of the first principal, Noel Hall, who was appointed by the Court of Governors, whose chairman was Sir Geoffrey Heyworth (later Lord Heyworth), to put into practice their broad intentions. It appears in a small book of three lectures delivered by Noel Hall to an audience at New York University in 1958 (*The Making of Higher Executives: The Modern Challenge*, Vol. 1, Ford Distinguished Lectures). The book has in it a great deal of wisdom. It is out of print but the college is arranging for it to be reprinted so that it will be available for those who are interested. Indeed, for a full understanding of Henley it is essential reading. It is the middle lecture which proved to be of particular assistance to many who were concerned with the early Henley ideas and came to understand the detail and the care that went into the preparation of the original college. The thinking in this lecture was part of early Henley and, published as it was in 1958, I did not have it in my hand in Australia but I did have it in my head. Subsequently, on countless occasions I was glad indeed to have it by me in all the colleges I later worked in.

In the men and women who had 'learned and practised their calling for from ten to fifteen years', we were looking for people who were doing well in middle management: who showed some signs in their employers' eyes of being capable of going up into more senior and perhaps even eventually very high positions. We wanted to form a group in which everyone would have left behind him the work of a junior manager, concerned more with the carrying out of instructions and geared to thinking of the day's and this week's needs. We looked for people who had already tasted responsibility, had already had to make some decisions of their own and answer for them, had begun at least to think ahead in terms of next year's needs and beyond, begun to think of their work as it fitted into the work of their undertaking as a whole and who had recognised the need for the integration of the various parts of an undertaking and, indeed, probably played some part in it. We wanted this feel of responsibility and understanding of what was involved in being a manager because it was the material on which members had some chance of building.

It was confirmed in the early years that this kind of person did seem to come broadly from a bracket of 32-42 years of age, so in our speech and in our handbooks we stated that we were looking for people who already held responsibility in their own field of work and were likely to be in this age bracket, although this was not always the case. We simply asked that if a nominator wanted to send someone a little above or below the age range, he should give us the reason before we interviewed the candidate. The variety in the group in those days was well spread. In each session between 1950 and 1957, when I left for Australia, the variety we wanted had been coming in and we were constantly getting sessions composed as follows:

First kind of mixture:

Civil Service	6	Each from different departments.
Nationalised industries	8–9	Sometimes more than one from the same nationalised industry, but usually each from a different nationalised industry.
Private industry	42-4	In a few cases a company was represented by two men, but this was rare. In most cases each man came from a different enterprise.
Overseas members (mostly British Commonwealth)	6	Might be from public or private sectors of the nominator's economy. The college essential was that each should have been born, educated and worked overseas and so would bring a different attitude of mind to his session.
Local government	1-2	A little irregular as the method of selecting local-government officials was developing gradually.
Fighting services	1-2	Never more than two per session.

Second kind of mixture:
Within the same group there was another kind of mixture:

Civil Service	The six men were sometimes generalists, sometimes specialists.

Nationalised industries	The eight or nine would come spread between area management, production, marketing, accountancy, occasionally research and occasionally purchasing.
Private enterprise	These varied a little, but were about: production 12, marketing 12, accountants 6, research 6, banking 6; directors occasionally.
Overseas	Six.
Trade unions	Between 1950 and 1957 no trade union had felt able to nominate a trade-union member.

The first kind of mixture gave each session a cross-section of members from each sector of the economy; the second gave each session of the same members a cross-section of the specialisations in which individuals typically at the time acquired their early and limited managerial experience. Extremely careful steps were taken, as the composition of each session was finally settled, to see that the members with different specialisations were distributed as evenly as possible among the six syndicates, each syndicate becoming a microcosm of the whole session. A small group of 10-11 members was thus well equipped to enable its members to combine and to help each specialist to overcome the difficulties he might be experiencing in passing from specialist to more general responsibilities.

In the days when the sole preoccupation of the college was in this particular level of person, Noel Hall regarded admissions as one of his prime tasks and had a registrar to help him discharge it. Inquiries about the college were legion. Outside commitments to meet and explain and discuss persisted, and he never ceased to respond. Somehow he managed to interview two hundred people a year at the very least, having the final say on whether individuals should be accepted or not; and he continued also to move among the sessions and keep a firm hand on every three-month course. When I say he had the final say in accepting and rejecting proposed candidates, this was one of those permissive pieces of legislation which were seldom used, as both nominators and the college came to understand that there were at least three parties whose responsibilities and convenience had to be taken into account: the nominator who could not, in the nature of managerial life, spare a good middle manager for three months at the drop of a hat; the individual, who had to leave his work and his home, and could not be asked to do so for three months at the drop of a hat; and the college, which had a specific responsibility laid upon it to secure in every session individuals of the level, and a group of the variety, which the Court of Governors believed to be indispensable to the pursuit of the college purpose. The build-up of a college relationship with its nominators was a crucial part of the build-up of the whole college. No wonder, in those early days, that the principal played such a strong hand in it.

The registrar's responsibility was to see that the whole relationship was fostered with the care that it obviously required. While it was true that the

Civil Service nominations were gathered for us by a single department, the Treasury, it was also true that as different departments nominated candidates through the Treasury for the college to interview, and they came and went through these early sessions, there was established between the college and each of those departments and ministries an individual relationship which neither the department nor the college hesitated to use if it so wished. This applied to the whole spectrum of relationships with each nationalised industry, with each large and each small company in the private sector, and with the departments of state, ministries and each local government authority – the channel of communication was from college to individual nominating unit and not through intermediaries.

In those early years, the college was able to take advantage of two things that operated in its favour. We were new – we were first in the field in Britain – and our members seemed to be satisfied with us, because the same nominators continued to use us, and we had fresh nominators appearing at the rate of ten a session. This was the first key, which led to the second because it resulted in our getting nominations in excess of the sixty-six we needed, though not in excess of the numbers we needed from which to choose the candidates who best suited the level and who gave us the mixture we wanted. The consistency with which we succeeded in getting both these could never have been achieved if people had not wanted to send their men to Henley. The requisite numbers of specialisation could never have been obtained and sustained unless we drew our candidates from a strong technological society. This is not to say that there were no mistakes. Some men and women slipped through the screening net who perhaps ought not to have been nominated or ought not to have been accepted at interview. Both sides made mistakes but there were not many of them. What did happen was that, for good reasons which the nominator usually explained to the college, a few people were accepted who were not quite up to the standard. It was no bad thing for a syndicate to have to 'carry' one such person in its number and give him a hand on his way: it was part of real life, and could help the individual build up his own confidence. The trouble began if there was more than one such person in a syndicate: if there were two, or far worse three, then the poor level of discussion dragged down the morale of the group, which could go very low indeed if weak men began to appear in the chair more than very occasionally.

The directing staff

The Court of Governors thought that the second key to the success of the cross-fertilisation theme that ran through the college concept (the first being variety in the composition of the sessions) was that it should get the right kind of staff. To throw some light on this, I must start by explaining the size of the directing-staff group that we had in the early days and the roles its members were expected to play, given that the first framework for the course of studies had been designed. The intellectual content of the course had been broken down into the divisions and sub-divisions required; it had been found that the assistance required from the community to supplement the internal contribution of the staff was readily available; and the *modus operandi* described had been put to its test in some twenty-seven sessions by the time I set out for Australia.

There were then seven members of the directing staff involved with the course of studies, this figure being increased gradually to nine as the nature of the task and the pressure on the staff came to be better understood. One of these seven was the director of studies, who was not a 'chief instructor' but rather our 'leader and chairman', who was responsible for seeing that the course of studies was integrated and unfolded before each session in the manner and at the tempo intended, and in seeing to it that the rest of the staff worked harmoniously together as a team. As our number grew from seven to nine, one member of the staff could be assigned to special duties which occurred from time to time and another could be on sabbatical. Two or three years after the college began, when Noel Hall obtained his first director of research (and he was subsequently joined by an assistant), we had two more men very much concerned with the course of studies, though not actually members of the directing staff. It is with the seven men, the director of studies and the six (known as DS) who were in charge of the six syndicates, that I am primarily concerned in this chapter. They had two basic functions: the first to prepare the course of studies for each session and keep it up-to-date, and the second to superintend the conduct of the course of studies in each session.

These responsibilities were interdependent. A DS could not play his part in preparing the course of studies unless he was constantly involved in the superintendence of the course which he had helped to prepare. He could not superintend the course of studies unless he had in him the knowledge that came from taking part in the preparatory process.

For both functions – preparation and superintendence – the subjects to be done in syndicate (most of the subjects in the course of studies) were divided up among the staff, leaving each DS with a particular responsibility for two or three subjects.

Preparing the course of studies

A fresh presentation of the whole of the course of studies was made in every session. In practice this meant for all of us a meeting about four times in each session, under the chairmanship of the director of studies, in which we reviewed the strengths and weaknesses of the block of subjects that had just been completed by the sitting session and compared notes with each other on how we thought these subjects had gone. It was everybody's business to keep watch on all the subjects and think about how they were going and what could be done to improve them. It was the particular responsibility of the DS in charge to keep a watch on the subjects for which he had been made responsible, to take part in discussing with his colleagues how they went and to take charge at once of putting into effect such changes as could be made between the time a subject finished in a sitting session and the time it would be required again in the next session three months later. Change in the presentation of the task where wording might have been found inadequate or ambiguous, adjusting the time allotment to conform better to the needs of a subject, usually inviting new speakers, new syndicate visitors, organising new outside visits and refreshing the literature with new or better material, and the resulting amendment of the paperwork, was the least that this job entailed. It is what I will, for the purpose of this account, refer to as 'short-term change'. This system of review with the director of studies in the chair, which brought into discussion, round a table, the DS who spent a good deal of their day with their syndicates, was a healthy thing and trained us all to see pretty quickly what could be done to improve each subject before it was required next session. It meant long staff meetings in an otherwise long enough day. It might sometimes be rough on individual DS in whose subjects there was much work involved in reorganising the college facilities attached to it, but it was not unmanageable. His colleagues, who were all in the same boat and under the same pressures, were accessible enough for consultation. The director of studies, and the director of research as he arrived on the scene, were there to help as well and an individual member of the staff could get out and take advice outside the college if he felt the need. What each individual had to understand was that everyone had to accept what everyone else actually did in the matter of revision so that every brief could be explained in each syndicate from a 'common staff mind'.

What surprised me as I gained experience at Henley was the help the DS could give members if he really took care to see that all the so-called 'facilities' were well chosen and briefed, the speakers, etc., etc. There was no lack of talent in the UK or any unwillingness to come down to the college to make contributions, often after dinner at night: one simply had to take trouble in finding the right man or the right place for a visit and then brief everyone concerned on the kind of opportunity members would probably want to take.

When it came to more drastic changes in the course of studies, which involved radical alteration in more than one subject, between subject and subject, which disturbed integration and which could distort the whole framework within which the course had been built up, this was another matter. Special arrangements had to be made and this usually involved the recruiting of an extra member of staff while a permanent member was detached to take charge of the working up of major change on this scale; and the forum for discussing and agreeing on such radical matters had to be kept separate from the shorter-term change I have just described. This organisational change usually took the form of the principal taking the chair and the DS putting on long-term, instead of short-term, hats – which is another way of saying that the same men carried the burden of the extra work but we simply 'reorganised' ourselves so that we knew what we were meeting to discuss. Meanwhile the superintendence of the course of studies in a sitting session had to proceed as though nothing was happening, which was hardly a novel situation for anyone who had any experience of administration. Eventually, long-term reform having been completed, the new course replaced the old.

I might add that the *short-term revision* was made possible by the flexible nature of the original framework for the course, which had many virtues. It was possible to amend any subject within the framework, without necessarily changing the others and without disturbing the integration more than a little. Even an experienced staff had more difficulty in finding time for *radical change*, simply because there were only twenty-four hours in the day and twelve weeks in the course; but we could manage both if the whole business of change was well organised.

Superintending the course of studies

I come now to this second half of the DS responsibility, which was the superintending of the course of studies during session. I am quite sure that the reader will have noticed how important it must have been for the DS to be involved in this if they were to discharge the first of their responsibilities for preparing and keeping up-to-date the course of studies, which I have just discussed. I sat on the 'edge' of my syndicate, a couple of feet away from the eleven members at the table. I had briefed the chairman and done my best to ensure that he understood what was required from him and refrained, as prescribed, from discussing the substance of the subject with him; and now witnessed my syndicate take charge of the subject assigned to them. I gradually learnt what help they were going to get from the reading and the various visiting speakers and so on. I knew how this particular subject fitted into the rest, of which they were not yet aware, and my job in the syndicate room was really to help them in the process of preparing themselves for higher responsibility. There was immediately a dilemma before one and if I discuss it first, this does not mean that I got rid of it in the early days of session: on the contrary, it remained with one all the time. The dilemma, briefly, was this – that if one believed, as we did, that this was a learning rather than a teaching process, that the men really were meant to make use of their own talent, and that we really did mean it when we said we delegated the authority to run a subject to a member chairman, that he should actually assume it, then just what were we supposed to do and when were we supposed to do it? Luckily, there were no golden rules about this and even if Socrates himself had drawn them up, I do not think I would have believed them! I had to have some rough code of my own and I think it was this:

1. I did not want to intervene if things were going well, and I did not.
2. If I was asked for a view, I would give it if I had one and refuse it if I did not know or if I thought that the individual or the group would do better to find it for themselves.
3. Sometimes, just because I was human, I would intervene because I had something to say that wanted to come out.

Working in this way one had to judge each situation as one saw one's syndicate, and the individuals in it, developing as the course unfolded. Much of the interest in Henley I found in living with this dilemma though I should add that the dilemma usually only arose in the formal work in syndicate. Most of one's interventions, points I wanted to make to chairmen, for example, were brought into conversation over a pre-lunch glass of beer in the bar, or other similar occasions when the individuals came and talked in one's room, or two or three of us lunched together. But the dilemma was often there: How best, if at all, to help? – a pondering, not an anxiety or a worry.

Wrapped up in the intellectual content of the course I have so far been discussing there was quite a different feature of one's work which was very much part and parcel of the DS responsibility. I was concerned not only with the substance of the subjects but also with the way the syndicate was working; this was another major interest for most of us. I was concerned, for instance, with the general atmosphere in the group. If they were to get the best out of each other, I wanted them to be relaxed but I did not want them to be so relaxed and comfortable that they became a nice cosy group. I wanted to become aware of any tensions there might be, to know whether the jobs we gave them were understood and accepted. Being involved in the group it was not easy for members themselves to think about matters like this. It was useful for them to have someone in the room who was standing back from the details, prepared to do what he could to help. I needed to see whether everyone was involved and interested, whether the discussion was on the ball, free, critical often enough, well shared out, whether they were wasting time. I wondered whether they would listen to each other, which they seldom did in the early days of any session. From time to time, someone would over-dominate the discussion and one could feel the irritation again, usually at the beginning of the session.

Usually it died out as an individual sensed what the group felt, or the chairman suggested it was someone else's turn to have a go. Sometimes, in the mixed groups we had, it was quite inevitable that someone should take the lead from the chairman, because at that point he knew more about what was being discussed, and it was a good thing as long as the chairman sensed when to take it back. I wanted them to be able to disagree without being disagreeable, but did not want them to go for agreement at all costs and let consensus mask genuine disagreement. I liked to feel that everyone would shoot out an idea in his head without fear that he might be thought an ass. I was particularly interested in the leadership of the group and in seeing that it was working in a natural and realistic way. I did not want even the chairman to dominate the proceedings.

I hoped I had an ally in the chairman, who might know more than I about handling people. Often he and some members of the group were discovering that the handling of groups or equals had charms of its own which were new to them, and I did not want to disturb the process of discovery in this any more than I did in anything else. What I did need for the dilemma part of the job was a good rapport with the men in the group,

who I hoped would know that when I did butt in, on whatever aspect of their work, I did so because I was trying to help. They might perhaps see that I understood a little of what was going on in the group, though I knew that a lot went on that they knew I knew little about!

All the above has been on the subject of working with syndicates. A good deal of time was spent, in addition, on the college occasions when syndicate papers were presented or subjects brought to college conference. At these the principal usually took the chair and our role was to attend upon him. Both types of occasion had their purposes and I believe the time spent was considered well spent. For most men it was an excellent experience to have to present their paper in a short speech with a time limit, in the presence of the men whose report it was. It was a good thing, too, for both the chairman and the members of his syndicate to practise getting on their feet in the larger gathering of sixty-six members and replying to a challenge, expected or unexpected, in circumstances so different from the small group of eleven members round the table.

It was good at the occasional conference to discard the formal speeches of presentations. We loosened up a little by devoting the whole hour-and-a-half available to an agenda on which the items related less to members' previous discussions, called for more preparation on the part of members immediately beforehand, and usually gave rise to more surprises to be played 'off the cuff'. Probably these characteristics justified the use of conferences in sessions of our size and met the needs of our managerial community at the time, but there was a snag in the presentations. Sometimes, but not always, some of the syndicate subjects tended to be exhausted by the syndicates round the syndicate tables. It was not always easy, therefore, to re-open the same subject for inter-syndicate discussion at presentations. We were aware of this but did not think it had reached a point which seriously challenged the way we brought our subjects to a conclusion.

I very much enjoyed all the syndicate part of this, but knew that I had some weak points. My particular feeling of weakness arose, I think, from my background and the fact that the field of general management in civil affairs was a vast one and had seldom involved me, at least at the levels I reached, in the detailed understanding of commercial and financial affairs met in civil life. I felt I should have liked to know more about the commercial and financial side of business, but I learned that you could not at the time find everything in one man, and that was why in early Henley we had:

1. A mixed DS team. We had a trade unionist/production manager with a lot of experience of both fields; a man with experience in the management of transport; a man just retired from the Indian Civil Service, who had the qualifications of a Bachelor of Science; an educationalist, and me.
2. We had to supplement the directing staff on every session with a small but constant flow of men with talents other than, or stronger than, or wider than, our own, who in our complex society we could get, and who, in their generosity, gave us so freely of their time.

With these we reckoned that we marshalled for members as much as we could in the way of new technology, new attitudes, a great deal of mature experience, and still left them ample room to discover so much for themselves and from each other. We DS were at the centre of the web and in a good position to see that this balance was kept if we remembered that, when it came to specialist knowledge, we were not trying to train specialists, but to help men to understand what different specialists could and could not do.

Research

The dictum of the first Court of Governors ran like this:

> It is considered that the staff of the college should be engaged on research as well as on teaching. Apart from the undoubted fact that teaching and research are good for each other, industry and the public service may well find it useful to have, as it were, a research station to which problems of administration can be referred. In this field the college will in course of time render a service no less valuable than its teaching by providing a store and clearing house of knowledge and experience.

Noel Hall did not rush into this. The method of instruction, he told the Court of Governors in his first report at the end of 1946, would require much original work on the preparation of material for the course and would involve at least applied research by all members of the full-time staff. He regarded it, therefore, as premature to 'outline a research programme'.

That was one reason for caution – he wanted to know more of what a research staff would have to do before he started to gather it around him. The other reason, I understand, was that in the aftermath of the Second World War he found it extremely difficult to find a director of research. Indeed, it was not until September 1951 that he secured the services of Mr David Clarke.

Meanwhile, the college had opened in March 1948 and the directing staff had been gathering the best material they could to assist members when they tackled their problems in syndicate. With the directing staff becoming more aware of members' problems and of the trends of thinking about them, partly from the members themselves and partly from the scholars and practitioners who were coming to Henley to speak, the new director of research found that the DS knew a good deal and knew something, too, from their own observation of the gaps in available material that they would like to see filled. So the college began to play a hand in preparing material of its own to fill at least a few of these gaps. Below is a list of those books and monographs that had been prepared by the time I went overseas in 1957:

Notes on Important Writers on Administration
Trade Union Law
Trade Union Organisation
The State and Collective Bargaining
Economic Controls
Statutory Instruments
Trade Associations and the Problems that Arise
Sources of Finance
The Joint-Stock Company
The Structure of Organisation
Accountability and Control
The State and Location of Industry

I should add that members expressed enthusiasm as the first few arrived, and from them and from other quarters outside came the request for the college to produce more over the whole field and to sell them.

The process, of which the above material was an important part, was known in early Henley as course development. This was a term which included all the reading material and other documentation gathered by the staff for reading lists which accompanied most subjects. It also covered all the rest of the work involved – for example, in getting to know the men who were knowledgeable in the particular fields in which we needed help, particular firms and other organisations which members ought to visit because of what they were doing or known to be planning, and particular journals to which new ideas were contributed, about which we ought to be thinking. In so far as any of this involved research by the staff it was *applied* research, that is to say, the gathering of material which already existed, putting it into a form convenient for the college purposes and presenting it to members who needed it and who in three months did not have the time to gather the bits and pieces together for themselves. In the early days of which I am writing, this was a fundamental part of the staff's job and in time both directing and research staffs got pretty good at it. Their job entailed being close to members where the management needs became known and whence help could often be obtained from members in getting access to the sources of information required in the gathering process. It was all accepted as part of the job of the staff but it was not fundamental research, which by definition set out to discover new knowledge – it was the gathering and presentation, and often re-presentation, of information which existed in a scattered form, highly inconvenient for busy men.

We thought of this applied research as legitimately DS business because its purpose was to strengthen the course of studies. The works I have listed above are good examples of such materials and we have seen that they were afforded a welcome. We were working in the early days of management education in the United Kingdom. But, as I left Pakistan for the Philippines in 1963, the college at Henley had acquired some financial help which enabled it to expand its research staff and develop its research policy. Now the effort of the existing DS and research staff could be reinforced and it seemed that the purpose of the latter was basically to

strengthen the established and essential process of course development. They were to help in the preparation of the course of studies, help to ensure that the need for change in it was accepted and the basis for that change rigorously worked out. They were to take a syndicate from time to time to ensure that they kept their feet on the ground but, being less involved with the course than the DS, would have more time to give to 'other things'. It was over these 'other things' that controversy arose in the college. I do not think any of the DS minded having in our midst a group of people whose *raison d'être* was to challenge our thinking. We were glad to have help if it was geared to development of the course. We were glad to see research men coming to discuss with us areas in which we had discovered research was needed, and to have research men amongst us who could tell us what was going on in the world of research and when we could expect to see the results. But where, if we embarked on fundamental research ourselves, would it stop and how would it be financed? Was not there a large-scale research effort beginning at last to unfold in the universities, and were they not much better equipped to undertake it than a tiny Adminstrative Staff College? This is the way I thought as I went to the Philippines in 1963.

Atmosphere

We needed an atmosphere in which members could and would talk freely and frankly with each other and could and would be critical of each other. I think we had such an atmosphere. In this brief note, I try to analyse what it was that contributed to it.

The conditions in which members lived

Members found that they were treated as adults. They lived in a large country property and in a neighbourhood which hardly anyone (other than the production man who missed the noise of his factory!) could possibly complain about. There were few rules – the discipline was very largely in members' own hands. Pretty well everything was done for them, so they were free to apply themselves to the demands of the college for their three-month stay. They were explicitly told that the place was theirs for those three months. They had been prepared in their minds at interview for this kind of situation and knew that they would get home for three or four nights every third week on a 'long weekend'.

The conditions in which members worked

At the beginning of almost every session there was an element of the tension that one finds in a group of people who meet each other for the first time and are not quite sure how they will match up to the standards of each other. This tension faded out in the first week or ten days as members got to know each other and became familiar with the kind of

people and work in which they were becoming involved. It would reappear in individuals as their particular workloads increased temporarily. This tension could be high but was mitigated by the fact that the individual and the syndicate were beginning to find their own internal strengths, and the syndicates were finding they could cope with each other on the college occasions. Much confidence, it seemed to me, came with this feeling of growing strength and it often helped an individual over a difficulty; the atmosphere improved with it, probably because members had been through something and come out of it.

Particular events in the course had their effect on the atmosphere. The first attempt to get agreement on the text of a group report often led a syndicate to stay up into the small hours. One could arrive the next morning to find that the syndicate had survived but as quite a different group with a much firmer and easier relationship between its members. Then sometimes a group would come out with a report which was transparently better than any of the others, or would emerge from an encounter with another syndicate by no means defeated in the argument. Sometimes a syndicate would be frustrated by the lack of progress in a subject or a draft on which they were spending too much time. The whole college might run into a sticky patch in the course where, say, there was an outspoken consensus that the workload, particularly the reading, was monstrous; it took the advent of a long weekend to save the day. This last we referred to as a sag in morale, the reasons not always being too clear. There was usually one such sag in a session and it lasted for about three or four days. They were the minor shades in college life.

I think one of the college values – which I do not remember ever hearing stated explicitly to members but which was implicit for anyone capable of recognising the undertones in an occasion – was the way in which Noel Hall tried to build on what the men had, and never criticised them in front of others for what they did not have or had not done. If a chairman at a presentation, for example, made a poor speech, he knew very well himself that he had made a poor speech and everybody else knew it, too. However, there was always something in what they had to say, even if it was only the effort they had put into trying to make a good speech, on which Noel Hall would comment briefly after every chairman finished what, to some, was quite an ordeal. Noel Hall's attitude in this played its part in the development of the atmosphere we needed, while in no way interfering with members' instincts to challenge an individual's thinking. It merely gave the member a chance to see that there were different ways of doing things and, we hoped, made him think how he would be critical of others. After all, we wanted him to see to it that his subordinates got something out of all this as well as he.

While on the subject of the exercise of members' critical faculties I think the critical strength grew rather than diminished as the groups got to know each other. We had our flurries from time to time, of course, and they could be tender ground in the early days of session; but I think as I watched the faces round my table that they rather enjoyed these flurries. If there was a weakness, then I think it was in me, in that the DS can do so much to challenge his syndicate's thinking, and can usually find a way of doing it, in or out of the group, without doing any harm to the process of growth. But it was a responsible job to be a DS and one was in a privileged position.

The supporting services

In some uncanny way the notion that everything was being done for the benefit of each session in turn, and that the place was handed over to it for three months as soon as the members arrived, permeated every corner of Greenlands where staff worked. No one ever said so in my hearing that I can remember, but everyone behaved as if they knew they had a part to play in building up the atmosphere; not just the directing staff in their face-to-face relationships with members during the course; not just the bursar, for all that he carried responsibility for the whole domestic apparatus and for so much of the members' well-being; not just the registrar, who was usually the first to make contact with a member and could do so much for him and for his session at that critical stage; not only the gardeners who tended the highly agreeable acres round the house, nor the typists who turned out the paperwork and seemed to know that it had to be immaculate and produced on time whatever the cost in effort; not only the college transportation staff who had direct contact with so many whom they fetched and carried in those days to and from the college railheads; not only the maintenance staff, the hall porters and telephone operators who worked to exactly the same high standards as everyone else. We all seemed to feel that we were involved in sustaining a standard of service that would show members that if we preached that the business of the administrator was 'to enable the work of a team to come to good effect in the achievement of some co-operative purpose' at least we had a pretty good go at practising it ourselves.

I think a good deal of this atmosphere was made possible because we had a building of our own, could engage our own staff, could offer them a continuity in employment in which a tradition of service could be built up. I daresay half the atmosphere the members brought with them but they also took something away with them when they went, which I used to think of as a bond, the strength of which surprised me when I encountered some examples. I am not going to quote the examples, fascinating though many of them are; I am more interested in this account in setting down my guess as to why there was a bond between those who went through Henley. I think it was because they had profited from each other's company, enjoyed it, and suffered a bit with their friends in the process of learning a great deal about their individual selves and about each other. No doubt some would deny that a bond could emerge from a three-month course. No doubt those who might agree with me on this would put the whole thing in a different way; but, without dragging personalities into it and embarrassing them, I am sure that the atmosphere in which we lived and worked had a good deal to do with the success that attended early Henley. Learning and re-learning are not always easy for the maturing man.

Appraisal and evaluation

By appraisal I mean the process by which performance was assessed within the college. By evaluation I mean the process by which the college performance was assessed.

Appraisal

There were two kinds of appraisal inside the college. One was the assessment which each member was in the position to make of his own performance. As we have seen, there was ample opportunity for the individual to compare his own knowledge, skills, experience, attitudes and personal qualities, with those of his colleagues if he cared to take the opportunity. It was inherent in the whole system that he should do this and the responsibility was made explicit in only the most general terms: basically it was implicit. For the DS to have pointed out a man's shortcomings in the presence of his colleagues would have been thought of as an infringement of the personality in Britain in those days and an arrogance on the part of the staff. The hope was that members could so easily see their shortcomings for themselves.

Subsequently, on a visit home between the Pakistan and Philippine assignments, the very cautious way in which the college was beginning to respond to the feeling that it ought to be more positive about this was to be seen. Any move in this direction, however, would never, it was thought at that stage, be more than the syndicate wanted to undertake. The staff role would be not to judge but to help members assess their own performance by open discussion in the syndicate.

On the other hand, the college would have been very stupid if it had been in any way reluctant to appraise the performance of individuals for its own purposes. We needed to know whether there had been any growth in the members who came to us and to cultivate a competence in measuring this; we wanted to make sure that our admission process was working and that we were accepting the right kind of people, who were profiting from the experience. The principal needed to keep a record for his own use against the day when he might be asked by an individual member's employer how the member had done while at the college. This was a request that could not be refused. What the principal would not do was submit any kind of written report on members' performance, believing that in so mixed a group no one could know enough about an individual member's work-setting to write the kind of report that would not be all too easily misunderstood and which might do much harm if left on members' personal files.

Evaluation

How, by the time I left for Australia in 1957, did the college at nine years old assess its own performance?

I think the first test was the market. The order book had been full from the beginning and the pressures were growing. Many of the original nominators continued to nominate, and new nominators were appearing at a reasonable rate. This was a partial test and seemed to show a measure of satisfaction in what we were doing. The Court of Governors, who had been cautious, had overcome their feelings sufficiently to let the principal go to Australia to discuss with the Australians their idea of having a similar college, which they would hardly have done had they been losing faith in their own institution. Visits by nominators to discuss the college and their own management-development plans and visits by the principal to companies were growing. We well knew that there was internal controversy about the college in some boardrooms. So it seemed healthy.

A good deal could be told from a sitting session. There were mistakes both in nominating and in our acceptance of candidates, but we thought there were remarkably few of these. There was a sag in most courses for a few days, somewhere in the middle of the course, but for the bulk of the time morale was good. The principal saw every member individually at the end of the session, responding if they wanted to talk and listening to their comments. He took up any criticisms they made if he was satisfied that they were really well founded. But he had a restless mind and was never satisfied. So he submitted the college to the scrutiny of a group of independent individuals who came down and talked it over; they told us to press on.

College relationships with past members

As I left Henley in 1957 for the beginning of my assignment overseas, the importance of this relationship was becoming more apparent. From the first the early sessions had expressed the desire to meet again, preferably at the college, and the college had responded by offering each session a weekend, about fifteen months after their regular session. Review courses had by 1957 become established practice. Members of each session were given the dates for their review course before they left the college; a brief was despatched well in advance. When they came back, there was a speaker to open the subject for discussion, there would be a few syndicate discussions and a college conference, all on a topic of current concern. About fifty out of a possible sixty-six usually returned. They quickly slipped back into gear in the relaxed atmosphere which was half reunion. It was a good opportunity for members and staff to take stock of each other and of the course they had attended.

Meantime, past members had formed for themselves, with full college support, a Greenlands Association. Any member was entitled to join and practically all of them did. The purpose was to support the college, keep in touch with it, and promote contacts between past members. As the number of past members increased, regional groups of this association emerged in most of the main centres in the UK and overseas. These were quite independent of each other, each conducted and financed its own affairs, invited someone from the college to visit them when they wanted to know how things were going, visited each other's undertakings, had an after-dinner speaker and sometimes a discussion, or just had dinner together. Twice a year was about the measure of it, though some met more frequently. Each group elected one of its members to a central committee which overlooked the association's finances, superintended through a sub-committee the production of a bi-annual journal which the college distributed to all past members, usually met at the college twice a year and talked things over with the principal. At the time, the existence of this association and the interest it displayed meant more to the college than I imagined. I rather took it for granted.

Neither the weekend 'review courses' nor the Greenlands Association journal could have worked unless the college had provided the association with an honorary secretary and editor to administer the assembly of information about past members, their career progress, movements and up-to-date personal and work addresses; to stimulate the writing of articles for the journal and see that it also included the available news of past members. The Greenlands Association evolved naturally and spontaneously; no one attempted to impose anything on past members.

2

EARLY MOUNT ELIZA –
THE AUSTRALIAN
ADMINISTRATIVE STAFF
COLLEGE, 1957-8

The idea emerges and is brought to action

The emergence of the Australian Administrative Staff College is marked in my mind by the care which the Australians had taken in examining the idea and in preparing the community for its arrival, and by the personalities of three particular men who played the leading roles.

The climate in Australia in the 1950s was ripe for the launching of some form of training or education of managers. The need to do something about it was the subject of some debate among senior administrators and managers in business and Government. Australians moving around the world were aware that others were thinking the same way and that some projects of an experimental nature had been launched. Some Australian undertakings had been sending men overseas for training, and these men were coming back and talking about it. These needed to be brought into focus and it was a Mr Geoffrey Remington who began to do this in 1952. He was a solicitor and a prominent and enthusiastic member of the Rotary Club of Sydney; and in the latter capacity began to think that this was a field of activity in which Rotary might have a part to play. He was by no means alone: he had many friends in Rotary but none of them knew exactly what should be done. He was a robust and cheerful personality, sensitive to what was going on around him, particularly thorough in his methods and very determined. He was the sort of man who took endless trouble in anything he did and whom other men in consequence were willing to trust and support.

He and his friends were very much aware of the reports being brought back from Britain about an experiment at Henley that seemed to be showing some success, and they began to think that the thing to do was to establish an institution that would 'train persons with capacity and experience to enable them to fill managerial positions of executive responsibility'. Mr Remington got in touch with Noel Hall, briefed himself thoroughly in what was being done at Henley, and explained this to the members of the Sydney Rotary Club. He became chairman of a committee which the club set up to consider whether the whole thing could be a legitimate Rotary project. He and his committee soon realised that if the project was to be a success 'the support of people in high places in commerce and industry and in Government circles would be essential', and he canvassed the idea that Noel Hall should be invited to Australia to explain at first hand what he was doing. He began to gather other substantial people around his committee, both from business and from government.

The Australian invitation to Noel Hall came in the summer of 1954 and there was at first a little hesitation about accepting it. The Court of Governors then still felt that the British College was an experiment and had a natural doubt whether British experience was adequate to justify assisting another country in thinking through its problems. However, the governors eventually agreed, and very warmly, and Noel Hall went out in September 1954 to explain what he was doing and to help the Australians think their problems through as best he could.

The Australian sponsors made extensive use of him, and he had a very busy five weeks in the country. They asked him to visit most of the main cities in Australia and made arrangements for him to talk in each to groups of administrators and managers, and for him to visit universities, institutions, associations, conferences and councils interested in management training and explain to them the nature of the British College. They so arranged his programme that three weeks of it were spent in Sydney. There, in addition to asking him to speak to a number of very full audiences, the sponsors took the opportunity of his presence to discuss with him in some detail the problems he had encountered in setting up and running Henley and their own ideas for an Australian College.

It was as a result of these discussions that the Australian sponsors decided that they would go ahead with an Australian Administrative Staff College. They liked the essential points in the Henley approach; the idea of trying to help men of action and responsibility to prepare themselves for higher responsibility; the idea that the sessions should be mixed groups gathered from government, from statutory corporations, as well as from business, and should be carefully selected; the idea that the objective should be 'not theory but improved practice'; the idea that the members should assume a major responsibility in the conduct of the work they would be asked to do. They thought that the Australian managerial community could support continuing sessions of forty people. They came to think that the Australian College should, like the British counterpart, be an independent institution free to develop on its own lines and they were indeed alive to the notion that it would need the support of a substantial number of influential people in all sectors if it were to be a success. They were also aware that a full-time principal would have to be very carefully selected. They refused to believe that lack of finance would be an obstacle to the achievement of their aim.

Noel Hall left on 12 October 1954, and Mr Remington and his Rotary

Club Committee followed up at once. A memorandum and articles of association were drawn up and the first signatures were appended to them a couple of months later. By February 1955 the college was formally incorporated, the company limited by guarantee and registered in the Australian Capital Territory.

Mr Remington had been at the hub of all these activities and a great deal of work had, of course, been involved. His main role had really been twofold: to take the lead in persuading people to support the idea of the college and to see, at each stage, that action followed discussion. He seems to have been very good at both. He would, for instance, take the greatest pains in ensuring that a man he wanted to gain to his side was really well briefed not only by himself but by others. He would think out what needed to be done to persuade a particular individual and then mobilise the right people – a long and exacting task. When it came to meetings he seemed always to be a jump ahead, to have thought out beforehand what was likely to arise and to be ready for it.

He seems to have had an aggressive streak in him which led him almost to invite confrontation with others of strong personality. In spite of this, I never met any Australian who would deny that Geoffrey Remington showed remarkable perception in selecting the kind of influential men needed for the success of the college; nor who would deny the untiring determination with which he set out to persuade these men to give their support to the projected establishment. Without these qualities of his, the Australian College might never have got off the ground. When I talked with him, he denied that it was an exhausting process. In fact I got the impression that he enjoyed it all enormously. He was steering the ship through rocks, and it was exciting.

He and his friends had one more task to do – to hand over the college formally and legally into the hands of a properly constituted governing council and satisfy themselves in the process that their ideas would be in the hands of men who would see that they were brought to action. The key to this was to get the right kind of council and especially the right kind of chairman. The potential members of the council were at hand not only from among the men who had been involved in and with the Sydney Rotary Club, but also now of course from among men from New South Wales, Victoria, South Australia, Western Australia, Queensland, Tasmania, and the Australian Capital Territory. It was a question of selecting the right men from them and persuading them to agree to join the council if elected. Mr Remington and his friends had no difficulty in assembling a strong council but there remained the question of a chairman. There Mr Remington made his last great contribution. He conceived the idea that Mr Essington Lewis of Broken Hill Proprietary Ltd should be invited to become the first chairman of the council.

The late Mr Essington Lewis was a powerful personality who dominated the industrial scene in Australia at that time. He was the head of the largest Australian industrial enterprise – there were few really big enterprises. He had played a large part in the mobilisation of Australian resources in the Second World War; for the government he was the embodiment of Australian industry. Because of his strong position, commanding presence and dominant character, few cared to cross swords with him.

There was no doubt at all that, if he could be persuaded to assume command of this new enterprise, he would see to it that the effort so far made by other people would be brought to fruition. Sir Daniel McVey, who had been very close to Mr Remington since the beginning and had worked with Mr Lewis in the Second World War, accepted from Mr Remington the task of trying to persuade Mr Lewis to become the first chairman of the council. After a little reluctance, due simply to the amount he already had on his plate, Mr Lewis said, 'Well, if you say I must, I will.' Thus the second personality appeared on the college scene.

The council immediately found itself dealing with the practical problems in developing the college – the examination of ideas that the sponsors had so far formulated, the raising of money, the selection of the first principal and the question of the scale on which the college should start. All these, of course, were interconnected and in all of them Mr Lewis played a strong and decisive hand. The council had little difficulty in endorsing the thinking that had been developed by the earlier sponsors, as most of them had been associated with their thinking for some time. It set up an executive committee to examine the main problems which it ought to be tackling and particularly the question of finding the first principal.

The executive committee embarked upon this task of finding the first principal by advertising. A large number of applications had been received and was being screened when Sir Douglas Copland, the Australian High Commissioner in Canada, wrote from Ottawa expressing an interest in the college and saying he would be glad to help in any way he could. Everybody in Australia knew Sir Douglas Copland. He was a man of powerful character, an economist and administrator who had occupied high places in Australia and had represented Australia overseas. He carried with him the authority of knowledge, experience and accomplishment. He was known as a controversial character with strong views of his own and a propensity for disputing with all and sundry, including established authority. He might be difficult to handle but this was the sort of risk that Mr Lewis enjoyed taking. The executive committee and council were unanimous that this was the man they would like to have and they offered him the appointment on 5 April 1956. I would hazard a guess that one of the reasons why Sir Douglas Copland accepted it was the fact that Mr Lewis was chairman of the council. Sir Douglas liked working with men of Mr Lewis's calibre and he knew him well. So one of the prime responsibilities of the council came to be settled, and a third personality appeared on the college scene.

From the moment of his return to Australia, in September 1956, Sir Douglas exerted a major influence on the thinking in the council. He observed that the council intended to start on a modest scale. They had begun to raise small sums to finance the beginnings. This was not Sir Douglas's idea at all. On his way home he had been to the United States and the United Kingdom and had formed the view that such things needed to be well founded. The people who were going to be asked to attend the college needed to be put in surroundings which would attract and inspire them. An atmosphere would have to be developed and this, to his way of thinking, could never be done in an environment which itself was unattractive. Towards the end of 1956 he found what he wanted in the Hotel Manyung at Mount Eliza. He had been asked to speak at a convention there, organised by the Australian Institute of Management. As a house for the college the hotel appealed to him at once. It was in an attractive position on the cliffs overlooking Port Phillip Bay, with views up to Melbourne 30 miles to the north and to Point Nepean to the south. It was set in beautiful grounds with its own sandy beach. The main buildings had adequate rooms for college use.

Most, but as far as I know, not all, the events which followed on Sir Douglas's return after that weekend in Manyung, are well known. The fact that he was bubbling with enthusiasm is on the record. The fact that the chairman and the council made a major change in their thinking, launched an appeal for funds on an entirely new scale, and in six months raised some £250,000 to buy it, is well known. They go to show that everyone in the upper hierarchy of the college at the time thought that Sir Douglas was right. But it is known that the owner of the Hotel Manyung, Mr Reginald Ansett, a well-known businessman, was not at all keen to sell. Was it Mr Geoffrey Grimwade, chairman of Drug Houses of Australia Ltd and a member of the council, who persuaded him to change his mind? Was his purchase – out of his own pocket – of the option to buy a highly crucial step in the process? Perhaps no one will know the answer to the full part Mr Grimwade played. Few, I imagine, would disagree with the view I encountered in Australia that Sir Douglas and Mr Essington Lewis were complementary to each other – Sir Douglas the prime mover, Mr Essington Lewis the powerful personality who launched the appeal over his own commanding signature. These men seemed to tower high in the minds of Australians. If you visit the Australian College you can perhaps see why if you look at their portraits which hang in the hall – two of the men to whom the college was to owe so much.

In the midst of this stream of thought and action Sir Douglas Copland found time to do many things, three of which were of major significance to the speedy establishment of the college. He handpicked his directing staff. He established them and himself in a small, scruffy but unforgettable office in Melbourne and got them thoroughly involved at once. He arranged for the Henley course of studies to be examined by his staff, with a view to discovering whether it was suitable to Australian conditions, and he reached the conclusion that, with some modifications, it would be. He thus provided the college with a virtually ready-made, integrated course of studies and was saved the time that would have been needed to create a new one. At the same time, before the raising of funds had been completed, and therefore before the possession of the building was assured, he decided in March 1957 that the college would open on 6 September that year. This decision the council took in its stride and, of course, it had the effect of galvanising the whole scene. Nobody was thinking of going back. On the other hand, everyone now had to go forward quickly.

So, by the time I arrived on the scene, on 8 May 1957, the conditions necessary for the early establishment of the college had very nearly been fulfilled. There was substantial support for it in all sections of the community; there was a strong council manifestly concerned to see that the college was a success; a full-time principal in action; and two of his eventual three directing staff were assembled and at work. We knew we were to cater for the needs of men with substantial experience; we knew that our sessions were to be composed of men with varied backgrounds from government and from business; we knew that we were to work for a session of forty people; and we knew that we had largely a ready-made course of studies. Sir Douglas was extremely busy playing his part in arousing interest in, and money for, the college. The purchase of the Hotel Manyung, later to resume its original name of Moondah, was about to be clinched. Altogether, morale seemed pretty high.

Sir Douglas had already made it clear to me that he wanted me to become a full member of his team. I was to be his director of studies and to have charge of an Australian syndicate when operations started. But the term director of studies meant no more than that I would have a co-ordinating function in a group which he wanted to tackle the course of studies as a team. We were to consult each other, to be in each other's minds over the whole field of preparation, which is what I was used to. Maurice Brown was a graduate in law of Melbourne University, with considerable experience in both government and university administration. Harry Slater was a Bachelor of Commerce of Melbourne University and a chartered accountant with considerable experience in private practice in accountancy, auditing, taxation and company secretarial work for a wide variety of manufacturing, trading and professional business. They were supported by a secretarial staff of four. The third Australian member of the directing staff, Harold Harvey, took up his duties in mid-June in time to play his full part in the first session. Harold Harvey's background covered twenty years experience in production engineering in the heavy electrical industry. He had eight years as Head of the School of Industrial Management at the Melbourne Technical College and six years in general management in the textile industry. So the balance that Sir Douglas was seeking in his directing staff came to be strengthened. All that I had to do when I arrived on 8 May was to join in. The door was wide open and there was plenty to do.

Nominations and admissions

Much of what had to be done can be grouped under the following headings: obtaining nominations; preparing the building to receive and sustain a group of more than forty people in residence; and preparing the course of studies. The difficulty, of course, was that all these things had to be done by the same very small group of men at the same time.

Looking at the question of getting nominations to begin with, we needed a handbook so that we could send to numerous potential nominators a description of what we were going to do, give them the dates of the sessions and some idea of the shape of the course. So near were we in our thinking that we found the staff had already had a shot at the first draft of a handbook. This was a rather tiresome document to prepare because it involved the settlement of so many issues before it was sent out. In fact it was so near the mark that we were able to go ahead and proceed with the business of getting our men. We wanted forty of them, the group to be mixed and as varied as possible. We had to get four men from the federal government service, four from different state government services, four from different statutory corporations and twenty-eight from private enterprise, each of whom we hoped would come from different industries or different types of commercial undertaking. We expected that a few of the people from the government services would have technical backgrounds and relied primarily on the private sector to nominate men with experience in production, marketing, accountancy, finance, banking, insurance and engineering, as well as some from general management; and we hoped that among all these there would be at least one representative of the trade unions. As a guide to nominators we said that we hoped to find the kind of men we wanted between the ages of thirty-five and fifty. We explained that we proposed to interview candidates before accepting them.

To be sure of getting a group of this kind, it is necessary to get more nominations than there are vacancies in any one session. Only then is it possible, by negotiating with a few nominators, to defer to a later session candidates of particular categories who appear in excessive numbers and substitute others to make good the mixture required; but we had no idea at the time what sort of pressure was going to be exerted upon us. There had been a good deal of publicity about us in the press; Sir Douglas had been stumping the country, addressing various groups and telling them what he was aiming to do. It is of some interest to note that we sent out no less than 760 letters to different organisations in the public service, commercial and industrial sectors of the Australian economy inviting nominations: they were all addressed to the top man personally.

But in the early days when the reputation of the college was still to be made, getting nominations was not as easy as it might appear. The receipt of a letter inviting nominations set up all sorts of problems inside the organisation addressed. The nominator may well be a man who is aware of the purpose of the college and he may approve of it; but he is faced, probably for the first time, with the hard reality of sparing a senior man for three months and this in itself is often quite a shock. Then he has to think whom he might spare and whether, in fact, it would be possible to spare him at the proposed time. He may be very keen to do something about it but quite often cannot. He may be a cautious type who prefers to wait and see how the college works before committing himself. He may have the hell of a problem deciding who should be the first to go. Or he may well be a man who has never heard of the college or one who thinks training is all nonsense anyway. So when Harry Slater and I carried the 760 letters over to the post one Saturday morning in early June, we did not imagine that we would get 760 nominations!

Meanwhile, Sir Douglas did not wait for replies to these letters. He was engaged in the campaign to raise money for the college and was meeting regularly the men who were in a position to nominate. Not being the man to lose an opportunity, he saw everyone he could and did a great deal of work on many people. Regularly throughout June and July he used to have someone to lunch about every other day in the Windsor Hotel. Very often he used to take me with him to talk during lunch about the college and the sort of things we planned to do, in terms which we hoped would convince the victim that he'd better part with one of his best men for three months starting in September. The pace was so hot that I never thought to keep a record of these lunches to try to equate the effort expended with the results achieved in terms of the contribution in men or money. But this was the boss on the job and it was quite clear that he regarded the responsibility for getting nominations to be his.

By the time we moved out to Moondah, in the latter half of July, nominations were coming in and we could begin to interview. This we did in Moondah whenever it was possible to expect candidates to make the journey to see the college; failing this, one, or sometimes two, of us made the journey to Sydney or Adelaide, or met an individual passing through Melbourne. There were only two we had to take without interview – one from Perth and one from Tasmania.

The object of the interview, of course, was first to let the candidate see the principal or one of his senior colleagues and hear from them at first hand what he was likely to be in for. We hoped that he would at least find out that he was going to be treated as a mature person, that he would be involved from the time of his arrival, and would carry a full share of the responsibility for the work. He would have a quick look round the college in which he would spend his three months (getting the feel of it at first hand was essential). The second object was to enable us to find out a great deal more about the man than we would get from any nomination form. We wanted to know as much as we could about the last ten years or so of his working life so that we knew what we were doing when we fitted him with his colleagues into a particular syndicate with a particular syndicate leader, and when we allotted him his chairmanships; we wanted to find out whether he had anything to say to us, or to ask us, and so find out a little of what we might expect from him. We were also on the look-out for anyone we thought might not profit from attending a session – the kind of problem which sometimes confronts a principal when the purpose of the college is misinterpreted or not fully understood by a nominator.

It was during the course of these interviews, in which I found myself heavily involved, that a number of things gradually became clear. We were going to get a group of very competent men, some of whom were particularly senior and were probably being sent as guinea pigs to size up the quality of the treatment, which was fair enough. All of them seemed to be willing to have a go, which was half the battle; and it looked as if we would get the full complement we sought. On the mixture we were not quite so certain. We were going to be strong in banking and finance, well-equipped with accountants and production managers. However, early in August, with only a month to go, it became clear that we were going to be short of marketing men. This last was an embarrassment inasmuch as we needed four at least and had a special role for them to play in part of the course. We made several attempts to fill this gap, but we never did, and we entered the session with the problem still round our necks.

We did not succeed in getting a trade unionist in the first session, though I am sure that Sir Douglas was far too wise a man to be disappointed at this. A good deal of discussion between the unions and the college must have been involved before his idea of persuading the trade unions to back the college could materialise. But, sure enough, there was a man there on the second session. We at the time were not to know it but this first nomination heralded a steady flow of trade-union candidates, which once again points to the remarkable perception the first principal of the college had; and the measure of goodwill between the college and unions was to grow out of his faith.

Apart from this it was all pretty good, we thought. The bulk of the nominations we got came from nominators who had themselves been involved in the sponsoring of the college. These were the men who knew what the college was intending to do and who had decided to put their faith in it and give it a start. Many of them had given generously of their financial resources as well, but they knew that the ultimate test of their faith in the college's potential was that it should get good members and they nominated accordingly.

It was all done remarkably quickly. It is not easy to spare a senior man at short notice, nor indeed for the man himself to break away from work and home at short notice. Administrators usually liked to plan further ahead. But everyone seemed to be prepared to make exceptions. Anyway, we got our first session of forty men. After one or two sessions, of course, one gets to know the kind of group that is likely to emerge when one invites nominations, but in the first session one has to plan on assumptions, never quite knowing until you have got them who is going to turn up. For the first three of these four months, at least, one was planning on assumptions that it would be 'all right on the night'.

Internal organisation and administration of the college

There was a good deal to be done to place the college on a sound organisational footing and Sir Douglas took the lead in all the important matters.

First was the question of servicing the council and standing committee which the council had set up to look after its business between council meetings. Sir Douglas took a strong view on this. He maintained that he, as chief executive of the college, should be placed in charge of the college records and that the secretary of the council and the committee should be a member of his staff. He thought that all college funds should be placed in his charge and that he should be responsible, in consultation of course with the chairman of each, for the preparation of the agenda for meetings, for the recording of their proceedings and for following up council and committee decisions. He preferred this to the system which was then operating in Britain by which the affairs of the council were handled by the chairman of the council and by a secretary who was a member of the chairman's staff. He had some difficulty over this at first but in the end the council came around to thinking that he was right, and Maurice Brown was appointed secretary to the council and the funds and the papers were transferred to the college, where they have been ever since. Sir Douglas attended all meetings of both the council and the committee, but he was not a member of either. He did not like this. I had nothing at all to do with it and at the time could not see that it mattered very much – a view which underwent change a good deal later on.

The arrangements for financing the college were placed on a sound footing from the start. The capital sum required for the purchase of Moondah and for the alteration of the building to suit college purposes was raised in the form of substantial subscriptions from a number of the larger companies in the private sector – the council sought no funds from Government – and the college was relieved of the burden of servicing loans. To cover the needs that were found to arise in starting the enterprise, a form of membership of the college company was created, which carried with it the financial obligation of a company sponsor to subscribe a total of £1,500 in three annual instalments of £500. In addition, each nominator was called upon to pay a substantial fee to finance the attendance of his candidate. So the college started completely free from debt of any kind and with a small reserve.

We had some difficulty and a few late-night meetings over the question of the internal organisation of the college. There were several functions to be performed. There was the council's business; the course of studies, its secretarial staff and the library, which fell into one convenient compartment; there was a need to supervise the arrangements for the admission of the members; and there was a wide range of duties to be supervised in the purchase of supplies of all kinds, in the kitchen and dining rooms, in the bar (which was called the Buttery), in maintaining the bedrooms, manning the reception desk and the telephone, maintaining the buildings, the garden and the vehicles and in keeping the accounts for all of it. Nobody wanted to be lavish but the standards should command the respect of the members and the service should be impeccable.

We were quite clear and agreed on the way to manage the course of studies. Under the principal there were the four members of the directing staff, our small team of secretaries and our librarian – and these were adequate for the start. It was clear, too, that as Sir Douglas was playing a major hand in explaining the college outside and in getting nominations and interviewing candidates, all that he would need to begin with was a competent girl to keep track of nominations, summon candidates for interview and keep the records straight with our various nominators. What caused the difficulty was the principle on which we should work in allotting responsibilities for our own internal administration.

Sir Douglas took the view that in an educational establishment there was no reason why the members of the directing staff should not assume at least some of the responsibilities for administration of the enterprise. He wanted Maurice Brown to look after the general administration of the college and Harry Slater to look after the finance and accounts, as well as for them to play their full part in the course of studies. I did my best to talk him out of this because I thought that members of the directing staff would be fully engaged in the course of studies and ought not to be involved in other work which would take a lot of their time. When their work in the course of studies allowed it, and between sessions, they would need to see and be seen and keep themselves up-to-date and they could not do this if they were tied by the leg. In the end Sir Douglas conceded my point, but only in a half-hearted way: we got an administrative officer, new lines of authority were not clarified, and as a result Maurice Brown and Harry Slater had a pretty heavy load to carry in the early sessions. I still think I was right and that what was really needed was an able administrative officer to relieve the directing staff for their own work. I am glad to say that they now have one.

To suggest that the responsibilities of the directing and administrative staff should be separated did not, of course, mean that they could or should work in compartments. In practice they have to work very closely together. The registrar has to see that each session is completed and hand the detail over to the director of studies at least a week before it is due to come in. Someone on the administrative staff has to see that the members acknowledge receipt of their joining instructions which tell them when to arrive; has to see that they are met at the airport and brought to the college; has to discuss the allocation of bedrooms to the members with the director of studies; and has to see that the administrative requirements of a tightly planned programme are met day by day. The morale of a session can be affected by a failure on the course of studies. Nothing knocks it back quicker than a failure in administration – a failure in the heating, poor food, poor service, or some lack of thought for the convenience of the members. There is no need to expand on the possibilities.

The course of studies and methods of work

As Sir Douglas was busy in playing his part in rousing interest and money for the college, and as he had looked over the course of studies previously, he had no wish to get involved in detail and wanted us to get on with it. I took the lead in this as director of studies; and if we overdid the extent to which we made use of the Henley material in the first two sessions at Mount Eliza, it was certainly my fault. We made use of the *framework* of the Henley course; of the subject headings inside that framework, which were the 'titles' to the management issues of the day that Henley believed at the time their members should be working on and which my Australian colleagues seemed to think would be suitable for their members; and we adopted the 'supporting subject' idea, which gave us the freedom to introduce a few subjects external to the general framework. But under all the subject headings I think there was sufficient freedom for us to change, modify or retain the 'brief' or 'task' on which Australian members would work.

What all this meant to a group of four men engaged in laying the first Australian course was that Henley probably did give them a start on most subjects, at least a fair chance to ensure that the subjects would 'integrate' with the Australian course, a fair idea of the time required to do each subject, and the supporting flexibility that I have just mentioned. How precious this help was to me I only found out on later assignments when I had to help start courses from scratch without any assistance at all. I suspect that Sir Douglas knew that there was some risk that there might be too much Henley and probably thought the price was worth paying if it ensured a quick start to the college. Meanwhile, the approach saved us an incredible amount of time and wear and tear. It meant, too, that it was possible for the DS to take over the subjects with which it was most appropriate for us to deal; the Australians to take over the subjects which were especially Australian in content and needed the more amendment; and I to take the rest, and the responsibility for the overall college timetable and the general co-ordination of our work. I had all the Henley documents and handed them over to my colleagues in terms of the responsibilities they had taken on, had talks with them individually about the purposes of these subjects and left them to put each subject into its Australian form – set the task in each, design the reading list, secure the reading material as best they could, invite the speakers to contribute to each at the right time, keep his colleagues in touch with what he was doing – while I did the same with the subjects I had taken on and worked out a timetable for the whole at the same time. Most of the things which mattered seemed to be on our side.

The 6 September was galloping up on us and there was not much time for leisurely argument. Sir Douglas not only believed in delegation, he actually practised it; we could use his name whenever we wanted to and he backed us up in whatever we did. We found that when we came to seek the co-operation we needed from the community for the course of studies, we got it without hesitation. 'Yes, Mr X will be glad to come and give a talk on such and such, and he will be glad to fit in with your ideas as to date and time' or 'Yes, you can send half a dozen men to visit my department or my factory on such and such a date and turn the place upside down if you like.' It was clear in the early stages that we were going to get the essentials we needed.

The Notes on the course and course of studies as these finally emerged and were put in front of session 1 were as follows.

NOTES ON THE COURSE

The course of studies

1. Administration is concerned with the unity and continued
    direction of the whole of an organisation, and the administrator
    normally has to deal with many aspects of it at the same time. Any
    division of the subject must in some respects be unsatisfactory and
    each separate part, considered in isolation, may appear to be
    unrealistic. But for practical study some breakdown is necessary.
    The college course is, therefore, divided into five main parts (I to
    V), some of these being further sub-divided, for the purposes of
    syndicate discussion. The accompanying list details these parts and
    sub-divisions and indicates the syndicate leaders in charge of each.

Principal subjects

2. *PART I* gives members of the college an opportunity of making a
    first comparative survey of the structures and administrative
    methods of the organisations with which they are familiar. At the
    same time it enables each syndicate to ascertain the knowledge and
    practical experience available among their own members.

3. In *PART II* those administrative problems are studied which arise
    under one managerial authority – in other words, all those matters
    which are internal to the work of a single organisation and can be
    controlled absolutely by the directing authority of that unit. These
    questions are examined from four angles, as follows:

    Subject II(a) – Management of the Individual, which comprises
    the place of the individual and the part he plays in the
    administrative unit.

    Subject II(b) – The Structure of Organisation and Inter-relation
    of Departments, which covers the way in which work is divided
    among departments and their sub-divisions and the manner in
    which satisfactory integration between them is maintained.

    Subject II(c) – Accountability, Delegation and Control, in which
    attention is turned to the problem of delegating authority from
    above and the methods available for controlling and assessing
    the work of the whole organisation and ensuring that accurate
    information, for the use of those concerned with policy and
    administrative guidance, comes up from below regularly and
    with the necessary rapidity. These questions lead naturally into a
    study of how the methods of delegation and control are

influenced by the manner in which a directing authority can be called upon to answer for the discharge of its responsibilities.

Subject II(d) – Organisation for Production, gives an opportunity to study a number of other particular aspects of Part II.

4. In *PART III* attention is turned to those activities of an administrative unit which, because they are partly dependent on the maintenance of suitable relations with other administrative units or persons, are not wholly within its own control.

Subject III(a) is devoted to a selection of the more prominent commercial relationships which are maintained by most of the organisations nominating members to the college.

Subjects III(b) and *III(c)* deal with other important examples of external relationships affecting administration, viz. organised labour, government and semi-government authorities.

5. It is in *PARTS II* and *III* of the course that the bulk of the detailed work will be carried out. At this stage members will be able to consider the uses and limitations of various specialised techniques in administration, not only in their own fields but generally. The work will include visits by specialists to the college and visits on the part of members, as representatives of their syndicates, to outside organisations.

6. In *PART IV* there will be a change of emphasis. The work in this part is designed to give consideration to the general interaction of the numerous problems of the administrator which have been separately considered earlier in the course.

In *Subject IV(a)* syndicates consider methods whereby management may keep an organisation and its various sections alert and vital, particularly when external stimuli of the kind outlined in Subjects IV(b) and IV(c) do not materially affect them.

In *Subject IV(b)* these interactions are considered on the assumption that all organisations are under the same economic pressures, but each management has to decide the steps it should take in the light of its own general circumstances to meet changes in the economic conditions under which it works.

In *Subject IV(c)* it is assumed that a particular firm or group of firms are required to carry out far-reaching changes in products or methods of production for reasons particular to themselves or their industry.

7. *PART V* will be a survey of the work of the session, emphasising the role and responsibilities of those who occupy the senior positions in organisations of different kinds.

Other subjects

8. The programme will be diversified by the study, in each syndicate, of the career and achievements of selected individuals eminent in administration in the past. Two separate studies are made, in the first and second halves of the course respectively.

9. A series of talks in the early weeks of the course covers some of the uses and limitations of figures when used for management purposes. A case study will be taken in this subject in the latter half of the course.

10. During the first eight weeks of the course, the principal will conduct eight lectures, followed by discussion periods, on 'The Australian Economy and its Relation to the World Economy'.

11. Provision is made for a short study of the problems which beset an administrator in keeping himself informed of the trend of current affairs.

12. Towards the end of the course a certain number of periods is allotted for consideration of a 'special' subject, usually of topical interest. The subject for study in session 1 will be notified in due course.

Syndicates

13. Each member of the college is allotted to one of four syndicates (A to D) in which the greater part of the work will be carried out. For Subjects II(d) 1, 2, and III(a) 1, 2, on the other hand, members will be divided up into specialist syndicates according to the subjects being discussed. For the study of Subject IV(c) members will be divided up afresh into modified syndicates.

Chairmen and secretaries

14. The college appoints, from among the members of each syndicate, a chairman and secretary for each subject. Their responsibilities are set out in the 'General Note for Chairmen and Secretaries of Syndicates' issued with this paper. Every member will receive, as the course proceeds, the papers needed for work on each subject. These will include a 'Brief', giving the range of the subject to be examined and defining the task selected for report, reading and book lists, and the names of visitors. Details of outside visits and particulars of other special arrangements will also be issued as necessary.

Briefing

15. The chairman and secretary for each subject will be briefed in advance by the syndicate leader in charge of the syndicate and will make plans to settle at their 'organising meeting' precise arrangements for dealing with the brief.

Directing staff

16. In addition to being generally available to the syndicate as a whole, the directing staff will be in frequent consultation with each chairman and secretary as the work on a subject proceeds and will be available to individual members of syndicate for personal discussion of problems which arise.

The Course of Studies

	Syndicate Leader in charge session 1
PART I Comparative Administrative Structures	Brig. Cornwall-Jones
PART II Internal Organisation & Administration	
(a) Management of the Individual	Mr Harvey
(b) The Structure of Organisation and Inter-relation of Departments	Brig. Cornwall-Jones
(c) Accountability, Delegation and Control	Mr Brown
(d) Organisation for Production	
*(1) Work Management	Mr Harvey
*(2) Research and Development	
*(3) Office Services	Not in session 1
*(4) Management Accounting	
*(5) The Personnel Department	Mr Brown
PART III External Relations	
(a) Commercial Relationships	
*(1) Consumers and Customers	Brig. Cornwall-Jones
*(2) Purchasing	Not in session 1
*(3) Sources of Finance	Mr Slater
II(d)/III(a) Review of Specialist Syndicate Work	Brig. Cornwall-Jones
(b) Relations with Organised Labour	Mr Harvey
(c) Relations with Government Authorities	Mr Brown
PART IV Constructive Administration	
(a) Imparting and Maintaining Vitality	Mr Harvey
(b) Adaptation to Economic Change	Mr Slater
(c) Adaptation to Technological Change	Brig. Cornwall-Jones
PART V The Administrator	Brig. Cornwall-Jones
Other Subjects	
Biographies	Brig. Cornwall-Jones
The Use of Figures in Administration	Mr Slater
The Use of Sources of Current Information	Brig. Cornwall-Jones
Special Subject	Brig. Cornwall-Jones

*Members having similar skills and vocational interest will be grouped together in specialist syndicates to consider a selection of these subjects, the choice of subject depending on the composition of each session. Each member will attend one only of such syndicates.

We had many problems in getting together the course of studies for session 1.

One problem, which was to recur in Pakistan and the Philippines, was the question of documentation. Given that the men would be strong in experience of their own, given that they would get new ideas and new attitudes from the thirty or forty visitors who would come and contribute to their work, and from the many types of organisation they would visit from time to time, they would still need to have books and journals. What was required was not a large library – forty men in three months cannot, and in practice will not, read for more than about three hours per day at most, and some of them, who have lost the habit of reading, would find real difficulty in doing even that. What was required, rather, was that the library should contain enough books or pamphlets or articles on every subject to satisfy ten men's reading at the rate of about three hours a day; that it should be of good quality and relevant; that it should be continually refreshed by getting new thought in and throwing old thought out; and that there should be enough copies to satisfy four syndicates at work on the same task at the same time. In practice, too, there usually developed a need for specially prepared material that would enable members to get down to business quickly because the kind of material needed was very often not readily available.

To collect a small library of this quality is a formidable task which obviously could not be accomplished in the time we had before the first session. We just had to do our best and in Australia this was not easy. We had the Henley reading lists, which gave a pointer to some of the books which might be useful; we had the minds of the principal and his staff, who knew their own fields and what Australian documents were available; we had the booksellers in the widely scattered main cities; and we had the libraries, which might be persuaded to lend. Anything else – in the USA or UK, for example – would take at least three months to reach us.

Time was a real obstacle here. What actually happened was that we used our wits and got what we could by searching the bookshops and borrowing from the libraries for session 1, while ordering what we wanted from overseas in the hope that it would arrive in time for session 2. I had a particularly difficult problem in finding the necessary books to support syndicate studies in biography when we wanted to be able to offer each syndicate a choice of several alternative characters. Each, whether chosen or not, had to be supported by sufficient books to provide ten men with a diversity of opinion on the individual, and these took a lot of finding. In the end we did not do too badly, though the pioneers of session 1 had to put up with some rather scruffy reading lists. We found a lady and got a librarian to train her in her job, and the service was pretty good. I had visions of a mass of reading matter scattered all over the floor of the Quiet Room as Margot Lamidey classified and catalogued frantically against the clock in the last few days.

We had a bit of trouble over the secretarial staff that would be needed to service the course of studies. Nobody could quite see why we needed four or five ladies, or how much the course would depend on them. However, as the documentation began to roll out and everybody came to see how important it was that this should be immaculately presented to members, this sorted itself out. I was very lucky in getting a first-class secretary in Miss Lola Brick, who was appointed course of studies secretary and was my right hand throughout my assignment as director of studies. She picked up the work very quickly and superintended the production of all the paper in a way that surprised sessions 1 and 2. Our aim was to have most of the subjects ready before the session started so that we would be free to give our full time to members.

As all the work of the course of studies went on and as we dealt also with the other problems involved in getting the college started we found time to talk over our jobs as syndicate leaders when the session arrived. In Australia the syndicate DS was referred to as syndicate leader. I am not going to repeat the full description of this which I gave in chapter 1. We were embarked on the first part of the syndicate leader's role in preparing the course of studies, and the Australians were finding out for themselves what was involved and, incidentally, seeing what the director of studies might do at this stage.

The all-important role of the syndicate leaders in relation to their own syndicates was also as described for Henley. The essentials, which one could get over so much better when one talked, were as follows.

The role was positive and not negative. Members were in charge of their own business, had to know what was required of them and what the college gave them to help them do the job; they looked to their appointed chairman to make all this clear and to tell them how he suggested they might set about it. The chairman was then in charge. The syndicate leader would be concerned to encourage initiative in the individual and in the group, to offer ideas on the problems that the group ought to be considering if they ran dry, to put them on the rails if they left them and took too long getting back, to challenge their ideas when this seemed necessary, to help them when they got stuck and generally to make the members feel that this was their session and their opportunity. They would have to discover for themselves when it would be wise to be active and when passive. They would find that they could help quite a lot in formal syndicate if their working relationships with the group were healthy, but that it would often be wiser to proffer help to chairmen and individuals outside the syndicate room in spare time, particularly when things were going awry and there was undue tension in the air.

Despite the pressures on us, or perhaps because of them, we were – in general – ready for the opening day. However, there was plenty to do as 6 September approached.

The last few days before the opening day

There was always a lot of detailed work to be done and these few days were no exception. The early subjects and other papers had to be in the hands of the typists and would be rolling out in their final form. There might still be two vacancies – there was one on session 1 – so we did not know the precise composition of the session until about a week before it started. Once this was firmly settled members could be allotted to bedrooms, some of which were large and had to be shared, who would share with whom arranged, and everything got ready on the domestic side. Arrival points would be known, and transportation arrangements made to fetch members from these points.

There was also a job to do which could take up to four days and could only be done by one mind. I shut myself away with the nomination forms and all the notes we had made at interview about each individual, produced the first draft for my colleagues to look at and to see which members I had allotted to their syndicates. They would have to look at them, needed to be satisfied that they had a really balanced group and that each member got a square deal in terms of the responsibilities that I had laid upon them. This last point would be extremely important to members, who would look at the results and miss nothing when they came to see how much it mattered.

There were a few simple rules to observe in settling the composition of the syndicates, each of which was to be a microcosm of the session of forty so far as this was possible. There had to be men from government, semi-government and private enterprise in each group. There were a number of Commonwealth and state representatives, who had to be shared out among the syndicates, and there had to be at least one in each. The available number of representatives from the private sector had to be shared, again as equally as possible, and each syndicate had to have its share of the available specialists (production, marketing, accountants, etc.). Overall the men coming from the different states had to be distributed as evenly as possible in the four groups. Perhaps the most difficult problem of all was to see that there was a fair balance between the syndicates in terms of capacity and quality. The draft, once settled with syndicate leaders, became the 'ordinary syndicates' and the basis for the remaining preparations.

There were rules, too, in allocating chairmanships and secretaryships. Not all the subjects in the course were of the same weight in terms of workload or of the same character in terms of demand on the syndicate officials. Some were heavy and others were lighter. Some required that the views of the group be crystallised in reports, some required the chairman to render account for the groups' work in a formal speech before the college; other subjects called for conference on the substance with no papers at all. Some came early and some late, and there were not enough to allow everyone a second chance. So there had to be some priorities in making the assignments and the director of studies had to be given a good deal of discretion. Broadly, each member had to be given one substantial chairmanship in his own syndicate and one secretaryship demanding the preparation of a report; no two members were to be called upon to work together as chairman and secretary more than once; syndicate officials should not be called upon to hold two offices at the same time; chairmen should be appointed to subjects in which they did not have experience. The task of assigning duties to ten men in four separate syndicates on the basis of priorities like these was an intricate staff job which took quite a lot of time and consultation. I did it for the first two sessions and so gave my Australian colleagues plenty of opportunity to find out what was important and what was not during those early sessions, thus to equip themselves to do it when I went away.

There were a few other papers which had to be issued centrally at the beginning and put together for members with the lists which emerged from the above arrangements. There was a college timetable, which would tell members what they would be doing throughout their three months; a note describing their jobs as chairmen and secretaries; and a kind of *Who's Who* telling them who we were on the staff.

These, with the papers for the first couple of subjects, were in their rooms when they arrived – just enough to show we meant business and were ready for them, and not too much to put them off. There would be an opening dinner that night at which the principal would speak, and thereafter we would get the men down to work with the minimum possible delay. That was the plan. The builders went out the back door as the first member arrived at the front, and we hoped we looked as if we had been running a Staff College for years.

I had found out a few things about Australians by then. I found, for instance, that if I took a step forward they would come a mile towards me but woe betide me if I stood still or drew back. I had found out that I could call Mr George Smith either Mr Smith or George but not Smith. And I think I got the idea one morning just before session 1 when I came in at the back door bent on something or other. A chap I knew was on his knees polishing the floor. He looked up and said, 'Hello C-J, how are you this morning?' I had a quarter of a split second in which to react. Goodness knows what I said but I knew it was all right. I had discovered one of the great delights of living in Australia.

Session 1 in operation

When the members came in on the opening day of the first session – a Friday evening – our overwhelming feeling was one of relief. At last, after all the preparations, the enterprise assumed the air of reality for which it had been created. The building became alive and was no longer a shell. From now on we would be concerned primarily with people and not only with ideas. We had slipped our moorings. The engines were turning. We were at sea.

The situation, of course, was not without its tensions. We knew very well, for instance, that everybody in the place would be wondering whether this new enterprise was really worth taking seriously and that a good many of them had been sent on the first session mainly to find this out. We knew that it would be quite some time before the group could become accustomed to the kind of work they were going to be asked to do and that there would be a tricky period while they were assessing the idea. We had yet to see whether an Australian group would accept it. The whole concept on which the original sponsors and the council had spent so much time, energy and money was to be put to the test.

I do not think this worried us excessively. We knew that the group was a good one and that the session would take a little time to discover that the work we had prepared for them, the way we contemplated they should do it and the overall experience they would get, were all relevant and would gradually be seen to be relevant. We were ready to spend a little time explaining the course and method to them on the first Saturday morning, but had them down to work the same afternoon. We had no doubt that Sir Douglas would strike fire into the group if that were necessary. We believed that we could capture their interest and, with that, their participation.

As to whether or not the college succeeded in capturing these in the first two sessions at Mount Eliza, the reader might perhaps be helped in forming an opinion of his own from the last two sub-sections of this chapter. I have no doubt in my own mind at all, but will confine myself here to a broad description of the opportunities the members of session 1 were given to improve their understanding of the nature and implications of the changes which were already taking place in their environment and to acquire fresh attitudes of mind. Thereafter, in the next section I shall switch to a report of a member of session 2 in which he describes the experience he had in passing through that second session in 1958. Together these may give the reader some further insight into the nature and purpose of the Australian Administrative Staff College and the relationship between content and method in its early course of studies.

On the first Sunday evening, Sir Douglas made his opening impact as the very definite leader of the college, and made it quite clear that the co-operation of the members was essential to the success of the work. The late Sir Richard Boyer, Chairman of the Australian Broadcasting Commission, had travelled from Sydney to give the session its first talk and to answer any questions they cared to put to him. He had given an excellent address and sat down to await questions – to find himself confronted with silence. This, to me, was quite a normal phenomenon at the first talk – the members usually take a minute or two before they take the floor– but Sir Douglas would have none of it. Down the meeting room from the chairman's table came the powerful voice of the principal,

'What's *wrong* with you?', and the session went into action! We all leaned heavily on Sir Douglas and his personality in session 1, and if there was anyone who brought the session through the first difficult period when the members were sizing up the college it was he. This, I suppose, is what principals are paid for, but it is good to work under this kind of lead.

Indeed, it was not long before Sir Douglas showed quite clearly that he would play a major part in creating the atmosphere in which change could be viewed as a part, and an exciting part, of Australian life. In his own field of economics, where he was a master, he may have been dogmatic and may have been unwilling to accept the challenge of other men's ideas, but the members forgave him this because he was throughout so genuinely and temperamentally concerned to challenge everybody and everything else. He proclaimed constantly that the world was the members' oyster ready to be swallowed by any Australian who sought adventure. He believed in an expanding Australia and saw the future of the country in proud and vivid terms. He was a pioneer himself and expected everyone else to be one too. He enjoyed the flavour of new things and did not suffer fools gladly. He was a challenge himself.

Session 1 unfolds

Part I of the course of studies was designed to start the process of persuading the members to describe their own knowledge and experience and get it into perspective by comparing it with that of their colleagues. It was an introductory exercise which demonstrated in a practical way the fact that the method would demand the participation of the individual – the exercise could not be done without it – and it started the group reflecting on the past and the present, which alone could provide the basis for the consideration in later subjects of current and future change. Its success, as in all subjects and particularly in this first, hinged mainly upon the quality of the chairmen and the willingness of the members to co-operate. We had taken some pains in selecting the former and, in spite of the doubts and wonderings inherent in the early days, we got the latter.

In most subjects in the next two parts of the course, the demand was that the examination of current roles, responsibilities, policy and practice should be critical and projected into the future. The individual subject 'tasks' persistently invited members to consider current and potential change and its implications, both in the internal administration of the undertakings represented in the syndicate (Part II) and in their relationships with other people, groups and institutions outside their control (Part III).

In Part II, for example, there was the opportunity to examine and compare the effectiveness of their own internal managements; the effectiveness of their employment policies and practices; of their efforts to organise work, to divide it up and reintegrate it; to delegate authority and reconcile this with control; to ensure that information passed up and down and across; to assess performance and keep relationships harmonious over time. This, of course, was ground with which the members were familiar, but not quite so familiar as they first thought, and which, therefore, kept them at a stretch. This was the more so because they were called upon to consider whether what they were doing could not be done better in both today's and tomorrow's circumstances. The fact that change was inherent in the work situations from which the members came of course conditioned their minds to this approach, but the fact that the college demanded they look into the future introduced an element of compulsion which insisted they take the opportunity they were offered. They could hardly avoid taking it.

Straddling Parts II and III was a series of 'specialist subjects': Production and Personnel in Part II, and Marketing and Finance in Part III. The specialists in these fields of work were grouped together to examine their own policies and practices, to draw the attention of the rest of the session to the main features in it which they thought were important and then face the latter's criticism. The intention was to give the specialists the opportunity to compare their own approaches to their own problems and then expose in college conference the areas of potential difficulty and conflict where co-ordination and integration were most likely to be needed from general management. The opportunity to recognise the need for change lay in the process of comparison which took place in the specialist syndicates and later in the college conferences.

The success of the process and the ability of the different kinds of specialists to see the motes in their own eyes as well as the beams in the eyes of their opposite numbers lay in the competence and numerical strength of the different specialists available in the session – in fact, in the response we had from our nominators and the ability we had to pick and choose candidates and so build up the kind of session and syndicates we wanted. The number of candidates required to make this possible in the early days of any college are seldom forthcoming and it is therefore seldom possible to get the balance one wants in specialists.

Thus, in session 1 in Mount Eliza, there was a lack of balance. Finance was strongly represented because from the first the banks and insurance companies supported the college strongly. There were enough men with experience in production and in accountancy and a few with experience in personnel work but we had not, as I have already said, succeeded in getting enough marketing men; and there were no people from research and development or from purchasing. The full sharpness of contrast and challenge which springs from a session in which the main specialists are represented in balanced proportions was therefore a little lacking. But this was marginal and the morale carried the members over this weakness in the structure of the group.

In the rest of Part III, the session was called upon to enter a wider field of inquiry, which introduced a broad concept of change. The opportunity, for instance, to examine the industrial-relations situation in its social and economic perspective, and to see what could be done to improve the relations between management and organised labour, was a study in change itself – how in the national interest to change a situation in which both seemed so often to find themselves on different sides. We were lucky in having men in the session who understood the strengths and weaknesses of the system in which industrial disputes could be settled or brought to conciliation or arbitration, others who had practical experience of trying to make it work, and those who came fresh to the subject and were well placed to challenge established attitudes.

In III(c), where the members were asked to examine the relations between business and Government and see what could be done to improve them, the challenge to change was a national as well as an industrial one. Here again there were men on both sides sufficiently equipped to probe a field which to many was new and who were perfectly willing to expose any inadequacies if they could find them. This is a difficult field at the pioneering stage when a college is itself exploring but we had one of those strokes of luck that one sometimes needs to set things alight. A Government speaker had taken the trouble to come from Canberra to talk on the subject. He had carefully prepared his talk, too – as indeed did 90 per cent of our speakers – and produced evidence to show that the Government had failed in its efforts to extract from industry advice which they wanted on a highly controversial and exceptionally important trade treaty which was, at the time of the session, under debate in the Federal Parliament. They had gone to the right place, given industry plenty of time and got no answer at all. The thought that their own house was not in order, that Government could not get industrial advice on a matter which everyone could see was of national importance, set the private-sector men right back on their heels. What was more important, it raised the level of thinking of the group and made them see that there *was* a need for change and that they were involved in it.

In Part IV, where the members were required to do a series of exercises in the handling of different kinds of change in the private sector, the opportunities to understand and exploit the changing environment in which they worked, as well as its implications for their thought and action on the job, were a major part of the whole idea. For instance, it was quite a shock for Australians to discover in 1957, when the whole country was surging forward, that there were occasions when continued success could breed complacency and subtly undermine vitality, and that general management ought consciously to plan to deal with them. It may have been a little unreal to separate the study of the implications of economic change from those of technological innovation as these so often go together, but there were difficult exercises in planning which made them think of the different forms change could take. The culminating 'special subject' in which the members were asked to examine the development of Australia over the next ten years was devoted to a study of selected areas of growth where change with changing circumstances was the main part of the problem. Its relevance was so apparent that it ceased to be a 'special' subject and was quickly absorbed into the permanent structure of the course.

These opportunities to understand the meaning of change and to work on its implications were supported substantially in several ways, a description of which will help to illustrate the dynamics of session 1.

Discipline

There was a discipline in the session from the start but the nature of it needs to be understood. The college laid down few rules. The members were asked always to be punctual, to accept the guidance of their syndicate leaders on matters of college procedure, of the administrative staff on matters of domestic convenience, and they were advised to remain in residence and make full use of their time except when they were away on long weekends – but otherwise little else was said.

If problems arose, as they sometimes did, the principle on which we worked was to explain the circumstances and work out the best solution with the members, leaving it wherever we could to them to decide what should be done.

But there were *built-in* disciplines which the members discovered for themselves. Each subject was done under a measure of pressure and there was always a number of subjects running concurrently under different chairmen, so the members soon found out that the schedule demanded careful planning of the work of both the group and the individual. As chairman the individual required the co-operation of his colleagues, which he would not get unless he was prepared to reciprocate when the role was reversed. Each subject had a deadline for completion, which demanded that the group focus its ideas without wasting time, and there was a tempo in the work. Except in the specialist syndicates, when each worked on separate tasks, all four syndicates were always working on the same subject and there was an element of competition between them. All groups were called upon to render account in plenary meetings for what they had done and there was sanction to the authority of the chairman. And, of course, the syndicate leader was present most of the time in syndicate and the principal in plenary meetings to lend challenge to their thinking and performance. All these things contributed to the discipline but it was not an imposed discipline. The discipline came from the members themselves. The test through which they came was that they maintained it.

Contributing visitors

Within this framework of discipline, one of the supporting features was the range of visitors invited to contribute to the work. The first category were men who came to offer their knowledge and experience to the session when it was working in a field in which the visitor was competent to speak. These people, who were more senior than the members and could talk with authority, added much to the session's knowledge and understanding but also did more: they brought their own personalities and their own attitudes as well as their views, and added to the vitality of the session. There were twenty-three of them in session 1, and they appeared at the average rate of about three per week, and always at a time which had been planned to fit in with the need. They were remarkably good at meeting the college's wishes in this respect. The members were on test in their handling of them because there was no reason why they should agree with the views they were offered. They often wanted to argue the toss with an individual who might or might not appreciate the process. I watched them all take advantage of this and learn how much could be got from these visitors if they handled them well. All the visitors were an indispensable asset to the session.

Another type of visitor was a man, usually a specialist, whose assistance was needed on some aspect of a particular subject. These syndicate visitors, and there were five of them who appeared from time to time during session 1, did not come to deliver prepared talks. They were invited to come and spend an hour and a half, or three-quarters of an hour, with each syndicate in turn and place their experience at the disposal of each group. The members knew what the visitor's field of experience was and had to prepare themselves to make the best use of busy men who had spared a day to help. This, too, was quite a test for the members because it is not always easy to set a man at his ease quickly and get him to give you what you want to take, particularly, perhaps, if he is a specialist who has a message he wants to get over himself. These visitors added to the members' knowledge and understanding, but their function really was more to let the members have the experience of meeting different specialists and to have the chance to practise their skills in handling them. They added variety to the course and hence a further stimulus to session 1.

The seminars – the series of eight talks given by Sir Douglas on Australia and the world economy – and the series of twelve talks given mainly by Harry Slater on the use and limitation of figures in management, were basically instruction intended to add knowledge and understanding that the members would need for the subjects in the latter half of the course. But they were much more than this. Spread out over the first seven weeks of the course, they gave the session two demonstrations of clear, logical and connected thought, each with its own continuity, which added considerable strength to a course which otherwise was meant to test the capacity of the members to move from one thing to another rapidly and without confusion.

The documentation of the various subjects was intended to support the members' attack on the course, introduce them to new ideas, give them the chance to discriminate between relevant and irrelevant material, and coax members back to reading if need be. For this kind of course it should be good, the quality and relevance being more important than the quantity, which should, nevertheless, be enough. The latest good thinking must be available. As I have said earlier, this is a difficult standard to attain or maintain at any time and it has to be remembered that this was 1957 when there was far less material available than there is now. But there was a cry, which still lingers in my ears, that we should try to gear the reading closer to the work we asked the members to do. Mature men with only three months to spare do not want to waste time researching like under-graduates. They want material on which they can get quickly to work.

Social life

There was, of course, a social side to life in session 1, which was as indispensable to health as it was to the members' attitude to their work. We had two tennis courts in the grounds and two golf courses nearby and many others within striking distance. We had the sea at our feet when it warmed up in the spring. We had the Buttery where we could get a drink now and again. There is no need to say how session 1 used these amenities, except that they did so thoroughly and never lost an opportunity. As a means of ironing out personal difficulties, of getting men to know each other better by meeting 'off parade', of releasing tensions and of keeping session 1 fresh, all these played a strong part in support of the work. There was, because of them and of the three long weekends, a balance in the life the members led.

Assessing performance

The prime opportunity the members had to assess their own attitudes lay in syndicate, where the individual had the chance to assess his own knowledge and experience and his own capacity to deal with people against those of his colleagues.

It was, I think, much more of a shock than most people realise for an individual, in Australia as in any other country that I know of, to find himself confronted with nine other competent men with whom he had to live and work for the greater part of three months. He had, of course, the strength of his own knowledge and experience, he had his own ways of dealing with people and he had his own convictions and confidence. But he did not know how these would measure up to those of his colleagues. This he had to find out for himself, and it was because there was so much for him to learn in the process of finding out that so much time was spent in syndicate.

Syndicate work

Life and work in syndicate revolved around the chairmen, who were appointed by the college and made responsible for managing the various subjects and rendering account for the results of their group's work in plenary session. Chairmen received their tasks from their syndicate leaders, were responsible for making a plan to enable a group to get to work, and for seeing to it that the syndicate made effective use of all the resources placed at its disposal – the experience and knowledge of men in the group, the visitors who came to help in one way or another, the opportunities members had to visit other institutions, the reading material and the syndicate leaders. There were seventeen syndicate subjects in the course, so each individual had one opportunity, and seven had two opportunities, to manage his syndicate, and all had the chance to observe each other's performance as chairman and secretary as the course unfolded. The process of learning was thus continuous and gradual, as it requires to be.

As the individual found his strength so the syndicate learnt how to work together and gathered a strength of its own. As the syndicates continued to assemble in plenary meetings, so the strength of each syndicate increased and the session developed a character and strength of its own.

In syndicate the opportunities were to acquire new knowledge and understanding and to acquire and develop the skills which men need if they are to live and work in the area of general management; the acquisition of the former being very much dependent on the development of the latter. New knowledge was available in abundance in members themselves. Now it was stimulated by the visitors, the outside visits, the reading material and the staff, but all these had to be brought together by the skill which the chairman and members of a syndicate developed in working together. The syndicate acquired new understanding by struggling with established and new ideas, just as they improved their own skills by struggling with the skills which they found in their colleagues. The gradual process of acquiring new knowledge and new understanding and developing skills was fostered by the structure of the course of studies. This started the member off on ground with which he was relatively familiar and led him on over ground which gradually stretched his mind, broadened his outlook and made increasing demands on all the syndicate members. It was in this process that a member had the chance to assess his attitudes, which few, I should think, could resist.

I have already described the broad nature of the course of studies and must now turn to examine the nature of the opportunities there were to practise the skills which we thought would stand the member in good stead in the future.

Practice in skills

The fact that we had arranged to place a fairly heavy load of work on the syndicates and that there were built-in disciplines which called for co-operation between members in syndicates, meant that the individual had to organise his time. He could not prepare himself to contribute to four or five different subjects running concurrently, attend all syndicate meetings and fit all this in to his own ideas about fresh air, exercise and sleep unless he did. It was intended to be so on the basis that a man cannot presume to manage other people unless he can at least organise himself and his own day's work. The member soon found that he had to do this.

He discovered, too, that the system would not work unless the chairman took pains to plan the work of the syndicate for which he had been made responsible and make it very clear to the individual members of the syndicate what he wanted them to do and when he wanted their contributions. A member was quite prepared to work but wanted a say in the general plan of action, wanted to be given something to do and to be left to work it up for the group without too much interference; he wanted to have his say in the group's discussions and he did not want to waste time. He knew he would have his turn as chairman and soon found out that if he wished for the group's co-operation then he would stand a better chance of getting it if he co-operated himself with other chairmen. So the group gradually became a team, under some compulsions, yes, but compulsions which members could have rejected, if so minded, but didn't.

And so, too, as each man's turn to be chairman came up, he began to develop his ideas and skills in managing the affairs of the syndicate. He had no power other than the authority of his office as chairman of a group of equals and his own capacity to lead and persuade; he had the chance to practise the art of doing it himself.

He had to keep a clear head to:

divide up the work

delegate

keep control

use other people's minds

hold the balance

cope with men who tended to over-dominate the discussions

draw out the men who were reluctant to contribute

deal with the men who would exasperate the group by hanging on to a point beyond all reason

distinguish between essentials and non-essentials

decide when the time had come to reach a conclusion on the evidence available because a decision was needed

clarify a confused discussion from time to time

bring the group back to the object of the exercise when they went off at a tangent

handle conflict of opinion and discover how to narrow down an area of disagreement

get the group's views down on paper

These we thought were skills which a senior man needed but which are not written in the books. They could, however, be practised and learnt by doing them and by watching other people do them.

The opportunities the members had in syndicate were reinforced by the syndicate leader, who was present throughout most of the discussions of his own group. He, of course, accepted the view that the opportunities were primarily for the members to seize themselves and he was concerned not to impede the process of gradual learning which I have tried to describe. But he was there also to challenge and stimulate as well as guide; a good deal depended on the skill he used in making clear what was required in each task, in keeping the group on the task, in judging when to intervene and when to leave the syndicate to work its own way through, in deciding how and when to help the group or an individual, and in suggesting what they might be missing as well as challenging their attitudes. We all had some quite substantial struggles with our syndicates as the session worked its way through the three months and we all played an active part when we felt we could and should. The conditions in Moondah, where the majority of members shared bedrooms with the members of other syndicates and where the whole session lived under one roof, greatly helped us, as we learned our jobs, in preventing any syndicates becoming the 'cosy group' which is the nightmare of all syndicate leaders. I would like to think that we helped them see some of the opportunities, not only in formal working hours, but also in the talks we used to have with individuals on other occasions.

I think that if opportunities such as these are presented to mature men in the way I have suggested, then most men take them. But they do not, of course, take them all.

A member's report on session 2

Each individual member takes what he needs and what he is capable of taking, and these needs and capabilities differ in each individual; facts which make generalisations about the impact on individuals pretty well impossible. But I think that the reader who has followed me so far deserves an illustration of what this can mean. I am lucky in that I can provide him with one that shows how one member approached this business of self-assessment in the early days at Mount Eliza. This particular member was inspired to record his approach some years after the session he attended at the college, and he has authorised me to use it. I have edited it but have not changed its substance other than by eliminating his name, which I do not think it is my business to broadcast. He was one of the forty-five members of session 2 who, like the forty members of session 1, constitute in my mind the real pioneers who marched behind Sir Douglas Copland, Maurice Brown, Harry Slater and Harold Harvey. This is what that member of session 2 had to say:

'It has just struck me that I should have done this a long time ago but the present time is appropriate to rectify that omission. In substance I think it represents what I thought then but it also owes something to my subsequent experience.

The heart of the experience for the participant is the opportunity it provides for self-assessment. This, of course, has been said before, perhaps to the extent of becoming platitudinous, but it does, in practical terms, cover an enormous range of matters of considerable subtlety and complexity. They are difficult to put into words without over-simplification and they are, I am sure, different in each man's case. They don't, it seems to me, stem out of the subject matter itself, although as I shall mention later, the subject matter is by no means irrelevant.

I learned quite a lot from the subject matter, but I learned and *remembered*, and I think put into practice, a number of things about myself, other men, and myself in relation to other men. I sharpened my appreciation of the importance of integrity in business and human relations, not in a sermonising way but in terms of its practical application. Different men may place their standards in this respect at all sorts of levels but I was greatly helped towards establishing my own at a point where I could better recognise them and attempt consistently to live up to them.

One example always comes to mind here. About 1956 I remember going along with a somewhat "snide" manoeuvre suggested to me by a very much senior officer, about which I had pangs of conscience on my own account, but with which I co-operated "in the line of duty". It did not occur to me strongly enough that the institution itself should have a "conscience" about such a matter. After session 2 I think I would have seen a matter like this more clearly and may either have convinced my superior that the proposal was beneath our dignity or, if necessary, have put my own future "on the line" in deciding not to co-operate in it. In fact, in 1960, a somewhat similar episode occurred and was resolved in a way which brought credit to the institution and all of us concerned in it.

I had "my nose rubbed" in the difficulties of communication. Night after night I went to sleep pondering why those other silly devils could not see the points I was so clearly stating, and coming to the conclusion that, for my own part, I could never take this matter for granted. I thought again and again about the situation I was finding myself in – what I should have said, what I would like to have said – and I seemed to discern in myself a growing ability to say in the first instance something closer to what I should have said. This can be a cause for some self-satisfaction and increasing confidence, but I hope also that it caused a realisation that the problem never disappears, and that the characteristics of oneself and the group and the interrelationship within the group constantly throw the problem up in a different and ever-challenging way. The situation in the meeting room, at plenary sessions, provided an excellent contrast. There is a great difference when one has to prize oneself off one's backside and try to say it right the first time, with little opportunity to come back again and say "what I meant to say was . . . ", without the advantage of being able to interrupt, or take more than one's share of the time immediately available, etc. Missed opportunities to speak represent a most compelling lesson to the member.

More correctly, it was the "mix" of opportunities taken, opportunities missed, opportunities put to better or worse account, that made the lesson. The balance of this mix would seem to me to have been upset if on the one hand too much informality came in to a presentation, or on the other if there had been a regular expectation that everyone should "have his turn". If the need for courage, initiative and self-discipline on the member's part had been reduced, the exercise could have been quite a different one. The experience of the modified syndicate also hammers home communication difficulties in other ways.

As a result of my experience as a member, I am much more *convinced* of the difficulties of communication as they apply to me *personally*, I am more alert I think in recognising in *actual* situations where a group is on "different wavelengths" (for example), more conscious of the need to attempt something constructive about such difficulties, than I personally would be if I read about communication, or even taught it theoretically, perhaps for a lifetime. I convinced myself about the necessity for a group of men to submit themselves to a certain amount of disciplined planning and orderly procedure if their joint efforts are to be fruitful and constructive. What a platitude! What is a "certain amount"? Of course this is *un*certain, and one must develop one's judgment in this respect. I think I was helped towards a better judgment of "How much?" in particular situations. I was less self-conscious thereafter in trusting that judgment – for example, in deciding whether, in the interest of more effective achievement by a meeting, the degree of procedural control to which I would subscribe would be greater than individual members would "like" if left to themselves. Whilst conceding the possibility that I personally might have had, and may still have, a tendency towards "over-control", I had drummed into me the necessity for this issue to be faced up to.

I was convinced of the need for knowledge in the team and especially "grasp" in the man in charge for the time being. What does "grasp" mean? It's not knowledge, it's not intelligence, although both have an influence on it; it can't be strictly defined, and it is relative anyway, but if there's not enough of it present in the man in charge relative to the job in hand, a group flounders. Of course, everybody knew that before – in theory – but we had ample opportunity to size ourselves up in this respect, and therefore perhaps better appreciate the scope of our own management prospects as they may or may not be limited by the extent to which we displayed this essential ingredient. We should have been better fitted to look out for it and perhaps also recognise it in men we might have to select for promotion. We should have been made more confident in insisting that A, if he hasn't enough of it, should be passed over, despite his seniority, his experience, his qualifications or his being such a nice bloke. We should have been made more confident in "taking a punt" on B's other qualifications for the sake of his possession of this elusive quality.

I frequently saw demonstrated the old truism that "it takes all kinds to make a world", and how men's strengths and weaknesses can be blended to advantage or compounded to disadvantage. This is, of course, open to observation anywhere but a syndicate seemed to me to highlight it, and one thing in particular which arises from this is a confirmation that self-development does not mean making oneself over in another's image. (In my own judgment it is most important to remember always the necessity to be true to oneself in any programme of self-improvement.)

The syndicate also seemed to me to provide an excellent running case study of delegation, or lack of it, in action. We saw many informative contrasts in chairmen, ranging between instructing, delegating and defaulting, with members of the team responding in a wide range of ways. We saw things go well, we saw things go badly; we personally relished the one and suffered the other. In the microcosm of the syndicate we were admirably placed to know or discover more of the influences at work in a much more concentrated way than is normally observable. I was confronted with the subtle difference between leaving men to use their initiative and leaving things to chance.

One last point may be worth noting before trying to sum this up. I was helped towards recognising some criteria for myself in respect of the value and danger of plain speaking in a group. My natural inclinations in this respect probably call for some tempering, but in the interest of timid and underconfident members someone must do something to deflate the pompous. Again the questions arise – how much, when, how and against whom?

Summary   Each of the foregoing is I think very important in itself but the most important point is the common factor in them all – judgment about matters calling for subtle balancing. More important still is that the process operated on my judgment of my own judgment.

Where did the subject matter of the course fit into all this? I remembered a lot of it, much was reinforcement of previous knowledge, in a great deal of matters I was brought up to date. Some other members have told me that they very frequently referred back to their college papers, but I must confess that I did not often do so. When I did, I have surprised myself by realising how little of the detail in some area I had remembered. What I did not forget is the syndicate experience and its impact on me – that went on and on, and enlarged itself.

Nevertheless, the subject matter was the task on which the men were engaged. If it is not up-to-date, topical, relevant, meaningful and challenging then the syndicate and everything else in the operation won't be "fair dinkum" and the processes won't work in the same ways.

What of the function of the staff? As I saw it, the staff had most successfully "held the ring" while we fought our own battles. They occasionally joined the fray – fair enough, they're human – but if they did so in circumstances where their position served as a shield either for themselves or for other members, the battle could lose its purpose and zest. Changing the metaphor, if anything in the nature of a college doctrine had been preached, if there had been any hint that things were so because somebody in authority said they were so, if we had been told in respect of the major subjects what the answer was (or even, I think, whether our own answer was more right or wrong), responsibility in the individual members and in the syndicates would have been undermined, and the necessity for us to exercise our own judgment could have been dangerously reduced.

One notable exception in some of the foregoing comment was the principal himself, Sir Douglas. He broke a number of the "rules" as I saw them, but I generally accepted that for the sake of the inspiration he provided. Furthermore, I saw the general tone of his approach as being "anti-establishment". If it had been the other way – and this may of course merely reflect my own prejudices – I would have resented it.

One final comment about the syndicate. It was not a *conversazione*. It was not just a discussion group, although it had many of the characteristics of one. It was essentially a *competitive working* group, made up of men who were also competing with each other within the constraints of group loyalty. For me, it had a "real life" feel about it.

I cannot emphasise too strongly that the impact on myself, as I saw it, took effect in a *practical* way, arising out of the practice which I had been given in the various situations with which I had been confronted. *Participation* and *involvement* were the essence of it.'

3

EARLY LAHORE – PAKISTAN ADMINISTRATIVE STAFF COLLEGE, 1960-3

The Beginning

The setting up of the Pakistan College is marked in my mind by the differences in the environment and in the circumstances in which the college was brought into being.

There were several differences, each of which had its implications. It was to be in one of those countries which were developing; it was set up on the initiative not of the business community but of the Pakistan Government; it was to cater primarily for public servants, at least in the first instance; the Pakistan Government wanted to make use of American as well as British experience in setting it up and was in a great hurry to get it started. The fact that the country was constituted in two wings, East and West Pakistan, separated the one from the other by a thousand miles of India, was another difference which gave an added interest to the whole experience.

One Professor Roland Egger, who was engaged in 1953 on behalf of the then Prime Minister of Pakistan on a survey of public administration had discovered that a few Pakistani senior civil servants were attending the college at Henley from time to time. It seemed it was he who first suggested that the Pakistanis might look into the idea of having an Administrative Staff College of their own, and see how far they thought that Henley or indeed any other foreign institution would be suitable for their needs.

This idea was picked up a year later in 1954 when Noel Hall, on his way back from Australia, spent a few days in Karachi, at the invitation of the Pakistan Government, explaining to gatherings of civil servants what he was trying to do in Britain. The Establishment Division of the Government of Pakistan was responsible for the training of Government servants and was involved in arranging this Karachi meeting. One of their officers, Mr A.D. Shaikh, was particularly concerned and became interested. The idea that his country might find in the Henley approach ways which might help to break down some of the barriers that existed between the different public services in Pakistan began to take root in his mind, and he made it his business to meet and talk with some of the civil servants who went through Henley during the next few years. He seems to have been one of those tenacious people who do a lot of hard work a couple of rungs below the top, and can seize an opportunity and hang on to it when they believe that they are on to something important. He had been involved, in collaboration with international agencies, in the development of a six-month training course for senior Pakistani civil servants in Los Angeles and this was about to bear fruit, but the Staff College idea stuck in his mind too.

When in 1958 he had an opportunity to visit the first course in Los Angeles, he got the agreement of his Establishment Secretary to his canvassing in the United States the idea of a Staff College. He visited a great many institutions and in the course of his travels met Dean Harlan Cleveland of Syracuse University and Dr Gant of the Ford Foundation in New York; in both these quarters he found interest. He returned home to Pakistan in September 1958 just before martial law was declared. The thought there prevailed that this might be an appropriate time to get the idea of a Staff College translated into action, if it really did seem to be suitable. With the help of the Ford Foundation in Karachi, therefore, the Establishment Secretary decided to send Mr A.D. Shaikh to Henley.

Mr Sheikh joined us in January 1959 as an observer and stayed for a full session until April 1959. He was completely free to see the session in operation and to talk to anyone about anything. Noel Hall gave him generously of his time. I knew what he was about, and he discovered that I had lived in his country for many years prior to Partition and that I had only recently returned from Australia. So we naturally found mutual interests and a great deal to talk about. We could easily agree that if Pakistan were ever to have an Administrative Staff College, it would be different from Henley.

Having picked up many ideas, then, he fell to writing a weighty report which he took back with him to Pakistan. With the help of this the Pakistan Cabinet Secretariat picked out many of the essentials in the Henley approach and related them to their own circumstances in a paper in which they embodied the stage of thought which had been reached in the middle of 1959. They saw, for instance, that in Pakistan as elsewhere the prevailing social order was changing rapidly and that with it the outlook, the tone and the methods of the institutions which served society as a whole were bound to change. The pre-Independence role of government was giving place to a more dynamic participation in the social and economic development of the country. The civil servant of the day needed to be as much an active worker in the moulding of a new social order as a business magnate, an industrial tycoon or a social leader outside.

This new kind of society could only become a reality if there was close co-operation between the civil servant and the men in trade, industry and the professions. They would have to work as partners in a great venture; but the idea of simply refreshing the outlook of the senior members of the

Civil Service of Pakistan (which had replaced the old British administrative class) would not be enough. The technician and the specialist, who had so far occupied a seemingly less important position in the social order, were gaining increasing importance and were bound to occupy as important a position, if not more important, than that being held by the non-technical administrator and the generalist. The generalists would have to specialise in some spheres of public activity if they were to make their full contribution to the development of the new social fabric. There would be a greater need for technical men to learn the art of administration if they were to be able to direct the affairs of their specialist departments, and there would be a much greater need than heretofore for the specialist and the generalist to get to know each other.

One way of doing this would be to create a forum on the Henley model where the two would meet and work together. But the Pakistanis saw quickly some of the differences there would be between the forum at Henley and the forum which would be necessary to meet Pakistani needs. The vacuum that existed in the commercial and industrial sphere of activities in Pakistan was only just beginning to be filled, and the number of men in the business sector with real experience of administration and management was not to be compared with the number of senior and experienced people in the Civil Service. The ratio of 1:10 would not be far wrong and in this setting the body of men who could attend the proposed college would necessarily be composed very differently from that at Henley. In fact, the proposed Pakistan College would predominantly, if not exclusively, be a Civil Service affair in the first instance, this feature only changing gradually as the private sector developed with the general development of the country. Both the Henley course and its method of work would therefore have to be substantially adapted. The size of the sessions would be much smaller – possibly about thirty – and it might be wiser to start the college with a pilot course in rented buildings on a non-residential basis, moving later into permanent residential accommodation which would be essential if the experiment succeeded. It would be financed by the Government and should, perhaps, be in Karachi.

Thus at Cabinet Secretariat level ran the thinking by the middle of 1959. Interest was growing but the Government of Pakistan felt the need for some further assurance that they were on the right track and wanted to have the benefit of both British and American experience. They turned again then to the Ford Foundation and asked Mr Culbertson in Karachi to invite Sir Noel Hall and Dean Harlan Cleveland to visit Pakistan so that the Government would have the benefit of their advice.

During their visit, which took place between 20 January and 5 February 1960, Noel Hall and Harlan Cleveland had a full programme discussing the idea with the President, some of his ministers and senior civil servants and others. In these discussions they found much to confirm the thinking that had already taken place and felt able to fortify the Pakistan Government in the conclusions which they were in the process of forming. Observing the determination of the Government to push the modernisation of Pakistan as rapidly as material and human resources permitted, they strongly supported the view that there was a very urgent need for an expanding number of broad-based executive leaders able to mould the efforts of the increasing types of the specialist that would be needed in a society thus straining to achieve the maximum rate of change. They confirmed the Pakistani view that any senior-executive training college in Pakistan would have to be designed to meet Pakistani needs and so would differ fundamentally from apparently similar institutions elsewhere in its purpose, its clientele and in the nature and content of its programme. They suggested that the broad purpose of the Pakistan College might be:

1. To consider the administrative problems involved in carrying out the ambitious development programme to which Pakistan had pledged itself.
2. To develop Pakistani awareness of the complexity of development administration; of the dangers to the national interest of meticulous attention to rigid procedures and traditions that inhibit rapid and pervasive change; and of the importance in this whole process of Pakistani initiative and enterprise.

They went on to suggest that these purposes could only be achieved if the members in the college were so senior that most of the teaching material was within their own experience, and most of the teaching would be done by and to themselves. They agreed that special attention should be given first to the needs of public administrators, expressing the hope that, in the interests of variety, a few students from private enterprise should be included in each session from the beginning. This was in the expectation that the numbers of the latter would increase as the private sector grew under the spur of the national development programme. They drew special attention to the importance of intensive research into the administrative problems created by Pakistan's own rapid growth and change. It was suggested that the research programme should be started immediately as it would be the key to the provision of self-teaching material for the college course of studies, as well as a basis for the development of a national doctrine on development administration. They thought that the courses themselves should not be of more than three or four months duration.

On this basis, Noel Hall and Harlan Cleveland gave it as their opinion that the Pakistan Government would be wise to proceed with their idea of establishing an Administrative Staff College. To make it a success they suggested – on the basis of experience elsewhere – that a number of indispensable ingredients ought first to be satisfied, namely:

1. There should be a substantial and manifest concern at the highest possible level for the success of the work of the college.
2. The composition of its governing body should guarantee that the college would be held in high esteem and be representative not only of Government but of other active sections of the national life for which the college would increasingly cater.
3. The location of the college, whilst sufficiently withdrawn from the

more active centres of governmental and business life, should nevertheless have good communications including ready access by air. The standard of accommodation provided, while not being lavish, should be such as to command the respect of all those living at the college, whether as staff or as participants.

4. Finally, the principal of the college – a member of the governing body and answerable to it in all matters except on the details of the intellectual life of the college – should be a man who had carried substantial practical responsibilities in the past, with sufficient intellectual capacity to inspire but not intimidate, and should be recognised by the prospective participants as one more experienced than themselves. It was also important that he should command the confidence of senior members of Government and of other important sectors of the national life whose confidant he was likely to become. He should, of course, be a Pakistani.

Once these essentials had been satisfied Noel Hall and Harlan Cleveland suggested in very strong terms that the most careful preparations would be needed before the first course began. The principal would need time to select and develop his staff, get his research programme under way and prepare the necessary teaching materials, and would need to make sure that nominations for the first course would be men of the highest quality, representing the widest possible diversity of experience. Noel Hall and Harlan Cleveland offered to help in the next stage by sending a senior representative from Henley and from Syracuse to help work out the general plan and prepare an outline of the course of studies – and they would provide further longer-term help if the principal thought this desirable when the time for the first course began to draw near. They suggested that the principal himself, when appointed, might like to visit both Henley and Syracuse; and they thought that in the light of the amount of work that would have to be done the college could be ready to open its doors (after the hot weather) in October 1961.

With their emphasis on Pakistani needs and offers of help these views were welcomed. On 23 February 1960, three weeks after Noel Hall and Harlan Cleveland had left, the Pakistan Government formally approved the establishment of a Pakistan Administrative Staff College; on 10 March, decided to appoint Mr A. Khalid Malik as its first principal and asked him to take up his appointment on 1 April. By 15 March General Sheikh, Minister of the Interior, who had been appointed chairman of the Court of Governors, then being assembled, had said that he would like the college to open in the autumn of 1960 – about a year ahead of the time that Noel Hall and Harlan Cleveland had recommended. With respect for this sense of urgency, but with misgivings that other preparations might be sacrificed in the interests of speed, Mr David Clarke, the Director of Research at Henley, and Dr J. Westcott, a senior member of the faculty of Syracuse University, were asked to report to Khalid Malik in Lahore on 21 May. Their task was to help him prepare a more detailed programme.

By 9 June, after some consultation and a great deal of reading, Khalid

Malik, Sir James Hardy (the Establishment Secretary), David Clarke and Jay Westcott had prepared a memorandum which contained (a) the draft of a college handbook, (b) basic data for the formulation of a dollar budget, (c) the draft of a letter calling for nominations for the first session, which it was then thought would take place from 3 October to 23 December 1960. These documents were based on the assumptions, which were clearly stated, that substantial manpower resources would be allotted to the development of the materials for the course, including the necessary teaching materials and a number of case exercises; that the renovation of the Punjab Club in Lahore, which by then the Government hoped to acquire for the accommodation of the college, could be pursued; and that the necessary staff and consultants would assemble by 1 September 1960. The draft handbook contained a list of the members of the Court of Governors; identified the individuals who were to be recruited to the staff; set out the objectives of the college, the level of men it was proposed should be nominated and a broad outline of the course of studies and the methods of work. It proposed also the setting-up of a research department and the establishment of a library. This represented the stage of thinking in Pakistan in June 1960.

There were still misgivings, at any rate in Henley, at the importance being attached by the Pakistan Government to an early start. It was also known that David Clarke and Jay Westcott were having some difficulty in understanding each other's different approaches but I had no feeling that these were going to create undue difficulty. Khalid Malik came on his visit to the college towards the end of June, stayed a fortnight and had a good look round. With Noel Hall's agreement he invited me to join him in Pakistan on 1 September, and I said I would. He then went to Syracuse. David Clarke came back from Pakistan a few days later, on 20 July, quite clear in his mind that the Establishment Secretary believed that the course he had prepared would be welcome to the Government. So we in Henley then thought we had a working basis and, to make my date with Khalid Malik on 1 September, I went off by air on 31 August. I had to leave my wife behind to clear up. She had a busy time!

When I arrived in Karachi in the early hours of 1 September I was greeted with an invitation from Mr Culbertson to stop over for twenty-four hours in order to meet him and his staff. I was glad I did; I not only met the Ford Foundation in the flesh for the first time but I discovered, to my surprise, that Jay Westcott was there and heavily engaged in the preparation of a fresh course of studies. From Mr Culbertson I got an idea of the part being played by the Ford Foundation in the developing world and particularly in Pakistan – an impressive picture from which I also got the feeling, which was to grow, that I was welcome as a member of a large, world-wide force of people trying to help in the developing world. He made another impact on me in the way he explained the Ford Foundation's attitude to the consultants it employed to provide this help. He regarded it as his responsibility to see that I was relieved, as far as it was humanly possible, of all administrative and financial worries so that I could get on with the job I had been engaged to do. Both he and his staff, and Dr Harry L. Case and his staff in Pakistan and later in the Philippines, did everything they conceivably could to maintain this attitude of mind in practice. It was certainly not their fault if I failed to do my job.

I had not known that Jay Westcott had been working on a fresh course of studies. I had come out with the outline that David Clarke had prepared in June, and I thought it was welcome to the Pakistan Government. Differences of opinion there would be but I had no idea that another attempt had been made at a new outline. I was very surprised to find that Jay Westcott was in the process of putting together a mass of material which would be brought to Lahore in the following two or three days for presentation to a meeting of the college governors. It was useful to know this and to talk to Jay Westcott, who had been working very hard throughout the hot weather and was obviously an exhausted man.

On 4 September I went up to Lahore, got a room in Falettis Hotel and met Khalid Malik again. There were many things on the principal's mind, the two most pressing being the course of studies and an important visit by the chairman of the governing body, who was coming the next day to settle the date on which the college would open. On the former, he explained that he was unwilling to settle on the outline that had been prepared in June because he felt it did not really cater sufficiently or directly enough for the needs of the students who would be coming. He hoped that I would be happy to work on the material which Jay Westcott had prepared under his guidance and instruction. As to the meeting with General Sheikh, he warned me that the chairman might still be anxious to start on 3 October, and told me he was worried at the idea. He had one member of the Civil Service of Pakistan, a Mr Mukhtar Mahsud, who had been seconded to him primarily to help in the acquisition and renovation of the Punjab Club. He hoped that Dr Karl Schmidt, the consultant from Syracuse, would be arriving at the end of the month. But the other Pakistani members of the staff were not yet in sight and he was obviously concerned lest too early a date should be set and so prejudice the success of the session. Both he and the minister would be looking to me to help settle a date which would be both practicable and take account of the desire of the Government to waste no time. He gave me a copy of Jay Westcott's outline, which I understood was to be followed by the supporting material in time for the governors on 7 September, and asked me to think it over. So I took it home.

It was hard for me to identify in Jay Westcott's outline the makings of a three-month course for mature men. It might be a list of lecture headings, in which case it would make no sense to me – who hoped to see a course in which members would themselves play a major part in the management of subjects of a different kind and one with not too much lecturing. If it was intended as a list of headings for subjects, using the word 'subject' as we used it at Henley and Mount Eliza, there was a huge job ahead of us in hammering the pieces into a different shape. I just did not believe that this could be done in the four months we had before the first session, and I doubted whether the result could be fitted into the three months we had for the course – much more like six months would be needed. But I must confess it was all very strange to me coming as it did from the mind of a professor who probably thought differently about the way we might help Pakistanis in the development of their maturing managers. Given freedom to knock headings about into subjects manageable by member chairmen, however – and Khalid Malik seemed willing to give me my head on this – I thought I could at least have a first shot at giving him what he wanted: 'A course that *was* about the issues facing Pakistani administrators/managers and that looked to the Pakistanis as if it was.' The question then became, 'Could I possibly do it?' I had never before set about preparing a new course from scratch.

General Sheikh was straightforward and fair when we met the following evening. He said he had been wondering whether it would not perhaps be rushing things a bit if he insisted on 3 October as the starting date, and asked Khalid Malik and me to say what we thought. I explained that this course material was completely new to me and that I would have a great deal to do in mastering the ideas in it and the rest of the material when it arrived from Karachi. I would have to break it all up into manageable subjects and would need at least a couple of extra months. Khalid Malik said that this made sense to him, particularly as his American consultant could not arrive before the end of September and would need to be involved in all this, and there was still so much to be done to the building. Then General Sheikh took the matter into his own hands and said that he would recommend to the board that 1 January should be the starting date.

At the time I thought it would be nonsense to press for more time. President Ayub Khan's Government was on the move and there was a real sense of urgency in the air. This was a tide which had to be taken at its flood. I have had a long time to think about it since that day. On balance, I still believe it to have been right. Meanwhile, it was good to be back in Pakistan after twenty years' absence. It was hot, it was dusty, but I was among people whom I regarded as friends, to whom I owed a lot. There were peons and bearers and khitmadgars, squash and billiard markers, malis, and all the rest; and I found my Urdu was still usable.

Getting staff and nominations

This was difficult in Pakistan. Good men were, of course, in short supply as everywhere else; they were particularly difficult to spare in the developing world because there was so much to be done. Some nominators, to whom the idea of developing responsible men in some kind of training institution was new, must have doubted whether they ought to be spared from the urgent tasks in hand. Some of the men themselves I knew were reluctant to leave work which they could see was important, and a few felt that there was a danger they might lose their jobs if they left them for even three months, let alone the few years for which a member of staff might be required. These factors were real in the public sector. They were real, too, in the private sector though in this the main problem was that private enterprise was too young and too undeveloped to nominate more than a very few candidates to the college. Most Pakistani firms in the East and in the West were family concerns struggling to establish themselves and quite unable to spare for a course the one or two men they had at or near the top. So, in getting his staff and candidates, Khalid Malik had to contend with some pretty real difficulties throughout my stay in Lahore.

Directing staff

When he had been in Henley, Khalid Malik had understood that he was going to get three first-class men; two of them would be general administrators of a quality which would command respect at once. He knew their names, and he knew the men. They would be able to master the essentials in the problems on which members would be asked to work and, with their experience, their characters and their personalities, would be well able to handle members in their syndicates. The third man was to be a competent research consultant who, it was hoped, would help lay the foundation for research which the college would need to do.

This looked like a good start but as the time drew near all three of these men, one by one, slipped from his grasp. Two were appointed elsewhere by the Government to work which, I can only suppose, was held to be more important, and the third (research) man after a lot of hesitation turned down the appointment and eventually went abroad. So, very late in the preparatory period, in the autumn of 1960 when we were all too near the opening date, Khalid Malik had to start all over again. Eventually Mr Hassan Habib and Mr Sibte Haider were appointed and arrived just before the first session started. Both came at extremely short notice, Sibte Haider having been instructed to join in circumstances hardly likely to induce any feeling of commitment to the college. The former brought twenty years of experience in the teaching of economics, in research and in the administration of education, while Mr Haider brought eighteen years of varied experience in administration centred mainly round agriculture and industry, and in the development of organisation and methods. So it was hard on these men, as well as on the principal, that they arrived too late to take part in the preparations for the first course. Khalid Malik had to rely on his foreign consultants to hammer out his first course of studies.

Members

Khalid Malik took sole charge of the admission of members to the college and set out originally to secure a group of thirty. Within this figure he thought he would be lucky if he could get four or five from the private sector; the remainder would come from the Government and public corporations. The basic qualification of admission was to be 'not academic distinction but practical experience'. The age bracket was to lie between 35 and 45. Selection was to depend on 'availability, suitability and the requirement of the college that there should be a well-balanced mixture of members with different working experience and from different regions'. All nominations were to be subject to the principal's approval and, where necessary, candidates were to be interviewed by him.

Quite early in the race towards the starting date, a decision was taken to reduce the number to be sought in each session from thirty to twenty. This was a shock to me, which I just had to take on the chin. It derived, as I understood it, partly from the thinking that it might be wise to start this experiment with a smaller group but more I believe because the Government came up against the real difficulty in getting nominations.

In the event the composition of the sessions over the first five sessions was not very different from what Khalid Malik seemed to be expecting. The best men were very good indeed; they had a wealth of experience, and the personality and the will to make use of the opportunities they found; and they had a willingness to help others. The bulk of the remainder were middle-of-the-road men; their experience was varied, as we wanted it to be, and they had the intelligence and the will to make use of the opportunities they found. The mixture was very good: East and West Pakistan were always represented not in equal proportions but in fair proportion given the number and level of administrators available in each of the two wings. There were not enough specialists because there were not enough about at the time, but the few specialists there were were vocal enough to strike sparks out of the generalists and demonstrate the need to close the gap in their understanding of each other and each other's role in a changing society. Occasionally a nomination came from the army and sometimes from a political background. Gradually Sindhi and Baluchi members joined the Pathans, Punjabis and Bengalis. The private sector had shown us a glimpse of the contribution it could make to the college when it was sufficiently established to nominate more men to take part.

During my stay I thought that this quality of session, small as it was, added up to a good investment of members' time but it was not a situation with which I was content. I did not like the process through which candidates were obtained or accepted, and I do not think that we as a college did enough to improve the quality of the candidates. Later on I shall have something more to say about the process of nominations, which is such a critical part of a successful Staff College. For the time being and for the working up of the course of studies, we had to work with what we had.

The development of the course of studies

I was with the Pakistani College for its first five sessions and just had a glimpse of session 6 before I left in 1963. To attempt to describe each of the courses for these five sessions would be quite outside the scope of this account. What I will try to do is to show the character of the first course and the reason why it appeared in this shape, and then go on to set out the major changes which were subsequently introduced in my time, which I hope will demonstrate the kind of balance Khalid Malik and his Pakistani staff seemed gradually to want from the British and American consultants they had engaged.

The course for session 1

Khalid Malik and I were alone at the beginning. We worked at the opposite ends of a large room. We were accessible to each other. We had no personal difficulties in working together either in this very early period or indeed at any time during my stay in Lahore so we could, and I think we did, share each other's thoughts on the development of the course as we went along.

We hoped (to say 'we assumed' would, I sensed at the time, be using too strong a word for Khalid Malik) that the members who would be nominated would be 'so senior that most of the material would be within their experience and most of the teaching would be done by or to themselves'. We assumed, and here the word is fair enough, that the sessions would be composed of members who would come mostly from the public services including the public corporations and that there was to be only a trickle of men from private industry and commerce. We first expected that there would be thirty on each session though this was reduced to twenty some time before the first session started. It was comforting to hear Khalid Malik say that there would be no difficulty in obtaining the assistance we would need from the administrative community outside.

On this basis I set about the first design of the first course. I brought to it my Henley ideas. I thought we should be concerned primarily with the personal development of the individual, and that this would mean trying to give him a better understanding of his country's problems, of what the Government was aiming to get done in the second Five-Year Plan; to give him a better perspective to think about the part that his own ministry department or corporation was playing in this Five-Year Plan and of his own personal part in it; to give him a better understanding of other people and their problems as a contribution to the immense co-operative effort on which the Five-Year Plan and so much of their country's future would depend. The course would have to challenge his experience and his attitudes of mind, give him fresh ideas and a much better understanding of himself which he would transmit to others, particularly his subordinates. Clearly in slanting the course towards the public service, as was expected of us, it would be imperative, if private enterprise as it developed was ever to become a real partner on a substantial basis, that there would have to be from the beginning a real attraction for private-sector men in the course.

There was nothing in this, that I could see, which conflicted with anything I had seen written about the purposes of the Pakistan College. Of what I was less certain, as my ideas of the course began to take shape, was whether all of what we began to think we wanted to do would be suitable to Pakistani needs.

The first thing, I thought, was to try and identify the main issues with which the senior administrators of the day were having to cope and which therefore our members should be asked to examine critically. There was a great deal of material which contained these issues and which I therefore had to read. There was the huge pile of paper which had come up in support of Jay Westcott's outline. There was the second Five-Year Plan itself, which was no mean volume, and there was the range of reports of specially-appointed Commissions examining the issues which President Ayub Khan's Revolutionary Government had set up with an eye on urgent reforms. It was from these sources in the first place that I began to collect the substance for this first course. It meant reading far into the night; but reading was not the only source.

In Lahore itself there were a great many senior administrators as it was the headquarters of the West Pakistan Provincial Government. The city was even then showing the beginnings of commercial and industrial development. All over the country, working for Pakistan, there was a host of expatriate consultants with keen minds and a deep interest in the prospect of change in the attitude of mind of Government servants. Almost everybody was willing to help when they found out what I was interested in, and I began to meet them. They did much to augment the flow of ideas and support or reject them as they emerged. Again they took a heavy toll of one's time.

Then, in the college when we had difficulty in identifying or working up the different subjects as they crystallised in our minds, Khalid Malik would invite senior men to come to the college and talk things over. He would get someone to come up from Karachi and stay a night to discuss a particularly difficult issue. He would make dates for me to go and see someone, and as I became more and more familiar with Lahore I made contacts and appointments of my own. It was a pretty rough month but by 5 October, when Karl Schmidt was expected to arrive, we had a rough outline of the course of studies ready as a basis for discussion. When Karl Schmidt did come it was not his fault that he never made 1 September. What I do know is that as soon as he found out when he was wanted, he uprooted his family and appeared in Lahore as quickly as he could.

Of course he did not like the outline which I had produced at all and in an ideal world, I am sure, would have liked to have started again from scratch. However, by this time it was clear to all of us that there was no chance of making radical changes in the work that had already been done if the college was to be opened by the end of the year. The outline Khalid Malik and I had drawn up had to be accepted and worked up for the course of session 1 as best as Karl Schmidt and I could manage. He assumed responsibility for the subjects in which he was interested as a political scientist, namely the main problems of national development, the three subjects on measures for the promotion of economic growth, on financial control, budgeting and accounting, organisation for development, and the planning and execution of development schemes. I retained those which interested me: key problems in education, the selection, training and promotion of men for senior executive posts, basic democracies and village-aid, accountability and relationships in the public services, the corporation as an organisational device for development, adaptation to change, food and agriculture, industry and the role of the administrator. With this division we could then go ahead with some measure of independence, which alone allowed us to work fast.

Interspersed with the problems we had in reading material, inviting speakers, ordering and receiving books and equipment, organising reading lists and outside visits, shaking the various subjects out into a programme, and settling down domestically, our days and a good deal of our nights were pretty hectic. But by 23 December 1960, which was the actual date that session 1 eventually started, we could present the members with the following:

NOTES ON THE COURSE

1. The objects of the college, as described in the handbook, are to provide the opportunity for senior executives to obtain a better understanding of the new vigorous environment in which they work, study the administrative problems involved in the National Development programme to which Pakistan is dedicated, examine some of the individual plans and projects now under way, and to develop their awareness of the complexity of development administration and the importance in this whole process of personal initiative and enterprise.
2. The course of studies and the methods of work have been designed to assist members to achieve these objectives.

I   The course of studies

3. In designing and selecting the subjects for study, the college has had to choose from a wide field. For the first session, the course of studies will be as follows:

Part I   National Development
4. This will be an introductory examination of the aims of national development and some of the main problems it raises.

Part II   Use of National Resources
5. This part will provide the opportunity of examining a selected range of important fields where it is essential that the best possible use should be made of available and potential national resources. The particular subjects selected for syndicate studies are all concerned with the use of human resources and will be:

II(a) : Key problems in education.
II(b) : The selection, training and promotion of men for senior executive posts.

II(c) : Basic democracies and village-aid.

In addition, under this heading there will be the opportunity to talk over with senior men of experience the use of natural resources and the application of science to the current and future development of these.

Part III Economic Measures for Promoting Growth

6. This part provides the opportunity for members to secure a background understanding of the principal economic policies which affect them as administrators. The subjects selected for syndicate study are:

III(a) : Policy alternatives for developing the economy.
III(b) : Resource allocation and its impact.
III(c) : Taxation policy and administration for development.

In addition, under this heading there will be the opportunity of discussing with a senior and experienced speaker monetary and fiscal policy and measures to achieve economic stabilisation.

Part IV Features of Administration of Special Importance to Pakistan

7. Under this heading the subjects selected for syndicate study are:

IV(a) : Accountability and relationships in the public service.
IV(b) : The corporation as an organisational device for development.
IV(c) : The system of financial control, budgeting and accounting.
IV(d) : Organisation for development.
IV(e) : The planning and execution of development schemes.
IV(f) : Adaptation to change.

Part V Major Fields of Development

8. V(a) : Food and agriculture.
V(b) : Industry.

Part VI The Role of the Administrator in the Public and Private Sector

9. This part will provide the opportunity for reflection on the work done in the session and the role, responsibilities and standards of behaviour of those who occupy senior posts in organisations of different kinds.

10. Throughout the course of studies there will be available to members a wide range of Pakistani and foreign newspapers and journals. These are provided with the object of encouraging members to reflect on their reading habits and the extent of the responsibilities an administrator has to keep abreast of events which may directly or indirectly affect his work.

II. Method of work

Syndicates

11. The greater part of the work will be carried out in syndicates. Each member of the college is allotted to one of these syndicates at the beginning of the session. For some subjects members will be divided up afresh into modified syndicates. Ordinary and modified syndicates are designed to represent as wide a variety of experience as possible. Each syndicate will work under the chairmanship of one of its own members. There will be a different chairman and secretary for each subject and they are appointed by the college before the course begins. It is their duty to lead the work of the syndicate on the subjects for which they are responsible.

12. The framework of study for each subject has been prepared in advance by the staff of the college. The documentation necessary for planning and carrying out the work varies from subject to subject. In each case it will include a brief, which outlines the general field of study and discussion and states the particular topic upon which a report is to be prepared. In each case also there will be a subject timetable which will give the total number of syndicate periods available for the subject and their distribution through the period in which the subject is before the syndicate. In most cases there will be reading lists, details of visitors who are to come and address the college as a whole, details of arrangements for visitors to work with each syndicate in turn and, in some subjects, arrangements for outside visits by means of which syndicates may obtain supplementary information to contribute to the work in hand.

The reader who has followed me so far can hardly fail to notice that the outline springs from the experience I had in early Henley, and from the reinforcement of that experience which I undoubtedly had in Australia. The changes I had made were to the intellectual content of the course, which I thought I had tuned in roughly to the Pakistan situation and to the fact that the first session would be composed of public servants. It had, I thought, two major weaknesses. First, to ask members to study in syndicate problems of economic theory, on which I had spent so much time with Mukhtar Mahsud and a banker from Karachi, was quite unsuitable. The other was that there had been no time left to allow for Syracuse making anything like the contribution they would have made if we had had the time which Noel Hall and Harlan Cleveland thought we should. If there was a third weakness, it lay in the fact that this course did not rise to the climax it needed if members were to go away with a feeling of satisfaction and achievement; the last three weeks did not keep the men hard enough at work.

In fact, the course worked quite well. It was a good session and the men made it work, but they did not go out to proclaim the college in the manner in which they would have if it had been a stronger course. This was the price the college paid for getting started in such a short time.

The course for session 2

Early in session 1 we were joined for three weeks by Dr Irving Swerdlow, an economist and a senior member of the faculty of Syracuse University. A robust and direct person, he spoke to the session on more than one occasion and moved freely amongst them: an excellent stimulus and challenge to their thinking at a critical stage. To Khalid Malik and members of his directing staff he proposed that the content and method used in session 1 should be diversified and enriched by the introduction of an economic seminar and a field research exercise. All this was done in a great rush because Irving Swerdlow had to return home. The outcome was that an economic seminar would be introduced in session 2 and a field research exercise in session 3.

The idea of planned economic development was taking hold in Pakistan and the economic seminar was to help members understand the concept of economic development and the problems that were involved in planning national growth. They would then be able to see what their country was trying to do and so get their own jobs into better perspective. This was the first objective. The second was to confront the member with an individual task in which he had to do a great deal of reading and research, produce a draft report on his own, take the views of his colleagues upon it and then complete the job and put his own name to it. The individual had a choice, selecting from a list the subject in which he would make his personal study. He had to make his choice in the fourth week of the session, when the economic seminar began. He was then given the task with a note introducing him to the nature of the topic and a substantial reading list. He was expected to present a draft of his report to his colleagues within four weeks. He could consult the staff in charge of the seminar as he went along if he got into difficulty.

The detailed planning of this first economic seminar was a major undertaking to which Karl Schmidt devoted a huge amount of effort. Well equipped as he was by virtue of his expertise in political science, thoroughly briefed as he almost certainly was by his university, he was not an economist so the preparation and conducting of this seminar must have drawn heavily on his own personal resources. He had to design no less than eleven talks and engage three outside speakers to cover fields where it was important to make men familiar with Pakistani practice. He had to design fourteen individual tasks for members, each with its guiding note and its reading list, and he had to get all this ready for session 2, which was to begin a month after session 1 finished. The headings for his talks and his tasks were as follows and will give the reader some idea of the ground he sought to cover:

Part I

THE ECONOMIC SEMINAR

The outline as presented to session 2

I. Talks/discussions conducted by Dr Schmidt.
    1. Economic concepts in national development   (2)
    2. Capital – savings – investment   (2)
    3. Production – productivity– and take off   (2)
    4. Money – price levels and inflation   (2)
    5. Tax policy and administration (panel of
        guest visitors)   (1)
    6. Capital formation and economic growth
        (guest speakers)   (1)
    7. Government's economic role   (1)

    (*Numbers in brackets are the number of 1½ hour periods devoted to each subject*)

II. List of subjects for individual study and report from which the students made their choice.
    1. The mix in a mixed economy   (2)
    2. The regulation of business   (1)
    3. The rate of capital formation   (2)
    4. The importance of social overhead investment   (2)
    5. Role of banking institutions in investment   (1)
    6. Foreign investment   (1)
    7. The role of foreign trade in economic development (2)
    8. Fiscal policy for development   (1)
    9. Role of markets and competition in economic
        development   (2)
    10. Direct and indirect controls   (1)
    11. Labour problems in economic development   (1)
    12. Programmes to increase domestic savings   (1)
    13. Rationalising administration   (1)
    14. Inflation   (1)

    (*Numbers in brackets indicate the number of students who chose particular subjects*)

To make the introduction of this economic seminar possible Karl Schmidt had to be withdrawn from the syndicate in session 1, of which he was in charge, two or three weeks after the session had started. He was replaced by a Pakistani member of the directing staff, who was still trying to find his bearings. Karl Schmidt did his best to ease him into his seat. The margins of session 1 were very narrow.

Subsequently, during session 2, there arose a controversy over the role played by the directing staff in charge of syndicates. We had two syndicates at the time in a session of twenty people. A directing staff (DS) took charge of each syndicate and, except for occasional changes for the sake of relief, stayed with it throughout the three-month course as was the practice in Henley and Mount Eliza at the time. In addition to the care of his syndicate, a DS played his part in preparing, before a session started, his share of syndicate subjects on each of which he hoped gradually to become better informed than his colleagues. The Pakistanis and the Americans disliked this intensely because they thought the syndicate was entitled to have at its disposal the man who knew most about the subject – the 'resource person' they called him. So they pressed for a change in the system. The DS in charge of a subject should, they thought, follow his subject from syndicate to syndicate, to place his knowledge at the disposal of each.

I was against this. I took the view that if the men had the experience we expected to find in them, for most of the subjects we invited them to study there would always be someone who knew enough about it to help his syndicate through the work. (The chairman would see that the group made full use of the other forms of help provided by the college – the reading material, the speakers, and syndicate visitors – and, of course, the DS's knowledge of each subject would be growing session by session.) He was, in any case, also concerned with ensuring that the purpose and place in the course of each subject was understood and the group held to it by its chairman; that the chairman had made it quite clear what the subject was about and what he expected of his group and each individual; that the chairman was making use of each man's knowledge and skills and of the contributions available from them if they really did the reading, if they listened to and discussed the contributions made by visiting speakers. The DS was concerned, too, that the relations between individuals in the group were healthy and the group was not taking the easy line. I maintained that the syndicate profited greatly from having a detached staff member in the syndicate who knew when to intervene and help and who knew when, in the interests of particular individuals or the group, they were much better left to find their way out. In short, we were not concerned only with the intellectual development of the man: we were concerned with his whole development. Now, I feared, the switch was in the opposite direction.

I was but a lone voice, however, and gave way because the Pakistanis claimed that my way would not work in Pakistan. Four years later, I discovered on a visit to Lahore that the battle on this issue was re-fought once or twice as the Pakistanis were still not resolved on what they were trying to do. From session 3 onwards, however, until the time I left, their way prevailed. I could just take it but I could see ahead to the time when there might be three or more syndicates and I continued to believe that it would be wrong. I also thought it would be deeply frustrating to the staff who had to pass from syndicate to syndicate on the same subject. Moreover, it would be very difficult to make satisfactory timetabling arrangements for bringing in the help which was needed from time to time to stimulate members' thinking and refresh the tiny team of DS. Finally, there was the danger under the new system that each DS would begin to think he was an expert and start to tell the men what the solutions were to the problems which we put before them. The men would go back with a college answer and be told by their bosses just where exactly they got off, and that would soon be the end of the college.

Preparing for session 3

For session 3 we further diversified the course by introducing the first field research exercise. We made room for it by pruning a little the time allotted to some of the syndicate subjects, by using the week allotted to the visits to the two wings of the country, East and West Pakistan, and by extending the course by three days. In sessions 1 and 2 the course had really been for 11½ weeks and in session 3 we made it a full twelve weeks.

This was another major undertaking we were able to introduce because the staff had been reinforced by the arrival of Mr Abdul Quyyum, who had attended session 2 as a member and had since come in as vice-principal, and a second American consultant, Dr Albert Gorvine, who had been engaged by Khalid Malik through Syracuse.

This field research exercise had two purposes. The first was to strengthen the members' analytical capacities by introducing them to the techniques of research and getting them to apply the results of this research to an administrative purpose. The second was to demonstrate the complexity of administration by getting members, while they did their research, to see the functions of a variety of agencies, recognise their inter-relationships and discover how far they were working together to the same administrative purpose. The administrative purpose to which the exercise in session 3 was geared was a study of the working of the ports of Karachi and Chittagong, the two ports through which all Pakistani traffic came and went and on which, therefore, a great deal of Pakistan's growth depended. The idea was that half of the session would study Karachi and the other half Chittagong, and their purpose would be to see how far it was possible to speed up the flow of goods in and out of each port in the safest, most economical and rapid fashion. A great deal of work was involved in the preparation of this exercise, and it was undertaken by Al Gorvine and Karl Schmidt.

Khalid Malik started things for them by securing the agreement of the principal Government authorities in each province for the holding of the exercise. Al Gorvine and Karl Schmidt visited the authorities concerned with the operation of the two ports and the various agencies that were concerned with the handling of goods. They explained what we wanted to do, designed the exercise in consultation with the authorities, and secured their agreement for the detailed investigations members would need to make. This itself was a major achievement because not all men who have a long and hard day's work are willing to submit to an investigation of the work to which they are devoting their lives – and this by students from a college who would in the nature of the course they were attending only be able to offer them a week. There is little doubt that Khalid Malik's preliminary preparation of the ground was decisive in securing open doors. Our hosts had dismissed from their minds the idea that this might in some sense be a committee of enquiry into their affairs and that the members

1 C.-J.

2 The Administrative Staff College, Henley, early days, 1950

3 The Australian Administrative Staff College, Mount Eliza, 1957

4   Members and staff, session 1, AASC, 6 September–27 November 1957

SESSION 1

6 September–27 November 1957
Principal: Sir Douglas Copland

SYNDICATE A	SYNDICATE B	SYNDICATE C	SYNDICATE D
W. G. Symington	M. R. Burnell	R. L. Patterson	J. G. Padman
N. L. Carter	K. H. Spencer	G. C. E. Berhitoe	J. L. Liebelt
J. G. Laurence	C. C. Weekley	L. Donaldson	D. R. S. Craik
F. McL Burgess	J. A. Heenan	J. H. Stephens	D. L. Dixon
R. A. Horsfall	G. H. Petch	R. D. Marginson	A. J. A. Gardner
L. F. Butler	J. D. Vicary	M. R. Pitt	K. W. Steel
S. G. Cousin	J. A. de Veer	H. H. Lack	W. E. R.
J. McConnell	B. White	R. G. Gifford	Alexander
L. K. Camron	J. W. Overall	H. R. Richardson	W. O. A. Astridge
G. S. Wright	F. C. Pike	D. A. Tate	G. Paterson
Brig. A. T.	*Mr H. W. Slater*	*Mr M. Brown*	J. M. B. White
Cornwall-Jones			*Mr H. A. Harvey*

5   Original library at Moondah

6 New Building, Mount Eliza, 1983

7 Dr A. J. Barnard, Principal, New Zealand Administrative Staff College, Wellington

8   Administrative Staff College of India, Bella Vista, Hyderabad

9 In 1959 a Review Course for members of sessions 1 and 2 was held: 50 out of a possible 65 returned. *Left to right sitting*: General Shrinagesh (Principal), H. E. Bhimsen Sachar (the then governor of Andhra Pradesh), Dr K. S. Basu (Director of Studies); *standing*: Balo Nehru, John Adams (seconded from Henley, Director of Studies, session 1), Akhtar Zaman, ADC, Potla Sen (later Principal), Ronnie Maulik, Shri Naidu (Registrar), Vijay Katoch. Four of these were former members of Henley

10 Prime Minister Jawaharlal Nehru with General Shrinagesh (Principal), during the Prime Minister's visit to ASCI, 23 October 1958

11 *Left to right*: Professor Doraiswamy, Mr B. K. Nehru, Vazir Sultan Tobacco Co. Ltd (Chairman), General Shrinagesh

12 Visit of Sir Noel Hall, Principal, Henley, seen here with General and Mrs Shrinagesh, Mr B. K. Nehru, Mrs Nehru, at a party in honour of Sir Noel, Jan–Feb, 1959

13 Meeting of the Court of Governors: Dr C. D. Deshmukh (Chairman), Mr R. L. Gupta (Principal), Mr M. L. Khaitan (Chairman, Bata Shoe Co.), Mr M. P. Pai (Chief Secretary, Government of Andhra Pradesh)

14   Pakistan Administrative Staff College, Lahore

15   President Mohammed Ayub Khan, General K. M. Sheikh and Principal Khalid
Malik, 24 December 1960. Opening day of the Pakistan ASC

16 Address by Field Marshal Mohammed Ayub Khan, President of Pakistan, at the inaugural ceremony of the Pakistan Administrative Staff College, 23 December 1960

17 Mr A Khalid Malik, First Principal, Pakistan Administrative Staff College and Mr N. M. Khan

18   The library, PASC, 1962

19   Mr N. A. Faruqui, Cabinet Secretary, addressing the members of session 5, 22 September 1962, PASC. *Right to left*: C.-J., Mr N. A. Faruqui, Dr A. Gorvine, Dr C. Birkhead

20　Sayeed Ahmed Khan course of studies secretary, 1962

21　Philippine Executive Academy, session 3

22　Dr Harry L. Case, Ford Foundation Representative, Pakistan and the Philippines

23   Pines Hotel, Philippines

24   An executive panel in action

25   J. P. Martin-Bates with Carlos Ramos, during a visit to the Philippines

26   Philippine Executive Academy—early days

were really only doing the exercise for the purpose of training.

The general structure of the exercise was to be: first, a period in the college during which members made a preliminary study of the role of the various agencies concerned directly or indirectly with the speed at which goods passed in and out of the port, and discussed the way they would set about their job on the ground; then a week in their particular port consulting the various agencies, gathering data and building up day-by-day their conclusions; followed by a period at the college when the teams would put together their material and conclusions in a substantial report. I think the reader will get a very good idea of the character of this first field research exercise and some feel, too, of the dynamics in it, from the description of their tasks which was given to members in session 3. The snags were as follows. It was a long and fairly 'heavy' exercise with a great deal of paperwork for the group and it drew into itself many people outside the college who were already very much involved and very busy. The member chairmen we reserved for it – probably two of the best men on the session – were therefore locked up in it for a long time. It was an exercise which it would be difficult to repeat in under five or six years and for which to find a replacement of equal quality would be almost as difficult. Nevertheless, as a one-off for session 3 it was first-class and as an example for the staff to aim at could hardly have been bettered.

Preparing for session 5

The third and last major change in the course in my day was the introduction of a seminar on development administration, which was brought in during session 5. The idea of holding this seminar arose partly from the belief that the members needed to be given a better grounding in the theory and practice of public administration in a developing country, and partly from the fact that some of the members in the earlier sessions wanted to make their individual studies in the field of administration, as distinct from economics which some of them found pretty difficult.

The development administration seminar was designed on much the same lines as the economic seminar. In the early days, it consisted of ten talks/discussions, ten different subjects for individual study, from which the member would make his own choice, present a draft of his views on it to his colleagues, take their views upon it, and finally produce a report to which he would put his own name. The whole session would attend the talks and both these seminars, but members would have the choice between economics and administration for their individual work. A general idea of the ground covered is set out below. We found room for it in the programme mainly by adding a thirteenth week to the length of the course. This seminar was designed by Professor Guthrie Birkhead, another senior member of the Syracuse Faculty, who arrived in Lahore in time to conduct it in session 5.

THE SEMINAR ON DEVELOPMENT ADMINISTRATION

The outline as presented to session 5

A.   Talks/discussions conducted by Dr Birkhead and Dr Gorvine

    I.   Theories of organisation

    II.   Public administration abroad
The dangers of comparisons
Institutional difference in governments
Departmentalism
Public corporations
Local government and local administration
The examples of personnel systems

    III.   The axioms of administration

    IV.   New ideas of administration

    Policy and administration
Conflict and co-operation
Authority and responsibility
Decision making
Specialisation
Decline of charisma

    V.   Two tools of administration
Research and statistics
Financial administration

B.   List of subjects for individual study and report from which members made their own choice

    I.   Fitting public corporations into Pakistan's governmental system

    II.   Recruitment and selection in Pakistan and the UK (or US)

    III.   The distinctions between the Pakistan and Indian (or US) budget process

    IV.   Power, authority and responsibility

    V.   Integration of the public services in Pakistan

    VI.   Performance budgeting

    VII.   Organisation of ministries and departments in Pakistan.

    VIII.   The role of local government in development.

    IX.   Comparison of Pakistan's system of entry training of public personnel with practice in other countries.

    X.   The work of F.W. Taylor

The following outline shows the course of studies as it had developed by session 6.

Course of studies

PAKISTAN ASC	*Abbreviated*
Session 6 2 February – 4 May 1963	*Title*

A. *Syndicate subjects*
Part I : *General administration*
    (a) Organisation Structure   I(a)
    (b) Internal Co-operation and Communication   I(b)
    (c) Personnel Management, Recruitment, Training
           and Incentives   I(c)
    (d) Delegation, Control and Accountability   I(d)
    (e) Project Planning, Budgeting and Financial
           Control   I(e)

Part II : *Programme administration*
    (a) Social Welfare   II(a)
    (b) Education   II(b)
    (c) Agriculture   II(c)
    (d) Industry   II(d)

Part III : *The role of the administrator*

Special Subjects
    1. The Constitution and the Basic Democracies   CBD
    2. Biography – A Study of Administrators   BIO

B. *Seminars*
Seminar on Development Administration –   ADM
    Theory and Practice   Administration
Seminar on Development Economics   ECO
                                        Economics

C. *Operations Research*
Impact of the Town on the Village   OR

Between these major adaptations to the Pakistan course, which we made while I was there, I was heavily involved in the following:

1. The adaptation of the course of studies to suit these major changes and the gradual handing over of this part of my responsibilities to Abdul Quyyum, who assumed them fully before I left.
2. The development of the syndicate work generally, and particularly in the development of those syndicate subjects of which I was in charge.
3. I had charge of a syndicate myself.
4. I was much involved in lonely attempts to boost attendance from the private sector.

Observations

As I left for home in February 1963, it seemed we had gone a long way from the time we laid the first course of studies before session 1 at the end of 1960 and the time we put the sixth course before session 6 in February 1963. This last, incidentally, was the first session on which we had thirty instead of twenty members. We had started with a course which was a little 'lightweight' and had a little too much Henley in its method. We had built on to it at least three of the main contributions which Syracuse sought to make and, if the two seminars, the field research exercise and all the syndicate work were pretty loosely fitted together, we did seem to have created a fair base from which the Pakistanis might work up a real Pakistani course. I had some concern on a few matters as I left.

I propose to close this chapter with some general observations on the experience as a whole and add a few remarks on the question of research to which Syracuse attached so much importance from the beginning. The fact that this is left to the end has nothing to do with the priority which I attach to it: it is simply that research in Pakistan at the time was an extremely difficult activity to get started.

The post of principal

Khalid Malik held the early sessions together because members respected his experience and his integrity. They liked him and wanted to make the college work because of him. But he was a gentle person, not sufficiently robust to give the sessions the lead they needed or to fight the upper hierarchy for the college's basic minimum needs in terms of people. What became apparent in the first two sessions was that he was a sick man, and his condition deteriorated during the early sessions. He was in very bad shape as I left and was shortly going on leave. There was to be a period of uncertainty and it was no business of ours to choose his successor. But it was our business as consultants to get our masters in Henley and Syracuse to make clear to the Pakistan Government that we had a big stake in the college and a keen interest in seeing that the ultimate and inevitable selection of a new principal was taken very seriously.

The directing staff

For the new principal there would be plenty of problems. Perhaps the most important was to ensure that the Pakistani directing staff were built up. This seemed to me to mean:

1. Getting the Government to accept that the college must be staffed by men with keen minds, much experience of administration and with personality; and that it would, in the long run, pay Government to release staff and members to the college.
2. Some continuity in the employment at the college of the staff would

be necessary if they were to play a real hand in helping to build the college; such continuity at the college would need to be encouraged.

Then, when all the consultants had gone home, the principal would be able to build a strong, live Pakistan College which Pakistanis would be glad to attend.

The composition of the sessions

As I have said the level of the men from the public sector was pretty good in my day. The best were very good by any standards, though there were not quite enough of these men on every session. The bulk were able to profit from the experience. While in a session of twenty men it is not at all intolerable and may, indeed, be advantageous if there are one or two 'weaker brethren', in the first five sessions this 'tail' was a little too long. Again, the underlying difficulty seems to have been the unwillingness of nominators to make the sacrifices which I have already mentioned, coupled with the reluctance of the candidates themselves to leave, even for three months, responsible jobs to which they were already committed. We should have been round the administrative departments in the public sector and invited some of the chief men to spend a weekend at the college to see what we were doing, in order to quicken the interest from which nominations flow.

The level of nominations from the private sector was patchy and the numbers, as we know so well, were very limited. What was vital to the future of the college, I thought, was to bend over backwards to get the private sector interested in all these early sessions. I used every contact I had among old Henley members, and wore out much shoe leather tramping the streets of the Pakistani cities doing what I could to get nominations. We also got a few people from the private sector to come and talk to the college, but something more needed to be done. Khalid Malik needed a senior, perhaps retired, industrialist on his staff to help in the preparation of the work the sessions were asked to do on industrial development, relations between government and business, and so on. One could feel the danger that if we failed to retain the interest of the private sector in the early days, we should wake up to find that there was no interest in the college, which would have become 'that Government place up in Lahore – no concern of ours'.

I have referred to the mixtures in these early sessions as often very rich indeed, always of course with the exception of the private sector. The variety of members' backgrounds in the public sector could hardly have been stronger for a college seeking to break down mutual ignorance and mistrust between people, seeking to broaden the individuals' sympathies, quicken their perceptions and promote better understanding of other people's ways of life and points of view. The widely separated East and West wings of Pakistan at the time were both well represented, as were central and provincial governments and a wide range of ministries and attached departments, Punjabis, Pathans, Baluchis and Bengalis. To anyone who knows anything of Pakistan, there were plenty of bridges to be built here, as indeed there were between the civilian administrators and the officers of the armed services and police. What was missing in the mixture would, we had to hope, in due course be filled as Pakistan's industrial and technological strength grew. Meanwhile, there were enough specialists to demonstrate that the days were passing when all the senior administrative positions would continue to be filled by generalists.

Individual and group work

On the whole I think most of us on the staff would have agreed that it was something of an achievement to have brought the course and its methods to the stage we had in two-and-a-half years. There was (and, of course, always will be) a lot that could be done to improve the course; important changes from session to session as the staff learnt its job; major alterations as the need for radical reform became clear. At the time I left, I thought we had seen so much change in our short time that it would have been good to call a halt to major changes, accept the general framework we had created and try to improve the details within that framework. An attempt to get agreement on the purpose, content, method and supporting facilities in each syndicate subject, in each seminar and in each field research exercise would not only have made for a much better course of studies but would have played a highly significant part in the development of the staff as a team. Probably it was a little early to hope for this though some of it would have gone on in the natural process of putting the course together with each session. Meanwhile, there were some particular things I thought needed looking at.

I had a feeling in my mind during those early two-and-a-half years with the college that there was some danger that the two different methods of work – seminar and syndicate – did not lie down very easily together in the same course. As these two methods of work overlapped for about four weeks, during which the workload on members was pretty heavy, I thought that the men would tend to give priority in their minds to one method at the expense of the other. The economic seminar called in the end for a report to which an individual would put his own signature. The syndicate work running concurrently called for a group report which the chairman of the syndicate would sign on behalf of his colleagues. I suspected that members would tend in these circumstances to give priority to the reports they had to sign themselves as individuals, at the expense of group work. This suspicion was terribly hard to quantify. Perhaps I sensed it simply because this was the way I would have been drawn myself. I express the doubt now not because I want to cut out the idea of individual work in a Staff College course but because I believed too much individual work might undermine group work, and that this was a matter to which the college would need to give a good deal of thought. As staff and members came to understand both these methods and their purposes, and became aware of the risks, I hoped the difficulty would be overcome. We were operating in the early days when we had not known each other's methods and were not aware of the hazards.

Presentations

I woke up too late to the fact that some changes needed to be made in the presentations, as we called them, which were the culminating event of most syndicate subjects. In the very early days, while I was working out the design of the first course and heard that the numbers in the session were likely to be reduced from thirty to twenty, I had some doubt whether these presentations would work at all in so small a group. There were two parts to them: in the first, the chairman presented his syndicate's report in a speech which had a definite time limit. The purpose here was to give the individual, in his turn as chairman, a chance to take charge of his group in the larger gathering, with perhaps some competitive element in the situation, and practise speaking in the presence of his own syndicate, some members of which might have found difficulty in settling the terms of the report being presented, and who might therefore be sensitive to the way the chairman put it over. It was thought that this would be a new experience for the men which they could only understand by 'doing'.

The second part consisted of a discussion of points which each syndicate had been asked to contribute and which had been put together by the staff on an agenda. The object of this was to give members a chance of managing their group when there was some uncertainty about the challenge which might be made to a group's thinking. The chairman was expected to play the leading role but he could call upon any member in his group whom he thought might have something to contribute. The member would naturally respond, and might or might not be prepared. Opportunities to contribute would arise and the individual, if he wanted to, could join in the discussion. The point was to give him the chance to overcome the difficulty of getting to his feet in conditions which were not quite so easy as in the more familiar atmosphere round a syndicate table.

These two purposes behind the presentation occasion were well founded enough in the larger groups in Mount Eliza and Henley, but in a college where the largest group was twenty they lost a good deal of their force. There was a difference in a syndicate of ten and a session of twenty in terms of the tensions present in the latter, perhaps just enough to confirm the belief that the men were getting some practice in overcoming personal difficulties in real life. I thought, therefore, that the occasions could be justified on these grounds. What astonished me in Pakistan was that the men pursued the items on the agenda at the length they did. There was seldom lack of willingness on the part of members to get up and speak, and the discipline was fair enough. The real weakness in Pakistan lay in the fact that none of us on the staff was good at taking the chair when it came to these discussions. There was no hope of giving the men practice in the skills I have just described if the substance of the discussion was not worth while to the men and was not well handled by the chair. My mind was not quick enough and these younger men never seemed to get any slower. The overall effect was that the presentations were not as good as they should have been; I should have thought of something quite different to replace them.

The absence of the syndicate visitor

This kind of visitor was invited to come and offer his experience to each syndicate in turn – spending about one-and-a-half hours with each group – it being left to the syndicate under its chairman to exploit the opportunity of his presence. The visitor was invited in the context of a subject on which the syndicate was working and he knew generally what that subject was; the group was, of course, told what his background and expertise were. So there was an incentive for them to get the best out of the man and there was an interest for the visitor, who was either a specialist whose particular expertise was required for the subject or, more often, a man more senior than any member. I knew that this was one of our very special tools in other colleges. It gave the men the opportunity of getting to know the visitor and his experience in the very intimate small syndicate group, but only if they had done their homework and thought it out. They had to have figured out for themselves what they thought he could contribute; they had to think out how best to put him at his ease to begin with and warm him up. They might well find that he had a message of his own that he wanted to get over and they could find it a bit difficult to get him to give them what they wanted. The extraordinary thing in Lahore was that I only found one Pakistani and one American who were prepared to adopt the role of syndicate visitor. Most of the people we approached strongly disliked the idea and preferred to be asked to give a talk to the college body as a whole.

Members got many other opportunities to cross-question different kinds of men. There were the guest speakers who, when they had given their talk, still needed handling in question time, which was very often the better part of the visit. On the outside visits three or four men could get a great deal from the people they met and bring encouragement to specialists in the pokiest of little offices, where hope of obtaining the interest of a 'senior administrator' had long since vanished. All these, coupled with the variety of new contacts which the men made in the villages and towns and the ports of Karachi and Chittagong, were part of the cross-fertilisation process; and the more intimate the occasion, the more effort the men put into preparing themselves for it, the greater the dividend they got out of it. Without them, the syndicate would have been cast back on its own resources: it had constantly to be refreshed.

Course development and research

I had at first some misgivings when I encountered Syracuse ideas about research. It seemed that the college was to become a leading centre for research into major problems of national development. The college staff were to be involved with Pakistani and foreign leaders in detailed studies designed, it seemed, for the furthering of knowledge about fundamental things like the motivation of development, its administration and its execution, with the expectation that their findings would be generally useful in other countries as well as Pakistan. I watched a huge library being assembled, which seemed unnecessary for the kind of operations I thought we were contemplating. Was the tail going to wag the dog?

Well, it might have I suppose but it didn't. When I visited Syracuse in 1968 they told me that when they first went to Lahore they thought American and British consultants would inevitably introduce ideas about administration which might or might not be applicable. Consequently, they wanted to rouse in the minds of Pakistani members a curiosity about their own administration, which would gradually enable them to build up a philosophy of administration of their own, based on the deepest possible analysis of processes in the Pakistan culture. They knew this couldn't be done quickly but they did want to help Khalid Malik lay some foundations from which this kind of research might eventually spring. Several attempts to get all this started were made but the idea was, I believe, before its time. There was an apathy first to be overcome. The Americans did not give up. They created the library on a scale and to a standard that would be required should such a centre emerge, the Pakistanis adding to it a fine collection of their own material, mostly in the form of Pakistan Government documents. The Americans offered in the seminars and the field research exercises the opportunity to absorb the value of analysis in tackling administrative problems. The standards set were high and must have left their mark on all who passed through Lahore. They brought out a few young Americans to research into specific Pakistani problems, demonstrations of what could be done; they encouraged the issue of publications based on research by both members and staff; and they did their best to guide and help such Pakistani directors or assistants in research as appeared from time to time. It was a long haul but alongside it there were scores of Americans in the fields and in the cities of Pakistan passing on the same kind of message – 'Analyse your problems, for goodness' sake.'

Before leaving this long-term aim, I should add that when I revisited Lahore in 1967 it looked as if the major research centre might yet take shape, again with the encouragement of Syracuse University but not this time in the Staff College. A research council had been appointed, the principal of the college had been made its chairman and a director of research had been appointed under the Establishment Division of the Government. It was intended that he should build up the proposed centre, which would serve the Government and all its training institutions, including the Staff College, in the conduct of the kind of research which the research council thought necessary. Perhaps one day it will emerge and be active.

Meanwhile, in the absence of indigenous research, the results of which are what really matter in a Staff College, the documentation of the course of studies was difficult. Members of the directing staff were responsible for their own area of work and their different syndicate subjects and for building the reading material to support them. For this they had the library, which included a great deal of American and some British thinking and a substantial flow of journals, from which one very often got warning of developing thought – 'early thinking' – which was often useful to a Staff College. But after them there was not much, as far as I could discover, to be obtained from Pakistan or from elsewhere in the developing world. I used western books, few of which were written for the specific purpose for which I needed them and in which, therefore, I tried to identify the parts relevant to my subjects to help members get to work very quickly. Whenever I could find material in suitable form I would extract and circulate it in a series we called 'Reading papers' or, failing that, try to fill the gap with a speaker or syndicate visitor. This was hard work in the early days of the college in the developing world. It was welcome news in 1967 when I found out that at last it had been decided that the lack of direction to the effort involved in documenting the Pakistan course could no longer be tolerated, and that the primary function of the director of research in the college and his two assistants was to be to help members of the directing staff in developing materials for the course of studies.

Before I put this chapter aside I must say a few words about the Henley and Syracuse relationship. Having worked extensively with Americans in quite different fields of endeavour, in both peace and war, it was a strange experience finding myself confronted directly with academics from an American university. I have quite a few friends in Syracuse; they did me a lot of good and I have an idea that I did not do them any harm.

When I left the UK in 1960, Noel Hall and I both believed that Henley and Syracuse were going to Pakistan as equal partners engaged to help the principal set up an Administrative Staff College in Pakistan.

As the early weeks and months in Lahore came and went, I began to wonder whether the first Syracuse men to come to Lahore really regarded the whole thing as an equal partnership. Sometimes I got the impression that they regarded themselves as being in charge of everybody and everything, including me. In due course we found that there was some foundation for this feeling, and our relative positions were then quickly put straight. Khalid Malik, I know, suffered a bit and so did Karl Schmidt and I until this was sorted out. But all of it I regarded as part of the difficulty in having so many people with their differing views trying to set up an Administrative Staff College. I guessed that Henley and Syracuse would have built a partnership in the end, or one or other would go. I remember thinking at the time the sorting out took place that it was really rather unfair to have put two men into the field with such different ideas on their relationships to each other. I was to learn much later that the financial arrangements which contributed to the early difficulties in Lahore had not been agreed to by the authorities in Henley.

Too much should not be made of all this. Misunderstandings, mistakes, at a higher level usually make for trouble lower down. Such things happen, do not always come to light and are not always corrected. In this case they did come to light, were corrected and so nothing prevented the Pakistan

College from opening on the target date, or later pursuing its destiny. On the contrary, I think in those first two-and-a-half years of its life, Syracuse and Henley did become an equal partnership and did help the Pakistanis to lay a base on which succeeding principals and their staffs could build, a course of studies which they could develop, some standards they would have to struggle to match; and if we left them continuing with the rather awesome demand for improvement, that I think was a demand which they welcomed; and it was certainly inherent in the whole idea of having a Staff College. The point I am making is that in the setting up of new institutions like this there will be difficulties; but difficulties are things that one quickly forgets and should not be allowed to mar achievement as it emerges.

So, a little proud at having helped this college off the ground, rather sad at leaving Pakistan and so many friends, never dreaming that we might get the opportunity of another visit, still less foreseeing the trials and tribulations through which Pakistan had still to pass, we took our departure. In February 1963 we boarded a train at Lahore station, crossed the border into India, changed trains at Amritsar and headed for Bombay and home – nostalgia *suprême*.

4

EARLY MANILA/BAGUIO –
THE PHILIPPINE EXECUTIVE
ACADEMY, 1963-6

How it started

Like Pakistan, the Philippine Executive Academy was founded on Government initiative and support. In this case, however, it was constituted within the state university – the University of the Philippines, which is a Government institution. It was conceived in the mind of a man who had himself attended a session at the Australian Administrative Staff College, Mr Carlos Ramos. Not only did Carlos Ramos conceive the idea but he fought it through to existence and was entrusted by the president of the university with the task of making it work.

The idea of introducing some form of executive training first arose in his mind in 1958 as a natural development of the work he had been superintending at the Institute (later to be known as the College) of Public Administration in the University of the Philippines since its inception in 1952. Here he had achieved a modest success. In addition to his normal business of teaching public administration, he had been offering short courses for supervisors and junior managers. He had been training civil officials as training officers, too, and had induced a number of Government agencies to start internal courses of their own; and in all of it he had begun to notice that the men who attended these short courses, particularly those who had been trained as training officers, were unable to get things started when they got back to their own departments and agencies. So it became clear to him that something needed to be done at a more senior level. He realised that the idea of training at this more senior level would probably need to be introduced and written into Government policy, so that he had some basis from which to work. In the summer of 1959 a new Civil Service Bill was introduced in Congress, and he managed to have a clause inserted which read as follows:

To help ensure the availability of a pool of trained administrators in the executive and senior levels and to improve further the competence and performance of executives in the different branches, sub-divisions and instrumentalities of the Philippine Government, the Institute of Public Administration of the University of the Philippines, with the co-operation of the Budget Commission and the National Economic Council shall organise and carry out a continuing programme of executive development.

I quote this in full because it shows that at the beginning Carlos Ramos was thinking only of a programme which would be devoted to the training of executives in government, and also because it mentions a 'pool of trained administrators' which, from the first, he had always hoped would one day emerge in the Philippines. He foresaw an elite group of competent civil servants at and near the top, non-political, non-partisan, enjoying a reputation for great integrity. They would form the hard core in all the Government agencies engaged on the development of the country and would be at the disposal of the President in his efforts to push forward reform, re-organisation and efficiency. This was a dream which to me had a familiar ring to it.

At the same time he persuaded the National Economic Council to incorporate in the 1959 Three-Year Programme of Social and Economic Development a recommendation proposing the creation of an 'Executive Academy' to achieve the purpose outlined in the Civil Service Bill which had by now become law. So the title 'Executive Academy' first appeared and gave him his launching platform.

It was while this was going on in the middle of 1959 that Carlos Ramos had occasion to pay a short visit to Canberra, which was to have a considerable effect on his thinking and on the kind of Executive Academy he was eventually to advocate. He went to look at the Australian methods of training in their public services and became aware, while in Canberra, of the existence of the Australian Administrative Staff College. He decided that he would like to attend it as a member and see what kind of a programme was put on for senior executives. He eventually attended session 4 in the last three months of 1959, and it was there that he formed the opinion that much of the method which Douglas Copland was using could be of value in the Philippines. He observed the level of men for whom the Australians were catering and experienced himself the value of the self-teaching process, in which members were involved. He liked the atmosphere in the college and the self-discipline that was inherent in the method. He saw the kind of staff Douglas Copland had gathered around him and the role they were playing, and he noticed that the college council had come to the conclusion that they could not get the kind of members they wanted for a period of longer than three months. Substantial adaptation of the Australian programme would, of course, be necessary to suit conditions in the Philippines but this could be worked out. So he returned to embark on a campaign to establish in his own country an Executive Academy which would draw substantially on the Australian/British experience.

Legal and financial backing

His next steps were to get the Academy formally established in law, and the finance to make it a possibility. This was a tough process in the Philippines. Carlos Ramos had to gain support from various branches of the executive, from Congress, and from the president and board of regents of his own university. His main problem lay in the fact that it was particularly difficult at that time to get the support of the Government for a new project. Everybody, every Government agency, had ideas of their own and they were not easily brought together. Carlos Ramos had to pursue his idea from one branch of Government to another; he had to draft his own legislation and find a congressman to support it; he had to keep almost an hour-to-hour watch on progress in and out of the Legislature, the executive and the university, if he wanted to steer his idea through the rocks which threatened the existence of new projects during that time. I daresay the pockets of resistance which he encountered from time to time were no more formidable than in other countries, but the campaign seems to have been arduous enough. It certainly required personality because the Filipino does his business on a personal basis. Fortunately Carlos Ramos and his staff were well equipped with the techniques required to do this. By the middle of 1962, the board of regents of the university passed a resolution, which had the force of law, formally establishing the Philippine Executive Academy in the University of the Philippines and under the Institute of Public Administration. A little later they had the satisfaction of receiving an allocation of Government funds which they thought would be adequate to enable them to make a start.

Carlos Ramos also hoped to secure the financial assistance of the Ford Foundation and to obtain from Henley a member of the directing staff who would assist him in setting up the academy. These two hopes resulted in Professor Ferrel Heady of the University of Michigan, and my wife and I from Henley, paying complementary visits to Manila in August 1962. Ferrel Heady's visit emanated from a meeting in Manila which Carlos Ramos had with Dr George F. Gant, one of the senior men in the Ford Foundation based at its headquarters in New York, to whose wisdom many of the developing countries owe so much. George Gant at once expressed interest in Carlos Ramos's desire to get financial help in starting the academy and promised to send someone to look into the idea in more detail. Ferrel Heady had arrived in response to this promise and was making a feasibility study of the proposed academy and one or two other projects which Carlos Ramos had in mind.

Mr J.P. Martin-Bates (who became the principal at Henley in 1961) and I had known for some time before these visits to the Philippines that Carlos Ramos wanted me to join him in Manila to help in the setting-up process of the academy. This we supposed was at the back of his mind when he came to Henley in Summer 1962 and Martin-Bates, he and I had a talk on the lawn. It transpired, however, that his immediate purpose was to propose that I go on a preliminary reconnaissance to the Philippines to discuss the kind of academy that he might set up, make up our minds if it was the sort of academy in which Henley's help might be useful, and see something of his country and his people. Joan and I had been thinking over the question of whether we would take on yet another overseas assignment and were pretty well agreed that we would. So we said that we would be happy to spend a few days in Manila on my way back from the United Kingdom to Pakistan, knowing that this might lead to a further secondment. Hence the visits referred to in the previous chapter.

Ferrel Heady stayed in the Philippines for a month, but I still had another six months to run in Lahore and could not spare Carlos Ramos more than five-and-a-half days. Both Ferrel Heady's report and mine were to be sent to the director of administration of the Ford Foundation in New York, which was financing both these exploratory visits.

In the short time I had in Manila it was impossible to grasp everything I would have liked to understand, but I think I succeeded in getting into Carlos Ramos's mind on at least some of the issues which I thought important. I spent most of my time with him and saw a good deal of Ferrel Heady. I attended a meeting of the Council of Administrative Management, had an hour with the president of the University of the Philippines and paid a visit to Baguio. Later, from Lahore on 5 September 1962, I sent in my report to the Ford Foundation in New York, making the following points:

Evidence of support for the establishment of an academy. I discovered on arrival that the Philippine Executive Academy had already been brought into legal existence by a resolution of the board of regents of the University of the Philippines. This I thought indicated a degree of support at the necessary high level which should be sufficient to ensure such essentials as the appointment of the full-time head for the academy, the provision of the necessary staff and the nomination of the right kind of men who would attend the courses. I found evidence, too, that the Government of the Philippines intended to provide some initial financial support and, presumably, to continue the kind of support that would be needed.

Constitution of the academy. The academy was to be created 'in the University of the Philippines' and 'under the Institute of Public Administration' in order to ensure a high standing for the academy on its inception. The acting head of the academy intended to advocate the establishment of an advisory council to the president of the university, composed of individuals of high standing and widely representative of those areas of the economy from which candidates would be drawn. Its composition would be such that its views on the direction in which the academy should develop would carry great weight and would be unlikely to be disregarded.

The full-time head of the academy. Carlos Ramos, who was already Director of the Institute of Public Administration, had been appointed as acting head of the academy until such time as the board of regents appointed a full-time head. The latter appointment I said would be of vital concern to the future of the academy. He would need to be a man who had carried substantial responsibilities in the past with sufficient intellectual capacity to inspire but not intimidate the men and women who would come to the academy. His selection should not be rushed but he should, if possible, be appointed in time to make some substantial visits to other institutions overseas and to play a part in at least the final preparations of the first session. He should be left in office undisturbed for at least five years.

Scale of the enterprise. Carlos Ramos was contemplating a college body of thirty members. I supported him in this.

Composition of the sessions. Carlos Ramos proposed to build up his sessions on the following lines:

1. As a guide, age would lie between 32 and 45 years.
2. The group would be a mixed one, representative of the departments of Government both at the centre and in the provinces, the public corporations, and companies in the industrial and commercial sector of the economy. The composition (in this case I use the term 'composition' to describe the level of members) of each session would make it possible to avoid elementary teaching as the members would have within their own knowledge sufficient material for advanced discussion. Once the academy was securely established, it was contemplated encouraging governments and businesses of other countries in South-East Asia to participate in it.
3. The academy would not overlap the more junior clientele who attended the courses of the Institute of Public Administration.
4. He hoped to establish the principle that the head of the academy would interview candidates before acceptance and have the final say on whether or not individuals should attend.

I fully agreed with this line of thought.

Permanent location of the academy. This Carlos Ramos hoped eventually to establish in the city of Baguio, 250 km from Manila, fifty minutes by air with a daily service. On my visit I saw one site some 12 km outside the city, which Carlos Ramos favoured at the time. I included in my report some essentials that needed to be kept in mind when selecting the permanent site. Meanwhile I agreed that temporarily courses could be run in a hotel in Baguio, and simply pointed out the danger that members might be tempted to waste time on other pursuits if the hotel was full of other guests.

Length of course. Carlos Ramos was thinking of three months and I thought that flexibility in settling the precise length — whether eleven or thirteen weeks or so — should be left to the full-time head, who would also be free to decide on the number of courses he should run in a year.

Development of the course of studies. This required the personal attention of the full-time head, and I laid stress on the need for his Filipino and foreign staff to assemble at the same time to set about the work that would be required to get ready for the first course.

Some useful preliminary preparations might be made by anyone arriving in advance of any agreed date, and I incorporated a note on what these preparations might be.

Meanwhile in the report I supported Carlos Ramos's idea of a programme on the following lines:

1. Full-time head and all staff assemble 1 July 1963 and should be given nine months to prepare for the opening date.
2. If these preparations were made, the Philippine Academy might open its doors to its first session on 1 July 1964.

There followed in the report a certain amount of detail about the Filipino and foreign staff likely to be needed, which I do not think it necessary to incorporate in this summary.

My general conclusion was that Carlos Ramos's project was one in which anyone who was invited to join was privileged to do so. I confirmed to the Ford Foundation that Martin-Bates was prepared to release me in time to arrive on 1 July and said that I was prepared to come for at least a year and quite possibly for longer.

Assignment agreed

As Ferrel Heady and I were so conveniently assembled together in Manila and were both talking with Carlos Ramos we were closely enough in touch with each other's thinking. I did not need to get involved in the early work he was then doing on the outline budgets for the academy's first three years. It was useful to know that the Philippine Government was showing signs of finding financial resources to help Carlos Ramos get started on preliminary work but the rest I could hear later on. Meanwhile Ferrel Heady knew what I was going to write into my report, and I gave him a copy of it in draft when I left Manila. He told me that his report would not be out of line with mine unless I changed my draft substantially, which I did not. Later Martin-Bates confirmed that his report did not conflict with mine, and it was gratifying to hear that the University of the Philippines received a Ford Foundation grant of $221,000 for the support of the academy. I left Manila for Lahore with some feeling of satisfaction. Carlos Ramos's work seemed to be moving towards action. I believed the building of bridges between the public and private sectors (which to me was a fundamental part of the Staff College notion as I understood it) would be of great assistance in a country like the Philippines, where the constructive interaction of both sectors would be so necessary if national development was to be accelerated. I therefore strongly supported the idea that the sessions should be mixed groups composed of men and women representatives not only of Government and Government corporations but also industry and commerce, though it was likely that in this case the Government representatives would be in the majority at the beginning. I noted that the level would be senior enough to have within their own knowledge sufficient material for advanced discussion. I understood I was to have one and perhaps two American colleagues. I told everyone concerned that I thought Henley would be able to help and went back to Lahore.

The detailed arrangements for my assignment were made in correspondence between General Carlos P. Romulo, the president of the University of the Philippines, Carlos Ramos, the Ford Foundation in New York and the principal at Henley in consultation with me. When I left Lahore in February 1963, I knew I was due to report to Manila on 1 July 1963, which gave Joan and me three months in the UK between assignments. The date was subsequently changed at Carlos Ramos's request to enable me to visit the Australian College on my way out and to see Harry Case and Ferrel Heady as I passed through the United States.

Staff and objectives

The head office of the Philippine Executive Academy was at Rizal Hall in Padre Faura. Here the Institute (soon to become the College) of Public Administration and the Philippine Executive Academy were established alongside each other. Carlos Ramos was head of both. To help him get the Executive Academy going he had assembled the following:

Director of studies:	Dr Abelardo (Bel) Samonte
Members of the directing staff:	Placido (Cid) Manalo, Jr, a civil servant with experience of the Philippine Government machine and the ideas under discussion for its organisational improvement.
	Professor Ramon (Monching) Garcia, a member of the faculty of the College of Public Administration.
Research associates:	A small team of Filipinas and Filipinos

Bel Samonte had just returned from attending a general management course at Henley, Cid Manalo had recently attended the equivalent in Mount Eliza, Monching Garcia was just off to attend a course at Lahore due to begin at the end of August.

Carlos Ramos's first American consultant did not materialise, but another in his place was expected to join us in two months time, and indeed looked in for a few days at the end of August to make his number. This was Dr Ray Randall, who was coming to us from an assignment in Jakarta which, to his distress, was being closed down owing to the internal troubles in Indonesia at the time. He was naturally much upset about this when he finally joined us in Manila. We did our best to help him settle down and while he was with us he was a challenge to our thinking. He did two very useful specific jobs for the academy but he was a sick man. He withdrew and returned to the USA in May 1964.

Meanwhile the Ford Foundation made it possible for Mr John W.L.

Adams from Henley, who had helped to start the Administrative Staff College of India, to join us for six weeks, as part of a larger Far East tour. His visit to Manila had been planned so that he would bring his intellectual and personal qualities to help us all at the time when we thought we would have begun to work on the course of studies. He was a staunch friend of mine and was an enormous help to me at this critical stage. It was a sad day when he had to move on to Australia.

As we settled down to work together Carlos Ramos made two points about the work we were going to do: first he wanted us as a group to see that everyone was encouraged to have his say; and second, that for a time the staff should regard themselves as exploring and not to think of themselves as making decisions, which he reserved to himself.

Very early on Bel Samonte circulated a memorandum about academy objectives. Here is the text of it:

Objectives of the Philippine Executive Academy

The Philippine Executive Academy has been established within the University of the Philippines, in response to a felt need for increased competence of general management at the top levels. Indeed, the effective administration of the nation's social and economic development programme requires capable, forward-looking administrators and managers in business as well as in government.

The Philippine Executive Academy is envisaged as a national centre where executives from various areas of the public and private sectors may be brought together for a free, systematic exchange of ideas and experiences through an integrated course of studies and research. As conceived, the Academy will be a community of practitioners, specialists and scholars dedicated to a mutual effort at increasing their capacity to cope with their respective functions and responsibilities, promoting better co-ordination and co-operation among them, and creating a strong sense of participation in the great task of nation building.

To this end, the Academy shall carry out continuing programmes of executive development. These programmes will take into account varied approaches and courses in the field that have been introduced in the United States, Great Britain, Norway, Pakistan and other countries. Such cumulative prudence and experiences, as adapted to the particular background, attitudes and environment, needs and problems of the Filipino administrator or manager, should provide the foundation upon which to build an institution that shall be the capstone of Philippine executive development.

In a developing country like the Philippines, the demands of management training are multifarious and urgent. The Academy shall therefore endeavour to meet such demands of middle and top management as prevailing conditions and available resources warrant. The feasibility of offering executive conferences and seminars for political executives such as department secretaries, under-secretaries, and provincial governors, will be considered. In any event, an *immediate* goal of the Academy is to formulate an intensive residential course designed for career executives who have assumed or are about to assume responsibilities of top-level management in departments, bureaux, commissions or agencies of the Government, in public corporations and private businesses.

It is presumed that those who will be selected to participate in this executive programme have had wide experience in their respective specialities or professions, as well as in administration. Thus, the Academy programme is primarily designed not to train participants in techniques or procedures in their special fields or departments, but to allow them to reflect and integrate their pool of knowledge and experiences, tested and enriched by an increased familiarity with the most modern concepts, approaches and developments in the art and science of administration. In so doing, they are expected to develop fresh, broader perspectives as they face the increasing burdens of top management and renew their confidence as administrators. It is indeed hoped that programmes will inspire them to develop a philosophy of management based on an inter-relationship of their varied expertise and experiences with the body of knowledge and values, trends and innovations that characterise a successful organisation and a progressive community.

More specifically, the basic executive course of the Academy shall endeavour to develop in the executive participants:

1. Broadened perspective based on a better comprehension of the economic, social and political environment in which they must operate as administrators;

2. Fuller understanding of the processes whereby policies at various levels are formulated, implemented and co-ordinated – through a better appreciation of the structural and dynamic aspects of modern organisation;

3. Greater effectiveness in making administrative decisions, formulating plans, achieving proper co-ordination and control – through the development of positive approaches and attitudes; sharpened conceptual, analytical and decision-making abilities; and improved skills in public and human relations;

4. Keener awareness of their respective roles in and responsibilities to their organisation, the Government, and the community as a whole.

Abelardo G. Samonte
24 August 1963

We discussed this and the ideas in it from time to time in the subsequent couple of months. Usually Carlos Ramos was himself in the chair, but not always. I felt as we went along that in some respect at least our ideas were in fact becoming firmer. It looked, for instance, as if there was a real consensus that our first priority was to work up a three-month residential course for what, in Government terminology, were called 'career executives' – a term which to my parliamentary democratic kind of mind seemed to exclude the politically appointed administrators who exchange places on elections. Special courses for the likes of these there would be, but not as a first priority. Indeed for all my time in the Philippines our target was the career executive.

Our ideas were firming up too, I thought, on the composition of the group. We were to try and get men and women from all three sectors of the economy. On the basis of thirty people in a session our aim would be ten from Government, ten from public corporations and ten from the private sector.

If there was doubt about this mix in Carlos Ramos's mind I understood it to be in whether or not the course of studies we were beginning to design would be attractive and valuable to men and women from all three sectors. It would clearly be up to us as a team to show that it could be. Carlos Ramos himself understood well that if we wanted nominators to spare these people to attend our three-month courses we would have to do a lot of explaining to their bosses beforehand; and if we wished the academy to succeed they would have to return after their course believing it had been a worth-while experience, saying so widely in the community. Our part in it would be hard work and no one thought it would be easy. As well as turning to the Philippine community for help, there were other sources, too, outside the Philippines that we could tap: Harry Slater from Mount Eliza, Al Gorvine from New York University and Professor Rolf Waaler of Solstrand in Norway, who came to help and to whose visits during my stay I shall refer briefly later on.

Getting nominations

In our attempts to attract nominations we described the composition of the sessions we were hoping to get in the following terms:

> The main composition should be at the assistant director level (just below the bureau director level) and their equivalents in the public corporations, in private industry and commerce and in other agencies of the Government. Perhaps a few bureau directors might wish to come on their own volition. Certainly some local government people might be expected and perhaps a regional director or two.

I said I would very much like to visit some of these people on their jobs. I was particularly interested in the Government agencies because I knew so little about them. Cid Manalo made arrangements for me to see four such agencies. From the men I met and talked with, I emerged with three substantial impressions:

1. The periodic substitution of a political appointee in the place of a
    career man in the top job of an agency was thought to bear down
    hard on the men at assistant-director level because it seemed to
    some that political influence penetrated everyone's life 'on the job'
    in the agency and resulted in unjust promotion and postings. Some
    could take this as part of life and laugh it off – the morale of others
    tended to suffer.
2. The bureau and its equivalent agency appeared to the staff to be a
    highly centralised unit of organisation in which the prospects of
    advancement for anyone were minimal. Once in a position as
    assistant director, or the head of a division which was the next level
    down, a man seemed to be stuck for ever.
3. The idea of improving the management in the public services was
    welcome enough but I was told that we would be wasting our time
    if we did not explain to nominators what we were doing. We
    needed to make them understand why they were sending people on
    our courses, tell their candidates the reasons too, and promise to
    back them up when they returned from the course. Otherwise those
    who came to us would continue to suffer on their return from the
    frustration which was the lot of anyone who came back from any
    course.

Most of these were in their late thirties or early forties and seemed, to
me at least, in need of the fresh air which would probably come to them if
they were to leave the narrowness of their own departments, find new
inspiration and generate new ideas and new attitudes of mind in the
company of a small mixed session of contemporary managers. The
nominators' problems would lie in understanding enough of the academy
to select people with the potential to make use of the opportunity and to
have a real interest in observing the effect the academy had on their
nominee – the two essentials from which all else would be likely to flow.

These brief visits pointed up the importance of getting on with the job of
selling the academy idea in the administrative/managerial community.
Carlos Ramos had already underlined this and was nudging me to go out
and meet senior people as much as I could, and to talk about what we
were going to do. By the end of August I had met about twenty.

I liked meeting and talking face-to-face with individuals whose interest I
felt I could rouse if they would give me a little time, and preferably with
those who would be likely to pass on their interest to others. I was never
much good at speaking before a large group, so my principal method of
selling the academy idea, when I had the chance, was by this individual
approach, to which I shall return presently. After my Pakistan experience,
the reader will not be surprised to find that I was desperately anxious for
the Filipinos to be heavily involved in this selling and recruiting activity. A
consultant has to take part but his colleagues, too, have to start learning
how to explain their academy themselves. So we made two attempts, in
which I hoped we would all be involved and be seen to be involved.

The first idea, which was mine, was that we would try to have published a series of articles about the academy. I had noticed that there were a few people of substance who had succeeded in having a series of such articles published in a well-known Manila daily newspaper. I set about writing these articles and told Carlos Ramos I was doing this. He could then decide whose name on the articles would best suit our purpose when he sent them in. I wrote eight articles and took a lot of trouble over them. They might have got into professional journals but there was no enthusiasm. I was after a wider public and for that they were held to be unsuitable; so that idea was a flop.

Then we found President Carlos P. Romulo, President of the University, willing to lend his name to a special kind of occasion called a Merienda. He would sign a letter, which we would draft for his consideration, inviting many of the good and great to such an occasion. The invitees, I was encouraged to think, would hardly fail to respond to an invitation from so eminent a person, so we would have a captive audience for about an hour with a chance to follow up afterwards over a cup of tea. Carlos Ramos and a few of the staff, including myself, would appear and explain ourselves – and what a lot of preparation went into that explanation! I have seldom suffered such frustration. In the first place, hardly anyone turned up, except a few already converted friends; and then President Romulo spent an hour explaining the many wonderful things which his university was doing, leaving hardly any time for us to talk about the academy. Did anyone tell him how important this particular Merienda was to the academy?

So I returned to my own conviction about the individual approach, with or without an invitation. Soon we began to draw rough lines between the public and private sectors and agreed that the Philippine members of the staff would visit the government agencies and public corporations; Ray Randall would explore interest in the private sector, visiting mainly American companies; and I would take on the British. Before he went home in May 1964, Ray Randall left us with the warning that it would not be easy to attract interest in the US business sector.

Eventually we had an average of twenty-eight members on the first three sessions. The balance between the three sectors was:

	Session 1	Session 2	Session 3
Government agencies	11	14	12
Public corporations	8	6	10
Private sector	8	9	7
Total	27	29	29

The process of nominations was:

1. Invitation to nominator from President Romulo of the university by letter to the head of the organisation.
2. Intense chasing of these letters by the PEA staff, virtually desk to desk.
3. Interview of proposed candidates at Rizal Hall.
4. Acceptance by the administrator.
5. Candidates reported at Baguio on opening date.

The course of studies and methods of work

The planning of the course was a little more complicated and took longer than I expected because our small team had to do many other things at the same time. It was not easy for us to share our administrator, Carlos Ramos, with others and difficult for him to devote as much time to the academy as he would have wished when he carried so many responsibilities. We were uncertain of the future plans for other management courses which we thought might help the same level of men and women, and perhaps there would not be enough people in the community to sustain more courses. We were inevitably involved in trying to explain our objectives and in getting nominations which, as we have seen, was not an easy business. We had to stake our claim for accommodation in the Pines Hotel in Baguio, explore alternative accommodation elsewhere in case the Pines cost too much, and do a lot of work on the permanent site requirements whenever the news came that a grant to build was near at hand.

All these needed a lot of thinking about as we forged ahead on the course, which meant meetings and outlines and hammerings till we had a general shape fitted roughly into parts. There was a lot of hard work and consultation as we got down to thinking through the different subjects, drafting the briefs, planning the reading, the visitors, and getting the whole fitted together into a timetable with such integration of subject matter as we were capable of achieving. Yes, we were under pressure during those eighteen months. From it all came the first course, which we laid before session 1 when it arrived on 8 January 1965 in the following form:

NOTES ON THE COURSE

I.   The course of studies

1.   Administration is concerned with the unity and continued direction of the whole of an organisation, whether the organisation is the Government as a whole or part of it, or whether it is a public or private corporation. The administrator normally has to deal with many aspects of it at the same time. Any division of the subject must be unsatisfactory and each separate part, considered in isolation, may appear to be

unrealistic. But for practical study some breakdown is necessary. The academy course is, therefore, divided into parts, some of these being further subdivided.

2. In the course of studies two main methods of work are used – the executive panel and the seminar. The procedures involved in each are described in the second section of these notes.

3. A list of the various parts and subdivisions of the course, showing which are carried out in executive panels and which in seminars and indicating the member of the directing staff in charge of each, is attached at the end of this note.

4. Panel work unfolds, mainly but not entirely, in the order in which it is set out in the note mentioned above. Seminar work is unfolded on a different principle, each seminar being fitted into the first seven weeks so as to provide members as far as possible with the background and the special help they need at the time they need it.

5. *Content of the work*

Part I is an introduction, which provides members with the opportunity of discovering the experience each panel has available in its members, of making a brief survey of some of the problems with which Philippine managers find themselves confronted, and of seeing how a panel subject works.

Part II is called the Environment of Administration and is conducted entirely in seminars. Each of its subdivisions is concerned to help members understand the relevance and significance of the political, social, technical and economic circumstances in which they work. As this understanding is necessary background for most of the course, much of it appears very early in the course; only the work of the national economy is spread out into later weeks to facilitate absorption by members. A good deal of healthy variety in the conduct of these seminars is to be expected, some being conducted by members of the staff and some by outside specialists.

Part III Internal organisation and management
In Part III are studied a number of matters which are internal to the work of a single organisation and, broadly speaking, can be effectively administered by the directing authority of that unit. These questions are examined from a number of angles.

III(a) Employee Motivation, Supervision and Productivity
A study which, as the title suggests, is designed to help members think about the people through whom they get their work done.

III(b) Personnel Management
A study of major aspects of personnel systems as deduced from the personnel policies and practices of the organisations represented, as well as from outside materials.

III(c) Delegation and Control
A study of the delegation of authority and the control that this involves.

III(d) The Improvement of Organisation
A study of the structure and dynamics of organisation; and the way people respond to organisational purpose and change.

III(e) Planning and Progress Implementation
A study of the way people plan in departments of government and in public and private corporations, the way they translate plans into active progress and the way they measure performance.

All the above Part III subjects are panel subjects.

III(f) Financial Administration
This subject will be run in seminar. It will be concerned to help the non-accountant acquire an understanding of financial reports and statements, and of the rules of sound finance.

Part IV External Relations
In Part IV, attention is turned to the fact that some of the activities of an administrative unit are not wholly within its control. Administrators in one unit have to maintain suitable relations with other administrative units, as well as various entities or groups and the general public. Out of these, two examples have been selected:

IV(a) Labour Relations
A study of the relations between management, on the one hand, and organised or semi-organised labour on the other. This will culminate in a role-playing exercise in which the panels will play the several parts of management, labour and government in negotiating a dispute.

IV(b) Relations between Government and Business
A study of the roles of government and business in which each panel will make a specific study of a defined aspect of national policy with the object of evaluating the existing arrangements for contact and consultation between government and business.

Part V Major problems of national development
In Part V there will be a change of emphasis. Work will be designed not only to study four selected problems of National Development but also to knit together in these studies much of the work that has been done in panels and seminars in the earlier parts of the course. The selected subjects are:

V(a) Starting a New Enterprise
In this exercise each panel will have the opportunity of working out a project for the establishment of a new enterprise, of their own choosing, in the private sector. It is presented as a typical feature of the current Philippine scene.

V(b) Urban Development
This subject, which will be a short seminar, is designed to introduce members to the problems of urban development in the Philippines. In the sphere of national development it is, perhaps, like the rest of Asia, one of the most formidable problems.

V(c) Selected Development Programmes
In this subject, the session will again be mixed in different modified panels, each such panel studying a separate subject thus:

V(c)(i)   Rice Production
V(c)(ii)   The Philippine Export Trade
V(c)(iii)   Transportation: Inter-Island Shipping

V(d) Field Research: The Development of Mindanao
An exercise, developed to study, in three selected areas in Mindanao, the factors which contribute positively to development and the factors which seem to impede it. To achieve this, each panel will, after some preliminary planning in Baguio, go to separate areas in Mindanao, work there for a week and report the results of their work on return. In the field they will be given some initial contacts and thereafter make their own way. They go simply as students of development.

Part VI Special Subjects
These, which support the general work of the course, appear in the first half of the three months.

VI(a) Biography
Each panel will make a study of an individual administrator with the object of discovering whether there is anything to be learnt that is relevant to those who bear responsibility today.

VI(b) Administrative Communication
A short seminar designed to crystallise members' thinking on the role and importance of communications, which will have been seen in many of the earlier subjects.

VI(c) Statistics
A short seminar designed to help members 'think statistically'.

Part VII The Administrator
A panel subject in which members will be asked to consider the character of the job of men who reach the top.

II. Procedure

Panel Work

6. The normal procedure for a panel subject is as follows:

    (i) Except at the beginning of the session, the chairmen and secretaries receive their papers some days before the opening of their subject. The secretary is responsible for arranging with the member of the directing staff in charge of his panel (DS) a time for briefing.

(ii) If reading material is distributed for the subject, it is put out in the library on the same day as the papers are issued to the chairman and secretary.

(iii) The chairmen and secretaries are briefed by the DS. The object of the briefing is to ensure that the scope of the task and the arrangements made are fully understood. Papers for other members of the panels are placed in members' boxes the day before the opening meeting.

(iv) After briefing, the chairman with the aid of his secretary is responsible for planning and directing the work of his panel. At the opening meeting it is the duty of the chairman to explain to the panel the scope of the task and to get agreement as to how it is to be tackled. At subsequent meetings, as shown on the timetable, the chairman is responsible for guiding and controlling the discussion so that the field of study is adequately explored and full advantage is taken of the resources available.

(v) In most subjects it is the duty of the chairman and secretary to embody the arguments and conclusions of the panel in a report, which is the report of the panel.

(vi) The report of each panel is circulated to all members of the academy and, in most subjects, a 'consider reports' period is provided so that each panel can consider all the reports and submit matters for discussion by the academy as a whole.

(vii) Finally, all panels meet in a plenary session at which the chairman, representing his panel, presents its report in a short speech. This is usually followed by a discussion of questions submitted by panels. Such meetings are known as presentations. The chairmen present the views of their panels in their speeches.

7. Some subjects end in conference to discuss questions submitted by panels. In these there are no presentation speeches. There are other modifications of procedure for particular subjects.

Seminars

8. There will be some variety in the procedures adopted by different seminar leaders; but the normal procedure will be as follows:

(a) A folder describing the purpose of the seminar will be circulated to individual members and should be read before the seminar starts.

(b) In most cases the reading material provided will be reference material which has been assembled to enable members to pursue the subject of the seminar later if they wish to do so. In some cases there may be a few reading papers which members will be advised to read before particular occasions.

(c) All seminars will be held in the meeting room.

(d) The work will in all cases be conducted by an expert or specialist who will seek to engage the participation of members in work in which their knowledge or experience are likely to be limited. Members will be expected to make use of the guidance and instructions received in later parts of the course.

9. The day-to-day work of the academy will be governed by the main timetable. Extracts from this timetable are made in the form of subject timetables to help members see the span and distribution of time available for each subject in a convenient form. If, to suit the convenience of visiting speakers, seminar leaders, etc., amendments have to be made to the main timetable, these will be distributed in the form of amendment lists to all members.

The course of studies

	Method	*Member of staff in charge – session 1*
Part I *Introduction*	Panel	Brig. Cornwall-Jones
Part II *Environment of Administration*		
(a) Administration & Policy Development	Seminar	Dr A. Samonte
(b) Accountability	Seminar	Brig. Cornwall-Jones
(c) Social, Cultural and Technical Factors in Administration	Seminar	Prof. R. Garcia
(d) The National Economy	Seminar	Mr H. Slater
Part III *Internal Organisation and Management*		
(a) Employee Motivation, Supervision and Productivity	Panel	Dr A. Samonte
(b) Personnel Management	Panel	Dr A. Samonte
(c) Delegation and Control	Panel	Brig. Cornwall-Jones
(d) Improvement of Organisation	Panel	Mr P. Manalo Jr.
(e) Planning & Programme Implementation	Panel	Mr P. Manalo Jr
(f) Financial Administration	Seminar	Mr H. Slater
Part IV *External Relations*		
(a) Labour Relations	Panel	Prof. R. Garcia

(b)	Relations between Government and Business	Panel	Brig. Cornwall-Jones

Part V *Major Problems of National Development*

(a)	Starting a New Enterprise	Panel	Brig. Cornwall-Jones
(b)	Urban Development	Seminar	Brig. Cornwall-Jones
(c)	Selected Development Programmes		
	(i) Rice Production	Panel	Prof. R. Garcia
	(ii) Philippine Export Trade	Panel	Brig. Cornwall-Jones
	(iii) Inter-Island Shipping	Panel	Dr F. Garde
(d)	Field Research: Mindanao Exercise	Panel	Dr A. Samonte

Part VI *Special Subjects*

(a)	Biography	Panel	Mr P. Manalo Jr
(b)	Administrative Communications	Seminar	Dr A. Samonte
(c)	Statistics	Seminar	Prof. R. Garcia

Part VII *The Administrator*		Panel	Brig. Cornwall-Jones

Baguio and session 1

When we left Manila for Baguio to hold the first session, we were about halfway through the three years we eventually stayed in the Philippines. From now on we could go up to Baguio for each session and when it was finished return to Manila to prepare for the next. My wife and I went up on the 28 December 1964, ten days before the session started. The academy staff arrived on the 3 January. We were all still hypnotised by the magnificence of the Baguio scene and hoped our permanent home would be built there. We had seen the site proposed for it 12 km outside Baguio and this had already been bought.

It was not long, however, before some doubts about Baguio as a permanent home began to creep into people's minds. Twelve kilometres was quite a long way on a mountain road and our members would need to find relief from the isolation in which they would be living. There were no villages nearby and one would have to go to Baguio for everything. I imagined the academy would need to secure directing staff who were prepared to serve it for some years if they were to help build the PEA up to the standard that it would need to survive. Would we get them if their homes were in Manila, their wives were accustomed to working and the only work available to them was in Manila, while the DS himself would be needed 250 kilometres and 1500 metres up in Baguio for six months in the year? This staff problem, plus the possibility that the water supply to the site might have to be pumped up the mountain side some hundreds of feet could be really serious threats to the permanent building dream.

Meanwhile, we decided to test Baguio, its road, air communication and its weather, and the practicability of running sessions in the hotel and moving ourselves up from Manila. We found some snags of course: we had to move the library up and down; and as we opened in Baguio the office in Manila had to be manned by someone competent to deal with the changes in the nomination situation. Neither of these problems was easy to solve but surely with practice such difficulties would be overcome. I went up to Baguio ten days before the opening date, for two reasons – first to work in peace on the allotment of members to their panels and to their responsibilities as chairmen and secretaries. The drafts of these had to be seen and checked by my colleagues and amended if possible in the light of their comments. Alas three members were then withdrawn at the last minute. The allotments had to be done again and checked in the very rush I had hoped to avoid. We started our first session with twenty-seven instead of the thirty we had hoped to get.

The second reason I went up early was to be on hand in case my colleagues needed my help on other matters. Carlos Ramos, for example, was down to address the session after dinner on their first night. Bel Samonte was to talk to them about the course of studies the next morning. Panel DS had to meet their own panel members and brief their chairmen and secretaries for the early subjects – there was a good deal of hard work in these preparations. An old hand who has seen all of this done by other people in other lands has a fair idea of what needs to be said or done to get a session off to a good start. So I wanted to be there, though nothing absolved my colleagues from the responsibility of putting into Philippine terms any advice I might give them. So we were all pretty busy in those last few days before the 8 January 1965. I attended all the academy occasions but kept clear of the panels when they started work while each DS was getting to know and help his own group.

I was clear in my own mind that I could not do justice to the job of a panel DS and that of a consultant at the same time. I just had to come to terms with this, knowing well that it would not be easy. As a consultant, of course, I could and did go into any panel I liked, subject to the normal courtesy of getting the DS agreement. I took one over for a single subject – the Export Trade – just to see what a Philippine panel was like. I saw them all together at presentations, conferences and other academy occasions, where I got a pretty fair idea of the quality of the small and larger groups of nine and twenty-seven respectively. This made up for what I missed in not being a panel DS.

My wife and I entertained all three panels in our house. I lunched every day with members and these kinds of occasions did a great deal to help me understand middle-management society in the Philippines. I dare say I learned most when I accompanied a panel on the field exercises in sessions 2 and 3. I have seldom laughed so much, for instance, as I did when individuals related and told me stories out of their own lives. Now and again I trod on a toe which seemed to me to be a bit over-sensitive, only to find in the end how generous a people they are in their forgiving.

Session 1

Session 1 had some encouraging features that are worth pointing out. Some really good men were on it who carried substantial responsibilities in their jobs. There was a good chance they would give a lead to the first session. They approved of the mixed group though they were not slow in recognising the need for a better balance in the representation of the three sectors. They reacted favourably to the way the course was organised and to the way members were required to participate in the management of the work they were asked to do. At the other end of the spectrum it looked as if there were going to be some who would not find it easy and had little to say, but it was not long before we found out that the majority were middle-of-the-road men who would be able to contribute. The members had to set aside some Philippine customs to fit in with the course we had prepared. They saw the need for everyone to be punctual on all formal occasions and thereby startled visitors who knew the unpunctuality of the Filipino. Gradually oratory was abandoned and replaced by short speeches. I cannot think what we should have done if members had found it impossible to accept the requests we made of them in these two respects.

I wondered whether a society which took such pains to avoid upsetting people would really be able to engage each other in discussions which would be free and frank and inevitably on occasions critical. Evidence that members were prepared to challenge each other in discussion was slow in coming but I hoped that here, too, it would become established practice.

I wondered how the visiting speakers we needed to stimulate the academy discussions would respond to requests to fly up from Manila. Most of them would be able to get back on the same day but for some it meant a night in Baguio.

The response in fact was very good indeed. When we could we would adjust our programme to suit their convenience and when they were able they adjusted theirs to ours.

From my Henley experience and from my standpoint as a consultant, who had been involved in the preparation of the course and attended panels from time to time and all academy occasions, I had plenty of opportunity to observe and I saw growth during the three months. Gradually men organised themselves better for panel meetings, discussions became more coherent and less excited, visiting speakers were seldom challenged on what they said but were welcomed, questioned and discussed later in panel. Gradually the raw groups looked like becoming teams, responding to those who gave their minds to their roles as they took the chair.

We in the academy were all learning. We felt that session 1 had been a modest success, but as they left on 31 March 1965 it was already quite clear that there was a great deal to be done by us in the six months we had before session 2 came in on 24 September.

Development

In the remaining pages of this account I try to draw together the issues that arose and had to be dealt with during the rest of my time in the Philippines. There was a great deal to be done if the academy was to survive.

Command and staff

There were two problems which caused me a good deal of concern. The first was the fact that Carlos Ramos had substantial other responsibilities in addition to that of establishing the academy. In my heart and in my head I felt that this was wrong. At least in its formative years I believed very sincerely that the man who was to set it up needed to put the whole of his thrust and drive into making it a success. He could only do this I thought if he gave himself to the academy full time. I did my best to persuade him to accept my view on this – to the point when sometimes I know I exasperated him – but he never did while I was with him. A full-time replacement for him seemed to be beyond the resources the academy could command.

My second cause for concern was the freedom with which men appointed to the staff in the PEA were expected to combine their responsibilities in the academy with other responsibilities outside it. It astonished me, for example, to hear quite early on in session 1 that as soon as the session was over our director of studies was off to Hawaii for six months on research, and that the other three members of the directing staff would be expected to teach part time in the graduate school; or in the case of Flaviano Garde to return to the National Economic Council and only be available to us part time. We were a tiny staff in any case. It became clear we had a great deal to do in the precious six months between session 1 and session 2, and it became equally clear that there were to be very few directing staff around to do it. Just the same as in Pakistan.

Nominations

Amongst Carlos Ramos's top priorities was a better balance between the three sectors and the elimination of candidates who were unlikely to take an active part in the work of their session. He reckoned he would be able to exert more influence on these two objectives if he had forewarning of the kind of candidates forthcoming. So he set out to get the president of his university to send, ten days after the end of the first session, letters that would galvanise nominators into action with a flow of candidates into the academy by the 10 June. This meant pretty fast work for our staff but ought to have given Carlos Ramos more time to visit nominators whose candidates had not come up to expectations. Alas the academy system was not yet geared to work at that pace. The letters went out all right – but were two months late. We lost that advantage and were thrown back on 'following up'. This tiresome process meant inquiring whether each letter had arrived, into whose hands it had actually fallen, walking in on chance to stir up action, making and re-making appointments with busy men, explaining, persuading, harnessing the help of members of the advisory council, talking to people over meals, getting introductions from friends to other potential nominators, and so on. Twice we had a bit of special luck when we met nominators who gave us two candidates each for the same sessions. This cheered us up, but throughout my time the getting of nominations was pretty hard going for all of us.

Short-handed or not we had to spread wider in the community an understanding of what we were about; and at the same time throw our energies into the improvement of the course of studies. Only if the courses were good and the members who attended them were prepared to say so openly would men and women want to come to them. The tension would go out of the admission system and we would be able to ensure at interview that the candidates we accepted were what we wanted.

The course and its methods

There was much to be done to the course and its methods after the experience in session 1. I will try first to show the changes we made to the methods and then later to describe the alterations in the subject matter in the course.

Panel work

Members spent a great deal of their time in panels so the success or failure of the panels as a way of getting work done in the Philippines was of critical importance. Carlos Ramos believed that the essence of the problem lay in those chairmen who did not take a firm enough grasp of their panels and in those members who, when not in the chair, were content to leave the work to others. He made clear his view that the responsibility for seeing that this state of affairs was improved lay with the panel DS. I thought he was right on all these counts. Eventually I left behind me a detailed note designed to suggest to panel DS what I thought needed to be done. I did not believe that guidance to members on chairmanship could be given by anyone other than panel DS. It is a continuing job through the session and can only be done by the man who is constantly with his panel, can watch performance, knows what he has said before and can decide as the experience of members increases how much needs to be said and when. Skill in chairmanship cannot be created all of a sudden by a couple of talks at the beginning of session. But I thought panel DS should:

1. Give the men some guidance at the beginning, the quality of which could certainly be much improved.
2. Follow this guidance up as the needs of the group were learnt – day after day and week after week.

I have divided this note into two parts. The first describes what advice a

DS might give his panel on chairmanship at the beginning of the session when he has them to himself in a panel room. The second part I have chosen to put into Appendix I, at the end of this chapter, where it can be read by anyone interested in following this up.

Turning back, then, to the guidance given at the beginning of the session, I thought that the essential points they should get across to their panels were:

1. Leaders or chairmen were appointed by the academy and were expected to lead their panels through the whole subject. For everyone this was a learning process. For some it could and did mean starting from scratch and ought to be thought of as an opportunity to acquire a new skill.
2. The chairman's first duty is to understand what the academy requires of him and what it has provided to help him do his job. The opportunity for satisfying himself that he understands both these things is at the briefing he gets from his DS. He has little chance of making good as chairman if he does not seize it at that stage.
3. The time between briefing and the first meeting with the panel is short. By then he, as chairman, must be ready to explain the task and suggest the way he thinks the panel should set about it. He has got to do some hard work and be ready for that opening meeting.
4. All panel tasks require that the chairman should divide the work between the members. He cannot do it all by himself so his plan must include the way in which he is going to apportion the tasks.
5. Everyone in the panel should be left in no doubt that the chairman not only needs but wants their help. He has to see that everyone gets a chance to make whatever contribution lies within their own competence.
6. The chairman's job requires skill which is to a great extent acquired by practice. He should be encouraged to give time to reviewing at the end of every meeting whether his plans for involving panel members are effective and whether results are being achieved in relation to the time scale he has set. The chairman really has to think.

Role of panel directing staff

The role of the panel DS is not so easy to describe. He is present with his panel at all times when it is sitting as a panel. He is not a member of it. He is sufficiently detached to enable him to follow the discussions and observe the performance of individuals and of the group as a whole. He is in fact in an ideal position to help if he feels he can do so without interrupting the process of growth. He has a choice between intervening during panel discussions or outside it. He may, for example, prefer to talk to a member over a drink or a meal rather than cause embarrassment by raising it in the group.

What kind of man was needed to play this DS role in those early days? He needed to have a personality of his own, a great deal of patience and two other qualities:

1. Experience as a manager or administrator such as comes to a man who has been responsible for the work of other people, and who has encountered other ways of doing things, other attitudes of mind; who has worked his way up, carried responsibilities which themselves had grown, all of which will have enabled him to build up a storehouse of knowledge and to be more mature than most members.
2. A growing awareness of the academic thinking that had begun to emerge from universities in many countries and an ability to bring some of this to bear on his panel discussions when he saw the two were related.

People with these attributes were hard to attract to the PEA, as hard as it was to get staff who were prepared to stay with the academy and help build it up.

Seminars

For the other method of work in session 1, the seminars, we turned to the community for leaders. The variety of expertise we needed could not be contained in the small team of DS we had.

The economic seminar. In the planning phase in Manila before session 1 started we thought very few of our members were likely to know much about economics. We ought therefore to enliven their interest in how their own economic system worked by explaining in a practical way the rudiments of some of the main economic theories and the relevance to Philippine economic development. So we searched for an economist who might do this for us. We found some men teaching economic theory in the universities but we needed a man with more than that – someone who by working in government or business had discovered how economics worked in practice, knew something of the problems the administrator/manager had to face and so would talk to our members in language they would understand. Alas, we found any such men were already deeply involved in the practising world and quite unable and unwilling to spare the time to prepare themselves and come up to Baguio six or seven times in so many weeks to lead this seminar. We particularly wanted the visits to be spread over the first half of the course and were in real trouble until one of us had the idea that perhaps the Australian College would help us out. Would Harry Slater come and could the Australian College spare him? We asked Maurice Brown, who was principal at Mount Eliza. We also asked the Ford Foundation if they would support this secondment if everyone agreed to it. They did and we breathed again. Harry Slater arrived three months before session 1 began, incredibly well briefed on the Philippine economy. He put the economic seminar on the map, setting the standard so that

Carlos Ramos could see what kind of person would be needed to replace him: in addition he volunteered to introduce in session 1 a financial seminar to help members understand and interpret financial reports and statements. With this, of course, Carlos Ramos was delighted, especially when it became clear that Harry Slater would be willing to come back and do it again in session 2 if his college were amenable. To this, again, everyone agreed.

Thus the Australian College and the Ford Foundation gave Carlos Ramos the breathing space he needed to find Mr Armand Fabella, who took on the economic seminar in session 3, and Mr Nuguid who took on the financial seminar. It was a remarkable achievement entailing great understanding on the part of the college at Mount Eliza.

The statistical seminar. We ran into much the same problem when we tried to find a leader to run a shorter seminar which would only entail three visits to Baguio. We needed a man who could inform our members of the uses to which statistics were being put in the Philippines, and warn them of some of the hazards they would encounter in using them. Morris Brodie, who at the time was director of research in Henley, used to introduce members there into this field in three talks which he embodied in a publication entitled 'On Thinking Statistically'. I had it with me. Carlos Ramos picked a statistician whom he thought might be suitable and we went through the book together. We thought Morris Brodie's thinking was relevant to the Philippines and that it could be used as material for the seminar Carlos Ramos wanted. But when the statistician came to try it out in the first session he found it difficult to avoid talking about the theory he had learnt in his college days. So it was not until session 2 that we found someone else who could begin to build a bridge of understanding between the manager and the specialist in this field.

The urban development seminar. I believe this was premature in the sense that no one was really ready for it – neither the staff members charged with the responsibility for studying the subject and its ramifications, nor the session, whose members were not used to thinking on the scale this seemed to demand. I felt I had failed to contribute to this myself and should therefore never have suggested its inclusion in the course. The decision to drop it was unanimous.

The communication seminar. This seemed to satisfy members' craving to be taught. I felt uncomfortable about it because I thought that the role and importance of communications was inherent in every subject we did and better learnt as the course unfolded, when the individual member could absorb what he himself needed.

Other seminars. I needed to learn about seminars and I picked up most of it in the Philippine Executive Academy. The main lessons I am sure were elementary:

1. The term can be applied to almost anything you like. They can be long or short. They can impose a lot of reading on members or not, and some writing too or no writing.
2. In a mixed session such as we had in the PEA a competent leader in

a field of knowledge can prepare the minds of members who come expecting to be taught and, whether they learn anything or not, make a psychological impact on the session, which is very important indeed.
3. To engage the attention of the Philippine managers, the leader needed to be either an applied specialist or able to explain theory to managers in language they could understand.

The introduction of case studies

Towards the end of session 1 Carlos Ramos wished to introduce a few case studies into the course. They would add to the methods a variety which would be refreshing, and they would sharpen up panel work by helping everyone see the value of probing more deeply into their own experience and into the problems we set them. The idea that the services of a consultant might be secured to prepare and conduct case studies for the academy was much in Carlos Ramos's mind at the time.

I was interested in these ideas and thought the advice of Professor Rolf Waaler might be useful at the stage we seemed to be at. Rolf Waaler had successfully combined the Henley/Harvard philosophies at his school in Solstrand in Norway and I planned to visit him. Carlos Ramos agreed and I spent five days with Rolf Waaler in Oslo at the beginning of June 1965. He gave me a great deal of his time and a lot of advice that would be useful. I embodied this in a report to Carlos Ramos and my colleagues, which is too long to incorporate here. Broadly what he told me can be summarised:

1. It would be unwise to rush the introduction of case studies in the Philippine course of studies: the finding of case material, the writing up of case studies and learning how to handle them takes much more time than one would imagine.
2. If we were proposing to engage a consultant we should be quite clear on the subject area we wanted the eventual cases to cover and to find out if the consultant would be willing to work in that area. Some men would like to work in their own field of experience because this would help them to discuss intelligently the material they would need to gather from their contacts and subsequently help in the handling of the cases in 'class'.
3. Before the consultant arrives it would be important to nominate two Filipino counterparts, young men, keen to be involved in this kind of work. They would need to have a knowledge of the fields in which the task was to be done and where the material was likely to be found, so that the consultant could get straight down to work.
4. A consultant should give a few demonstrations in the handling of cases. But it would be important that he ensured that Filipino members of the staff were involved. The handling of cases was very much a personal matter for the individual, and the Filipinos must develop their own methods which would not be the same as the consultant's.

5. With regard to the length of cases Rolf Waaler was much in favour of short cases, by which he meant two to six pages. He felt it would be wrong to start with long cases because the material is very hard to collect, they are expensive to prepare, and may overwhelm the student.

6. With regard to the handling of cases Rolf Waaler told me that in the early days of a session in Solstrand the directing staff would take the chair, never the members. Later, when members understood what was involved in a case and were willing to try their hand, then only might Solstrand allow them to do so. A case should never be part of the chairman's responsibility in panel.

7. There was no need to be too rigid about relating cases to particular subjects. It was useful to run cases which were relevant or partly relevant to a panel subject while that subject was being studied. On the other hand, it was quite a good idea to run some cases of which the relevance would only appear later. Sometimes, too, they could be used simply for variation and refreshment. Occasionally, a case which one had thought quite good just does not work and the reasons are difficult to discover. There is no need to feel frustrated if some sessions do not take to them as quickly as others.

I hoped these notes would be helpful and handed in my full report on 10 June in Manila. From all the talk that had been going on before I left there on 10 April, I thought there was a fair chance a consultant might emerge. I did not believe it would be difficult to find two young enthusiastic counterparts from the ranks of the Filipinos who had attended the annual courses in the Philippines or business schools in the United States. But Carlos Ramos wanted to move faster. What he did was to select a few ready-made cases from those available in Manila, persuade some men in the community to come up to Baguio and run them, and gradually involved members of the staff. In all, six cases were laid before session 2 and six before session 3.

I attended them all. They were not invariably well conducted but, when they were, members put their minds into them and obviously enjoyed them. There was a different flavour about them, a change from panel and seminar; but on the basis of six cases in three months I do not feel able to say more than that I hoped it would be possible for Carlos Ramos to press on with this experiment. Sessions 2 and 3 were different from session 1 and from each other, but all three sessions to my mind needed help in developing their analytical capacities.

The field research exercise

The reader will recall the enthusiasm with which the first Pakistan exercise designed by Karl Schmidt and Al Gorvine was received. I took this enthusiasm with me to Manila and found an immediate interest. What we did not discover so easily in the Philippines was a project with as good and clear a purpose as in the first Pakistan case. To ask a group of administrators to examine the ways and means of speeding up the flow of traffic through their two major ports, as we did in Pakistan, was one thing; it had a cutting edge which interested members, and it took them far away from Lahore. In the Philippines, Mindanao was regarded as the highlight of promise in national development at the time and was a natural choice for my colleagues. The purpose of the exercise there was that the men should examine the factors which might be helping or hindering the growth of three areas of land in that huge island in which the development of the infrastructure, agriculture and industry was at an early stage: this was quite a different thing. The purpose was less clear to members and the exercise might well have been a failure, particularly as it demanded a great deal of paper work and long days in the field, followed in the evenings by drawing threads together for the report and discussions they would have later in Baguio; it was a heavy exercise and occupied a big part of the course.

In the Philippine case, the three chosen areas of Mindanao were Zamboanga, Davao and Iligan. In each case it was judged to be a success. I believe the reasons were:

1. We had reshuffled the panels. Members disliked this at first but in the course of the exercise found refreshment in the change.
2. Work in the field seemed to appeal to the Filipino just as it did to the Pakistani.

In both countries there was a short sag in morale as members re-adjusted themselves on return to the academy but once this was over the whole session seemed to come together because each panel had received the same stimulus.

One of the difficulties in most field exercises on this scale seems to be that you cannot repeat them. They place too heavy a burden on the local officials in both government and business. So there was no question of returning to Mindanao for session 2 or session 3. We had to go elsewhere and this meant re-designing and working up new exercises. This was a major undertaking and led Carlos Ramos to invite Al Gorvine to come and do this for us in the summer of 1965. Again the Ford Foundation helped us out. I cannot imagine how we could have otherwise had a field exercise at all.

I accompanied one of the panels on each of the field exercises in sessions 2 and 3 and saw a new province each time. Sometimes the administrative arrangements for the men were good and sometimes they were not at all good, but it never seemed to matter very much. If there had been a little inconvenience, discomfort, even poor food, a panel seemed to me to come out a stronger team and this I thought was worth a great deal. It was in direct contradiction of what I had read, that the Filipino manager does not take to team work, which was nonsense. Gradually, too, I daresay we were introducing more and more members to parts of their own country they may not have seen before. Gradually, as the academy appeared in more provinces, more and more people were becoming aware it existed.

APEX (Alumni Association of the Philippine Executive, Inc.)

Towards the end of a first session, members sometimes express the wish to form an association of some kind to keep in touch with the academy/college after their return to work. The Philippines were no exception to this, though it was not until the end of session 2 that APEX was brought into being. The opportunity must have been unique as practically all the past members lived in Manila and could more easily assemble together than others scattered far and wide in a huge country like, say, India. APEX has since become part of the academy scene, to which Carlos Ramos attached much importance when I last heard from him.

Miscellaneous notes on the Philippine Executive Academy

C.-J. left this part of his book unfinished. He did not write the last part of this chapter as a complete sequence, and he intended to draw the ends together in conclusion. I thought it best to end with a few paragraphs he wrote after the completion of session 1 and then to add as appendices some of the most valuable and enduring pieces of his own composition:

Joan Cornwall-Jones

Main changes to be made to the course

Summed up briefly, the main things to be done were:

1. 'Stiffening-up' panel work. This was essential. What was required of the staff to ensure this? What could be done to improve chairmanships and the documentation of the course which would help to enhance the quality of panel work?
2. Introduction of some Filipino case studies.
3. Attempt to correct too much theory in some of the seminar leaders.
4. Re-define the purpose and re-design the exercise in field research.
5. Work to improve Part V subject Starting a New Enterprise. In this context, I was already beginning to feel the need for an industrial production/marketing man on the Philippine Executive Academy staff to keep the course of studies tuned-up to the requirements of the private sector and to help in this exercise in particular. This was a need which Carlos Ramos and I discussed and which, ultimately, led to the appointment of Mr John Landgrebe who was familiar with the Philippines and with Martin-Bates. John Landgrebe joined the academy as a consultant just after I left and brought his influence to bear on session 4.
6. Eliminate Part V subject Selected Development Programmes and substitute a new subject directed towards investment.

This was the raw material with which we were to develop the course of studies and get it ready for session 2. The new material had to be designed in the form in which we needed it; the old material had to be improved as much as was possible in the time. Then the two had to be moulded together in a new timetable leaving enough time to invite and fit in the speakers we wanted to come and support the programme on particular days and at particular times.

The other side of the coin

On the way home, I reflected on the extent of the progress we had made in the academy so that I could tell Martin-Bates on arrival. It was a good discipline at that particular moment because when one thinks, very properly, about what needs to be done to improve an enterprise one tends to forget what should be said in its favour: I thought there was a good deal to be said in its favour. We did not reach our full target of thirty men but to get twenty-seven I thought was an achievement. There were some very good men among them, the majority were well up to it – only the 'tail' was a bit too long but I believed that this could be corrected.

Against all the odds, there were seven men from the private sector and with them an acceptance by the academy of the principle of the public-sector/private-sector mix. To expand the private sector intake would be difficult, but it had become the academy's target and the members appeared to welcome the idea of the mix. They seemed also to enjoy the structured course and the discipline in it, and I think they understood that our interest was primarily in them. They had worked very hard and their morale throughout had been very good indeed. The only 'sag' occurred on their return to Baguio from the Mindanao exercise – it was hard for them to pick up again after sixteen days in the field.

The hotel, which at the time was hardly the place to build up a tradition of service, was not as bad as I expected. The men seemed to have decided to make it work.

I felt that Henley had a good deal to offer the Filipino. In the developing world it seemed to me that there was a compelling need for men to learn to work together more closely; the system we introduced put members under *sufficient* pressure to help them bring the best out of each other; and the process they went through made them organise themselves better, helped them with the difficulties they found in reconciling Philippine cultural traditions with modern organisational life. But to achieve this the staff had to be a strong one in terms of character and experience, as well as knowledgeable about theory and practice in administration.

Appendix I – Panel work in the Philippines

Just before I left the Philippines I wrote a few notes for my colleagues on the work of the staff in panel.

In panel

If I were a panel DS, what would I really be looking for in a Filipino panel room, after my three sessions?

1. I want my chairman to lead, skilfully. It may not be good at first. Do not worry, it can be made to improve gradually. One man learns from another. In the desire to let everyone have his say, chairmen hold back too much and do not lead and guide; they lose sight of the purpose of the brief or of a particular item in a discussion; they are scared of interrupting men because they have not the skill to do it. In their desire to be impartial they are weak in seizing opportunities to develop a discussion; they let a discussion meander on. They learn by doing, and others in the panel will help, but I must learn how to intervene sometimes myself to quicken the learning. Most of my guidance to chairmen, however, must be done outside the panel, consistently all through the session.

2. I want the group to get better at seeing the essentials in a discussion and discarding the inessentials. Panels are not good at this. Individuals will bring up small things, special to themselves, and cannot see very well what is important and what is not. I must intervene to make this change take place gradually over the twelve weeks. It can, you know, if you watch it and get to sense what the essentials are.

3. I want my group to get much better at using ideas, which they are given in seminars or talks, in the subjects they do in panel. Groups are not good at this. They do not seem to realise that seminars and talks are geared in to panel subjects and are meant to help panels in panel work. This ability to associate one idea with another is of profound educational importance to any manager. I must see it happens. So I must attend all seminars and talks, hear what is being given and see that they use what is relevant to their brief.

4. I want to coax my group – all the individuals in it – to read. They do not, you know. Most depend far too much on the newspapers. I want to change this. I want my chairman to distribute the reading material and insist on his colleagues reporting back only what they think is relevant to the task and doing it briefly. I want my chairman to interrupt such reports, when he recognises a useful and relevant point is being made, *then and there*, and get it discussed so that the group *use* what they are getting and begin to see how valuable the reading material can be. So, I must know what is in the reading material myself and challenge them if they are not using it. But I must be sensible about this because we are coaxing men to read, who mostly do not really read. One cannot expect too much and can only see gradual improvement. One man who does it well can be such a help.

5. I am very keen that my group should learn to work together and agree on all they can agree upon, under each other's leadership in turn. A consensus of opinion is so often essential in ordinary work and I do not think panels are very good at this at first. Individuals tend to stick to their own ideas and dislike giving way, whereas in life if action is to result from discussion there often has to be a compromise. At the same time the last

thing I want to see is an individual with real convictions, on a subject that matters, give way just in the interests of getting a consensus. This stifles a man's spirit. I must therefore develop in myself a sense which will tell me when a man is giving way when he should not and insist they argue out disagreements when they are worth while, and if necessary reflect disagreements in their reports. So often when men really face issues on which they *think* they are in disagreement, they *find* they narrow the area of disagreement by analysing the reasons for the views they hold.

6.   I want my group to get really good at organising work, and they are not very good at this on the whole. I must talk to my chairman if he does not organise his subject well. If his plan at the beginning is not a good one, I must tell him, outside of course, where it seemed to fail. If he has not come prepared for any period, and his men do not know where they are going, I must take him aside afterwards and tell him what was wrong. I must not be impatient about this but I must keep it up because otherwise it will never improve.

7.   I want to make full use of the fact that we have government and business men on the course and do all I can to see the different sectors understand each other better. I feel I ought to be able to do this better than we have done in the past, and I think I will achieve it if I intervene sometimes and get the men to work out *why* particular things are done this way in the public sector and that way in the private. One must compare first and then have a mind to enquire into the reasons for similarities and differences. It is these reasons that make for real understanding.

8.   I do not want anyone in my group to be left out or to feel left out. This does not mean everyone has to join in on every point, but it does mean that everyone should get the chance to participate, be encouraged to participate over the course, and join in as much as he reasonably can. In this I must be sensitive to individual attitudes and capacities (which means simply I must know my men) and I must recognise that some men will hold back a bit in the early days, others will talk too much, some will have little to say on one subject and maybe more on a later one where they have more knowledge or experience; some may be weaker than others, and so on. But one has to watch and see everyone is engaged and involved as much as possible.

9.   Another all-pervasive kind of thing to watch is the extent your panel 'looks beyond and ahead' when thinking or discussing anything. A manager when he thinks about things should be alive to their significance to other things, to their effect on what is going to happen or what may happen. He cannot afford to limit himself always to the immediate situation. A policy or practice or a decision which may be all right for today may not be adequate for next month or next year, or may have effects beyond a particular situation. Something he finds out may have a wider significance than may appear at first sight unless he develops this sense of thinking beyond or ahead. One can intervene sometimes with a 'How about the future?' or 'Does that make sense for all time?' – just try and cultivate a new way of thinking.

10. This leads to the problem of change. So many things change – the needs of men and their expectations, the climate of opinion in the country, the growing opportunities, the economic situation, the boss, the organisation or relationships – that a manager needs to be prepared for change, needs to judge between the changes he would like to see and the changes he can hope to make. I want to see my panel members eager to think about change, eager to change when they believe it might be done, always intent on detecting changes that may affect their work, receptive to new ideas that may help make for change where it is needed.

11. I am most of all concerned to see that each man in my panel gets better in doing all these things. I must therefore know his background thoroughly at the beginning, get to know him well, watch the way he is getting on, and not be afraid to talk with him if I think I can help. I can do much, if I really make a study of this and think out how to do it. There is no need to hurt a man if you only want to help – if the men *know* you only want to help. If I cannot do it myself for some reason, I can get other members to help perhaps.

12. In all these matters in panel, one has to remember that although one is on the watch for things like this, it does not necessarily mean that the DS will have to do anything about a particular thing at a particular time. The best thing of all is that the group should discover their own inadequacies and put them right themselves. But I think I have come to the conclusion in three sessions that panel DS ought to be fairly active in these matters because groups do not seem to realise their problems until they are pointed out.

I do hope you panel DS will improve on these ideas yourselves and determine what things you had best be on the look-out for in your Filipino panels. These are just some of my observations and there must be many other things you can think of. Keep these beside you in panel perhaps and train yourself to think this way till it is part of you and you do not need any notes.

The drafting and finalising of reports

This has been quite a problem in the Philippines. Panels often do not like the look of a first draft and tend to stay up late at night too many times helping the chairmen and secretaries make a better job of them. Directing staff have a difficult time deciding how much to intervene at this stage.

1. You have no hope of getting a good draft placed before a panel:

(a) UNLESS the secretary, or the secretary and the chairman, can 'communicate in writing'. This is a thing which every manager ought to be able to do but many are not good at it. You are therefore always very much in the hands of the secretary and chairman and cannot expect all your geese to be swans. But the standards should improve. As a good secretary comes along and makes a good job of it, others begin to see the standard and during the whole twelve weeks they *will* improve.

(b) UNLESS the secretary has the 'report requirement' always in his mind and makes notes that he can see will be useful to the report *as panel discussions proceed*. He has got to be quick enough to intervene if he is not clear what view the panel decides to adopt so that he can get it clear.

(c) UNLESS the chairman sees to it that the panel's views on points are made clear by the panel as matters proceed and the secretary notes them down. This is not an easy thing to do but chairmen must develop the capacity to do it. Sometimes when things get difficult chairmen can say, 'Well, leave it to us – we will do our best to reflect your views in the draft', and then hope they can make a good job of it.

(d) UNLESS, before the draft is written, the chairman tells the panel broadly how he intends to lay out the report and the main points he intends to put in it. If he fails to do this, it is the secretary's job to remind him to do it because the secretary needs it done.

2. If, in spite of this, you do not get a good draft, then the panel has to buckle down to it and help out. In the early stages of the course this is a good thing. It helps make the panel into a real group, just the act of going through the travail late at night. The need for this may recur once or twice during the session as drafts come up which are wide of panels' ideas. But it should not be the regular pattern. You want to work for a situation where the draft will be somewhere near the panel's views and where the tidying up can then be left to the chairman and secretary to do on their own, in the evening before the final reports go to the typists. If you never get to this point, the panel will have far too many late nights and will not be devoting the time it should to other subjects.

3. If things are not going well in your panel in this respect, at the end of, say, three weeks, then why not have a post-mortem and analyse the reasons why a particular report went wrong? You could drive home the points I have made in paragraph 1 above and everybody would learn how much needs to be done to prevent the whole panel getting involved. You do not want to prevent the group helping a chairman and secretary when they are in real trouble but they would be the first to agree it is bad management for the whole panel to be involved all night with every report.

4. As regards intervention by the DS at the report stage, the first thing is that the DS should see that the chairmen, during the discussions, are doing what they ought to be doing *vide* paragraph 1. Then, if a draft emerges which does not satisfy the panel, he can watch the panel's reaction and if the panel members are dissatisfied and make some constructive suggestions, I should leave them to it. If the panel is at a loss, then why not voice your own opinions? You can start by reading to them the requirements of the report as stated in the brief and ask them if the report really fills the bill. You could go on to point out some of the issues the panel discussed and which are not there. I have sometimes suggested a

framework for a report when I saw what they wanted and just could not get around to it; and I sometimes helped them to express a point which I could see they could not articulate very well. But I do not do this too much because I do not want to get myself into a position where they come to rely on me for what they really ought to do for themselves. I do not think I have ever stayed up with them late into the night, on a report that is.

1966

Appendix II – Note on technical assistance: the consultant's role

In the middle of 1964 Carlos Ramos and I ran into some difficulty in our relationship. He thought I was overpressing him to do something he did not want to do. He had the idea it might help if I wrote him a paper describing what I thought my job was. I did so in great haste before I left for Japan.

1.   The consultant must not only know but must understand that he is coming to an independent sovereign state. Some consultants do not really make this part of themselves before they arrive. You see it in things like grandiloquent programmes worked out with the greatest of good intentions. Too many advisers, enthusiastic about their experience, are inflexible in understanding that this may not be exactly what is required. This can be learnt, though it takes time and is wearing to both host and guest.

2.   The role of a consultant is to advise, and advice can be accepted or rejected. This sounds easy but is not because, for instance

(a)   The line between host and guest is not all that easy to keep clear. In the gestation period of a new project one is often asked to do more than advise, because there is a shortage of staff to begin with, or people are not used to working together and do not communicate and the adviser believes his advice has been accepted, and so on.

(b)   Although one tries to restrict oneself to advice, in fact it is hard to avoid playing a part in the making of policy. When one gives advice you have to watch yourself or you go beyond your role.

(c)   It is sometimes very difficult to reject advice when there is faith and vigour in the advice and the host is not quite certain himself.

3.   These sort of things I find hardly ever happen if relations between the host and consultant are strong and free and happy. We can both recognise and articulate instances where the lines are getting crossed and laugh over it. Assuming an adequate degree of competence in the adviser (a big assumption), this in fact is the core of the matter. The question is how do you get this state of relationships between people who live normally at opposite ends of the earth.

4. Obviously the adviser should know as much as he can about a country before he goes to it. I have some priorities in mind:

(a) You need to know how your hosts think, work and behave and so how to behave yourself. This sounds simple but it is not. I had no idea, for instance, before my first ever visit to the Far East, how different people's attitudes are to time, how they are accustomed to reach decisions, how they react to pressure, how fast they want to go and how they themselves achieve objectives. I made at least one mistake which wasted a lot of time. This area of behaviour seems to me to be easily the most important.

(b) Then you may think you have acquired a fair knowledge of the overall system in which a 'new' country has to work. When you get there, however, they are inevitably different from what you thought. You are usually working under pressure of some sort, or think you are because that has been your way of doing things, but there is so much to understand about an entirely different constitutional system, a different administration, a different economic situation, and you have such a short time in which to make a contribution. True, you have your indigenous colleagues to work with but they may not know what you really need to know.

(c) Then there is the fact that affairs in any country are not static. They are moving all the time and changing under your nose. There is a history and a current thinking which you have to catch up with in addition to mastering the law and the practices.

5. In a perfect world where there might be plenty of time, and one could have improved one's understanding of these things before one left the shores of one's own country. But these assignments always seem to come up at short notice and one never has time. I think what I would have appreciated would have been (i) a couple of talks with men in London who knew the Philippines and what I would encounter and could tell me how to behave; and (ii) perhaps more of an organised induction on arrival. But after eleven months I doubt whether I would have understood much of the significance of what I was being told. One probably has to learn it oneself. It is a great help having lived for years in countries other than my own but even so I sometimes forgot that there are other ways of doing things than the British way.

6. I have some observations on Anglo-American collaboration in senior-management education institutions. There are differences in approach (in the university men I have worked with) and there are different temperaments. It is important to distinguish between the two. There is no reason at all why the differences in approach should not be reconciled and no need for the host to worry too much about them if he knows what they are. In fact, I think he stands to profit if they can be reconciled, as I myself have profited from the challenge and refreshment of American attitudes and the rigour of their discipline in the intellectual fields.

The practical problems which I see, and which I think have been my problems, are:

(a) The United States university man, and for all I know all university men, want to teach. The Henley man wants to let the men teach each other. This is an overstatement but is near enough. Both have to learn that the problem is not 'either-or' – it is how best to combine the two ideas through the hard grind of co-operation.

(b) The American seems (I have too few examples to justify the statement) to want to 'hit the man hard' with a lot of high policy stuff at the beginning of the course. I have been educated in the belief that one gets more strength by building upon the experience the men have when they come and stretching and widening upwards as I go. This has to be reconciled, if not by agreement then by the decision of the host. It is a bit tough in the argumentative time but not serious if you know what's happening.

(c) The university man, I should think in any country, divides his work up in what academics think of as respectable ways. His disciplines are accepted all over the world. A Henley man divides the work up in a way which seems to be completely foreign to the university. He slashes across all the accepted boundaries and makes divisions of his own because he has a different purpose, and has only got three months, and believes as much in the method as in the intellectual content of the work for results.

7. These are the things which can be settled. There remains the question of temperament and personality. The ability to sit down and talk without losing your temper – when as I have already said there is already some international competition in the air and the field is controversial – is quite vital. Each time one fails, it is worse next time and all of it bears on the host as well as the nervous systems of the consultants. Tolerance seems to be a very important quality, only equalled perhaps by a sense of humour.

8. How does the host reduce some of the risks he must run in trying to get the right man? This is a very difficult problem. Some of the points I have noticed are:

(a) It is difficult for both sides to know what *is* required. On the one hand, the field may be new to the host and on the other the consultant will find it difficult to see how much is wanted of him. Time is required to get mutual understanding and both must, of course, make allowances.

(b) The host cannot travel too much to interview people so he has to rely on other people's advice, who again may not quite realise what is required.

(c) The 'right' man is probably in short supply anyway.

9. It is too easy to say that the host should make clear what he wants

and the guest should absorb this. They should but it is not easy to be precise, and still more to be confident of personal qualities. Too often choices have to be made, or just are made, in too much of a hurry. In trying to jot down quickly now the thoughts that seem to me to be important I shall miss a lot but here are some:

(a) Previous experience abroad *ought* to make a consultant more adaptable to a new environment.

(b) Known tolerance in the sense of being able to deal with other people as equals, and a sense of humour I have already mentioned.

(c) Can the host get a really *frank* statement of a man's strengths *and weaknesses* from someone the host knows?

(d) Time for the consultant and his family to adjust themselves to the idea and equip themselves to understand.

(e) If some kind of course can be given a man before he leaves, and a small planned induction course on arrival, these would help but the variety of needs must make this difficult of accomplishment.

10. I hope these points will be of some use to you in your immediate task. They cannot I am afraid be a fully considered view. I am still 'learning as I go'. Personal relationships seem to me to be the key to success, but these must spring from respect for competence. Absence of this I know very well can destroy the whole relationship.

Appendix III – Notes on the PEA by Rolf Waaler

These are notes on the Philippine Executive Academy made on 1 February 1966 by Professor Rolf Waaler in answer to questions posed by Carlos Ramos. Professor Waaler stayed with the Academy for two months – 7 December 1965 to 7 February 1966.

General comment on quality of the course

'A good foundation has been laid. What I have read is generally well done, conscientiously done: sometimes more specifically and more detailed than usual in Solstrand.'

Developmental advice on the methods of work

At the time of Rolf Waaler's visit the academy was using the panel as the backbone to its methodology; in addition six seminars of varying length and under different leadership, and six short case studies.

What Rolf Waaler seemed to me to be saying as we started off on 1 February 1966 – my last session in Baguio – was:

(a) We should seriously consider using more variety in our methods because too many of our members were weak in knowledge and experience.

(b) Consider using some more seminars; he gave us some illustrations of different kinds of seminars that he thought might be useful.

(c) We should be encouraged to get on with the gradual introduction of more case studies.

(d) We must experiment in the course or we would never get improvement. Static behaviour in relationship to a course of studies and to teaching methods will lead to deterioration of the quality of the course.

Quality and composition of panels

The programme as it is offers the private sector less of interest than it offers the government.

Rolf Waaler has seen in the composition of session 2 that there were eighteen public service (agencies and corporations together) and twelve private sector. Why not change this to fifteen in each so that the private sector can see they are on equal terms? If then we also supplement the course of studies so that it meets the special needs of private industry, the PEA would be 'on the map' as serving both categories: an essential with the possible arrival of a Harvard AMP, or PEA may end up an educational institution for Government – which would be very unlucky indeed.

Rolf Waaler went further about the composition of the Filipino sessions in saying in another passage that we might even change the balance to eighteen private sector and twelve public. The quality, especially regarding dynamics, is usually high in the private sector. Members from government usually seem to be more static; and the background and type of jobs usually held by private-sector representatives are more varied than that of the representatives of government.

Finally:

1. The quality of the course stands and falls with the quality of the participants.

2. Staff work, even on a very high level, cannot compensate for poor quality among the members.

3. To get the PEA accepted by Government as an excellent developmental venture is therefore essential. This is the only way of getting more applicants than the PEA can accept, which again will permit the PEA to be selective and get the right variety (diversification) in the composition of its panels. It is not only the individual qualification of the participants that decides the quality – it is at least as much the right composition of the panels.

5

INTERLUDE:
AUGUST 1966 – DECEMBER 1969

JOAN CORNWALL-JONES

During our last few months in Manila in 1966, Dr Harry L. Case, the Ford Foundation representative, discussed with C-J the idea of his writing a book about the Staff Colleges because of his involvement with so many of them; and after much heart-searching C-J agreed. We left the Philippines in July 1966. C-J had decided to undertake a journey round the colleges to bring himself up-to-date. He had also agreed to carry out a feasibility study for the Thai Government on a Staff College there.

We began by taking a holiday in South East Asia and Western Australia, after which we went on to the first college at Mount Eliza.

Developments in Australia

C-J worked with the directing staff and heard about new thinking and ideas in the eight years since we had left. The number of members from overseas had grown and included, among others, managers from South East Asia, Africa, India, Pakistan, Afghanistan, the UK, Papua New Guinea and Japan. C-J talked late into the night with Maurice Brown (who had become the principal), Harry Slater, Jim Stewart (member session 2, now on the directing staff), and other staff. The college's progress between 1958 and 1966 is best summed up in Maurice Brown's words:

A body with growing traditions of quality has come into existence and has come to stay. Through the support of our sponsors and other people interested in administrative performance we have paid our way. Understanding of the college's purposes is growing, in Australia and beyond: our nominators want to go on nominating and the list of nominators is growing. We are being drawn increasingly into consultation about the setting up of other comparable bodies, here and abroad; and the college is developing a life and climate of its own. We are engaged in a rigorous review of the content and method of our course (research and development is as important here as it is anywhere else), and we are looking out for things we might usefully do which have not previously occurred to us.

I am often asked how one assesses the results of a venture like ours. We argue among ourselves, of course, about the validity of various measures of success. Looking at the process as a whole, however, I would say that the people who have passed through the college have had an opportunity to acquire a quite substantial body of information, an insight into their own strengths and needs as managers, and a better perspective in which to practise their craft.

C-J's notes suggest that the main new venture was an intermediate course of four weeks for junior executives between the ages of twenty-five and thirty-four. This course was to give the promising younger administrator an opportunity to build on his own experience and that of his fellows; to reach a better understanding of his work and that of his superiors; to face some of the problems, principles and co-ordinative techniques which form the basis of administration, to gain instruction and practice in some of the personal skills the administrator needs; and to get an appreciation of his own role and that of his enterprise as part of the community as a whole. Candidates for this course should have shown evidence of promise as administrators, and have had some experience of junior executive work. No formal academic standing was prescribed. The college selected forty-five members for the session. Where practicable, candidates were interviewed by members of the directing staff and the selection conducted so as to include the widest possible diversity of training and experience. The maintenance of a suitable balance in the composition of a session was of vital importance. The method of work was similar to that of the advanced course.

We spent about five weeks at the college and then visited Sydney, staying with Keith Steel (session 1), general manager of the Australian Mutual Provident Society and later chairman of the council of the Australian Administrative Staff College.

During our travels, C-J felt it important to meet as many past members of all the colleges as time would allow. He saw this as maintaining both the interest of the members in the institution of the college and building a link between the college and the members. In Melbourne and Sydney the association arranged reunions for C-J and invited former Henley members resident in Australia.

C-J wanted to go to the Eastern Region of Public Administration Conference to keep in touch with the latest developments of management and public administration in Asia. Iran was to be the host country for the Fourth Conference of EROPA, of which Dean Carlos Ramos (Philippines) was the secretary-general and one of the founder members in 1958. We left Sydney by sea for Bombay, and flew on to Teheran.

EROPA's objectives are: (i) To promote the adoption of more effective and adequate administration systems and practices in order to advance and implement the economic and social development programmes of the region; (ii) To develop managerial talent, especially at the executive and middle-management levels. When the conference ended, we travelled via Afghanistan to spend a week in Lahore and promised to return the following winter for two months.

Thailand

At the request of Martin-Bates (Henley) we next visited Thailand. On 25 December we flew to Bangkok. The Lufthansa plane was decorated with Christmas trees: we were the only passengers! Mr Pathom Jarnson, Director of the National Institute of Development Administration (NIDA) was at the airport to meet us. For two months C-J met many senior officials in the Government and managers in the private sector, and consulted with Minister Bunchana Althokor, rector of NIDA, about plans and ideas. He also visited various parts of the country and saw several of the industrial development schemes. He met financiers in the Thai Bank and other commercial ventures. He then wrote a short paper, 'A bird's eye view of the Thai Society', as background to his report to Minister Bunchana, Martin-Bates and the UK Ministry of Overseas Development. The Thai College seemed unlikely to start for some time as a great deal of planning would be needed on finance, buildings, staffing and finding nominators and other basic ground work which all the other colleges had undertaken before their inception. One of C-J's conclusions was the importance for course members to be proficient in English. In a letter to Martin-Bates in February 1967 he wrote:

> It was not until quite late in my time in Bangkok that I had myself come to realise the importance of this. I had been given to understand that the course would be in Thai and I now wnated to challenge this. In the private sector, I had gained the impression that up-and-coming Thais were realising that if they wanted to get on, they had to learn English. I knew it was more difficult in the public sector, where men had little practice in speaking English. But if the Civil Service and the public sector were prepared to spare a dozen Class One Officers for each session, would it not, for instance, be possible to give them instruction beforehand in English? It seemed to me to be a contradiction to start a College which aimed, above all things, to develop a manager, to broaden his outlook and at the same time to deny him so much of the broadening influences which were available from other countries, including the United States and the UK, by way of library material and visiting academics. I think both Minister Bunchana and Pathom Jarnson were impressed with the idea.

When the feasibility study in Thailand had been completed, we flew to Bombay to return to Europe by sea, staying in Spain for a few weeks. C-J had had little rest since 1960. He needed time to sort out his thoughts and papers before returning to Henley for the summer.

Lahore

In October 1967 once more we set off for Pakistan. On arrival in Lahore we stayed in the Ford Foundation flat for two months. Mr M. N. Abbassi, principal; Mr Hassan Habib, vice-principal; Mr Nasseem Mahmood, Mrs Satnam Mahmud and Dr Guthrie Birkhead of Syracuse University, were all still at the college. Whilst C-J was working I visited the craftsmen whose cottage industries I had helped develop from 1960 to 1963. They had made good progress in their work. The main crafts were textiles, metal work and rush matting. All of these were now being marketed in the big cities in Pakistan. I was able to do some work with them in the short time we were there.

The course in progress at the college was the first Regional Co-operation and Development course, which came about as a result of the Baghdad Pact, later CENTO. The RCD brought together Iran, Pakistan and Turkey. President Ayub Khan in his autobiography, 'Friends Not Masters', refers to RCD as follows:

> A major benefit of the pact was the Association of Friendship which we were able to develop with the Governments of Iran and Turkey. It was on the basis of this Association of Friendship that we were finally able to evolve the scheme of Regional Co-operation and Development. . . . . I worked out the concept of RCD on two assumptions: the first was that, irrespective of size, each member should have an equal say in any regional alliance. (Any arrangement in which there is a dominant partner would run into difficulties.) The second assumption was that we should exclude politics and military affairs as far as possible.

The course syllabus was:

Part 1 General Administration

(a) Organisation theory and practice, with particular reference to the Governments of Iran, Pakistan and Turkey.
(b) Personnel administration and human factors.
(c) Budgeting and financial control in Iran,Pakistan and Turkey.

Part II Foundation Lectures

(a) Development economics
(b) Development administration
(c) International relations

Part III Programme Administration

(a)   Economic planning and development in Iran, Pakistan and Turkey.
       (This includes subjects like agriculture, industry, economic
       development, planning, population policy, etc.)
(b)   Local Government
(c)   Education
(d)   Organisation in action and the role of the administrator

Part IV RCD concept, structure, organisation, progress and future
prospects.

Part V Field Tours in Pakistan, Iran and Turkey.

The college was flourishing. We had enjoyed seeing old friends again and
being back in a country in which we had made our home for many years.

Hyderabad – The Administrative Staff College of India

We left for Delhi just before Christmas at the invitation of Mr R.L. Gupta,
the principal, to spend a session in Hyderabad at the Administrative Staff
College of India, which John Adams of Henley had helped set up in 1957.
As far back as 1947 the Indian Government had heard of the proposed
college at Henley and had become interested in the Henley philosophy.

In 1953 a committee of the All India Council for Technical Education
recommended that an Administrative Staff College of India be established.
The committee was representative of both Government and industry. Two
of its members visited Henley that year.

A Court of Governors was set up under the chairmanship of Dr John
Matthia, a former Minister of Finance in the Central Government, at the
time he was a director of Tata's and vice-chancellor of the University of
Kerala. Towards the end of 1956, General S.M. Shrinagesh, who had
retired from the army as Chief of the General Staff, was appointed as the
first principal of the college.

Hyderabad, in Andhra Pradesh in south-central India, was the city
eventually chosen for the college to be established. It is situated more than
700 miles from Delhi and Calcutta and about 400 miles from Bombay,
Madras and Bangalore, the other main industrial and commercial centres.
Bella Vista, which had previously been the palace of the Prince of Berar,
the Nizam's eldest son, was made available. In 1957 General Shrinagesh
visited Henley and observed a session in progress. The Indian College
opened its doors in December of that year.

Before going to Bella Vista at the end of 1967, C-J saw as many as
possible of the founder members who had been involved in the creation of
the college and who could give him a background to the current political
and economic state of India. We went up to Chandigarh, the new capital
of the Punjab, to meet General Shrinagesh, the first principal, who had

now retired from the college. He and C-J not only had the colleges in common but also the old days in the Indian Army.

Over the New Year we flew to Nepal for a few days. We were fortunate in meeting an old friend in the Minister of Defence, Giri Parsad Bura Thoki, who had been in the battalion with C-J. (Since then, Nepal has founded its own Administrative Staff College in September 1982.)

We arrived at Bella Vista, Hyderabad, on 9 January, four days after the start of session 31. Mr R.L. Gupta and his staff welcomed us. Dr G.R. Dalvi was director of studies, Mr R.J.M. Shelton of Urwick Orr, UK, the Ford Foundation consultant helping with the new consultancy project. We also met Dr C.D. Deshmukh, chairman of the Court of Governors.

Over the eleven years since 1957, the college had gained a reputation and become accepted by Indian management and administration. Like most of the colleges, ASCI was independent, being funded by subscription from the private sector of industry and commerce but with Government contributions related to the number of participants from Government service.

The senior programme, modelled on Henley, was the main course in 1964. In 1965 the college started expanding and diversifying. The main factors contributing to this were the Indian Government's interest in developing management, coupled with a substantial grant from the Ford Foundation.

C-J worked at the college for three months. Towards the end he wrote two papers which set out candidly his views on what he had seen and heard. The first was 'The Senior Course at Hyderabad in Session 31'. On his return to England he prepared a shorter version, which is part of this chapter. The second paper was 'New Ventures'. This is included unabridged together with a programme of the courses the college would hold in 1968-9, which shows the great variety of courses introduced in the first ten years of this college.

I am indebted to Dick Shelton, the Ford Foundation consultant, who has given me a great deal of help in sorting out C-J's Indian Staff College papers, and to John Adams of Henley. They have both written papers on the college's history which will be of great value when the full story of the Indian College comes to be written.

'THE SENIOR COURSE AT HYDERABAD IN SESSION 31' by Brigadier Cornwall-Jones (1968)

In studying the environment, the course confines itself very largely to the internal problems of India. These are so vast that this is, no doubt, on the whole right. But might not the college begin to get the men to think a little more about India's relations with the outside world as well? For example, her financial relations with the lending countries and the international institutions, and the problems of her overseas trade?

May there not be a case for the re-organisation or re-grouping of subjects? This would require a lot of thought and I know that some of the staff would like to do something in this field. I hesitate to make any confident suggestions in the Indian context, but what seems to be needed is that the ideas in these subjects should be presented in an order which would enable the men to build up their thinking on a more systematic basis. Would it possibly make more sense to start with a subject on motivation, to go on with personnel policies and practices and then turn to organisation, integrating modern thought on these various subjects in a more systematic way?

A great deal has been done to teach the use of financial and non-financial figures and inculcate the need to measure work wherever you can. There is so much to be done in these fields that the work has, of necessity, to be distributed over a good deal of the course. But I have a feeling that it is at present so scattered that its impact and meaning is less than it might be if the material under both these headings could be a little more concentrated. There is room for improvement in some of the attempts to make men aware of some of the mathematical techniques, but it seems to me that this is mainly a matter of planning.

The claim that part of the course provides members with an integrated view of the management function is fair enough, but in session 31, at least, it seemed to be weakened by the treatment that was accorded to the subject, Adaptation to Change. I believe this has been done well in other sessions and I think the field of study is a good one. But a field of study like this requires much discipline, which seemed to be lacking in session 31. Perhaps this is an instance where a more positive and involved attitude of mind was required of the directing staff?

The rest of the subjects are perhaps fair examples of synthesis, though I had a feeling that Starting a New Enterprise might be toughened up and I wondered why in Public Relations there was no liability to render account for the work done — as far as I know this is the only subject so treated in the course.

The Climax. Any course needs a good climax and in a ten-week course where it is important to maintain the interest of the men and prevent them beginning to think too much too early about going home, a good climax is terribly important.

At present, the senior course relies on the cumulative effect of a number of subjects of approximately equal weight and interest — Starting a New Enterprise, Adaptation to Change, Management Development, a business problem, a rather long drawn-out study of the Five-Year Plans and the study made of leadership and direction. I think the senior course needs in its concluding couple of weeks a single subject with a particularly strong Indian flavour and appeal. This, which could only be introduced at the expense of something else, would I think add to the strength of the climax.

New Ventures

1. These include:

    (i)   A number of short courses designed to improve the performance of matured specialists in their own specialism (five already tried out, two proposed).
    (ii) An experimental short course for mature people on the managerial grid.
    (iii) A short course for young entrepreneurs.
    (iv) A proposed seven weeks course for junior executives.
    (v)   The consultancy service.

2. The ideas behind (i), (ii) and (iii) above seem to be:

    (a)   to contribute to pressing needs;
    (b)   to help sharpen the expertise of existing staff;
    (c)   to contribute to the finances of the college.

Individually they all make sense to me. The college problems seem to lie in deciding how many of these they can run and how often they can run them within the available time and accommodation, and in relation to the overall financial situation. Pressing upon the college also will be the question which is inherent in most courses and already apparent at least in the specialist courses, namely, how much time they require to do a good job: which seems, in practice, to me, how much time is necessary to teach and how much should be devoted to seeing that the teaching goes home.

3. The idea behind the junior executive course seems to be:

    (a)   to contribute to a need;
    (b)   to strengthen the finances of the college.

The problems confronting the college seem to me to be whether this is really a responsibility of the college or to assume in the light of the fact that it is one of the main responsibilities and skills of the Institute of Management; and if the college is committed to it to find the staff and time to plan a course in a field which is entirely new to them. Whatever may be done must be a very real success from the start.

4. The objects of a consultancy service, as I understand them, are:

    (a)   to provide a comprehensive service to both the public and the private industrial/commercial sectors;
    (b)   to provide a strong source of up-to-date material for all the various college activities;
    (c)   to assist in keeping the staff up-to-date;
    (d)   (I am less sure of this) to assist in the design and conduct of some of the courses.

I am merely interested myself in this as a means of strengthening the courses and building up the strength of the staff. I am aware, of course, that the whole process of working towards these objectives is still being considered and worked out. Meanwhile, I note:

(a) If the Senior Course is to remain, improved no doubt but in anything like its present shape, and if there is to be any form of interchangeability between the staff who serve it and the consultants in the Consulting and Applied Research Division (CARD), then the latter will require mature and experienced people.

(b) If the consultancy division is to have on its staff this kind of mature man he certainly will be in a position to carry out the kind of applied research that the Senior Course will need and feed it into this and other courses. This will only happen if there are enough consultants of this calibre with time following an assignment who can reflect on their new knowledge and transfer it to the training side.

(c) While I like the idea of a mature man from the directing staff undertaking occasional consultancy assignments to refresh himself, with the consultants relieving him in his DS job while he is doing it, I don't think it should be assumed that all the men who are interested in joining the directing staff will necessarily be interested in consulting work, or indeed, that all consultants will want to do the DS job or will have the necessary skills to do it. All this, of course, simply means that the interchange of men and ideas will need the most careful planning – a fact of which everybody, I think, is conscious.

(d) Assistance in the design of some of the college courses, if this is one of the functions of the CARD, does seem to pose a pretty formidable problem for the men running CARD. Will they not be involved primarily in seeing that the consultancy service is a really competent one and in feeding any material they acquire to the training side?

18.3.68

Administrative Staff College of India: Courses, 1968 & 1969

Senior Executive Course

Session XXXI	19 January	— 28 March	1968
Session XXXII	14 June	— 22 August	1968
Session XXXIII	17 January	— 27 March	1969
Session XXXIV	13 June	— 21 August	1969

Review Course

For Session XXIX	8 April	— 13 April	1968
For Session XXX	3 June	— 8 June	1968
For Session XXXI	7 October	— 12 October	1968
For Session XXXII	2 June	— 7 June	1969
For Session XXXIII	6 October	— 11 October	1969

Junior Executive Course
Session No. I | 26 October | — 23 December | 1968
Session No. II | 23 October | — 20 December | 1969

Profitability Accounting Course

Course No. III | 8 January | — 16 January | 1968
Course No. IV | 9 July | — 17 July | 1968
Course No. V | 3 January | — 11 January | 1969
Course No. VI | 8 July | — 16 July | 1969

Managerial Grid Seminar

Course No. I | 17 March | — 22 March | 1968
Course No. II | 16 September | — 22 September | 1968
Course No. III | 3 March | — 9 March | 1969
Course No. IV | 22 September | — 28 September | 1969

Marketing Management Course

Course No. III | 5 February | — 15 February | 1968
Course No. IV | 11 February | — 21 February | 1969

Materials Management Course

Course No. V | 2 April | — 11 April | 1968
Course No. VI | 8 October | — 17 October | 1968
Course No. VII | 1 April | — 10 April | 1969
Course No. VIII | 9 September | — 18 September | 1969

Production Management Course

Course No. I | 3 August | — 12 August | 1968
Course No. II | 17 March | — 26 March | 1969
Course No. III | 5 August | — 16 August | 1969

Manpower Planning Course

Course No. II | 28 February | — 4 March | 1968
Course No. III | 1 September | — 6 September | 1968
Course No. IV | 27 January | — 1 February | 1969
Course No. V | 9 September | — 15 September | 1969

Course for Young Businessmen

Course No. V | 26 August | — 14 September | 1968
Course No. VI | 1 September | — 20 September | 1969

Quantitative Methods Course

Course No. II | 10 December | — 18 December | 1968
Course No. III | 9 December | — 17 December | 1969

Personnel Management Course

Course No. I | 12 November | — 23 November | 1968
Course No. II | 4 November | — 17 November | 1969

United States

C-J had a visit to the United States planned for the autumn – from 23 September to 19 October 1968. Ten days were spent in Syracuse with Guthrie Birkhead reviewing the situation at the Pakistan College.

There were briefer visits to Ithaca, Michigan State University, Washington and Princeton to meet former colleagues. A significant day (17 October) was spent at the Ford Foundation in New York. The generous help given by Ford in Pakistan, the Philippines, India and later in Ghana is clear from the relevant chapters in this book. On 17 October the position in the first three countries was reviewed, as well as East Africa and Thailand. C-J's notes, made before his visit, as a basis for discussions with Mr Rocky Staples, head of Ford's Asia division and the Pacific, are important and revealing.

> Ford Foundation have put a good deal of faith and a good deal of money into these staff colleges. We believe it to have been a worthwhile effort. If the Foundation finds that this faith has not been misplaced would it not be reasonable for them to take some really direct interest in Henley itself? What my Principal, Martin-Bates, would be interested in is this: (i) Would the Foundation be prepared to support Henley by financing the salaries of two extra staff members who would give the Principal the strength in men which would enable him to offer help to the different colleges and meet the demands from new countries which continue to arise? (ii) Would the Foundation be prepared to support the secondment to the Henley staff of an occasional American professor who would really get to understand what Henley is about and at the same time be a great stimulus to Henley? (iii) Would the Foundation be prepared to support the idea that we should try and create a flow of American nominees to the Henley course, which my Principal thinks he could get if he had the opportunity to come out and explain himself to American businessmen? We would like, for instance, to have up to one American in every syndicate and if the Foundation really is out to promote better management in Europe, is not this one of the ways that they could help? (iv) In short, would not the Foundation be prepared to invite the Henley Principal over to New York to discuss these propositions with them?

Unfortunately this never materialised. We returned home from the States on schedule and renewed contact with Henley. C-J heard about the starting of another college at Achimota in Ghana. There was talk that he might be invited out as a consultant. He wondered if it was not time to retire and let younger men take over.

Principal's Conference

Martin-Bates recorded:

In 1969 C-J was asked if he would undertake the onerous task of acting as Secretary to the Meetings of Heads of Administrative Staff Colleges held at Greenlands on October 13th to 17th. His experience of War Cabinet committees and his first-hand knowledge of all the Colleges at home and overseas made him the ideal person to do this job. He produced a 24-page document at the end of which everyone said he captured the atmosphere as well as the substance of the meetings, and in addition made a substantial contribution to the success of the Conference.

The document is too long to produce here, but it still has much relevance today and is available for inspection.

Present:
Dr F. Akbari
  Dean, Faculty of Public and Business Administration,
  University of Teheran, Iran

Mr Maurice Brown
  Principal, The Australian Administrative Staff College

Mr J.P. Martin-Bates
  Principal, The Administrative Staff College, Henley-on-Thames,
  UK

Mr Khalid Power
  Principal, Pakistan Administrative Staff College

Dean Carlos Ramos
  Dean, College of Public Administration,
  The Philippines and Philippine Executive Academy

Mr N.P. Sen
  Principal, Administrative Staff College of India

Mr E.A. Winful
  Director, Ghana Institute of Management and Public
  Administration

  Secretary: Brigadier A.T. Cornwall-Jones

In attendance from time to time:

Mr John Adams, Deputy Principal, Henley
Mr Henry Taylor, Director of Special Projects, Henley
Mr Morris Brodie, Director of Research, Henley
Mr Ben Aston
Mr Andrew Life

Mr Winston Rodgers
Mr Aris Presanis
Dr Robert N. Rapoport, Tavistock Institute of Human Relations
Mr Harold Bridger, Tavistock Institute of Human Relations
Mr Roger Mottram, Industrial Training Research Unit, University
    College, London

Some of the main subjects discussed were development and research,
content and method of main course, role of syndicate directing staff, case
studies, evaluation of courses and members, integrative exercises, operational research, the distinctive contribution of the Staff Colleges,
diversification, optimum size, finance, and inter-college communications.
One day was spent in London visiting the London Business School and the
Royal Institute of Public Administration; the Minister of Overseas
Development, Mrs Judith Hart, joined the heads of colleges for lunch and
discussion; and the governors of Henley gave a dinner in the evening. After
the Conference, having seen a good deal of Mr E. Archie Winful, the
future principal of the Ghana Institute of Management and Public
Administration, it became apparent that C-J was wanted in Ghana. So,
from the middle of October, he worked on preparing himself to go there —
reading about the country and its people and finally planning a course of
studies. We flew to Achimota on 30th January 1970, where we stayed for
six-and-a-half months.

6

EARLY ACHIMOTA – GHANA INSTITUTE OF MANAGEMENT AND PUBLIC ADMINISTRATION, 1970

How the idea emerged

Late in 1966 Mr A.L. Adu, who had been secretary of the Ghanaian Cabinet in President Kwame Nkrumah's time and was currently Deputy Secretary-General of the Commonwealth Secretariat in London, came to think that Henley ideas might be of use to his countrymen in Ghana. It was believed in Henley that it was his interest that led to the proposal that the Government in Accra invite Mr Martin-Bates, as Principal of Henley, to come to Ghana and discuss the establishment there of a Staff College bearing some similarity to the Administrative Staff College at Henley.

In response to this invitation Martin-Bates spent 12 – 13 December 1966 in Ghana as the guest of the Institute of Public Administration and the National Liberation Council. The preparations for this visit were carefully made. Martin-Bates gave a public lecture on higher education – primarily on Staff College work – which was well attended by about two hundred people, including many of the senior officials in the Government and a good many industrialists. He had a private audience with the Head of State, and Chairman of the National Liberation Council, General Joseph Ankrah, when the role of the college in helping to rehabilitate the economy following the overthrow of the Nkrumah regime was discussed. His detailed discussions about the college were mainly conducted with Mr Victor Mamphey, the principal of the Institute of Public Administration, and with members of his staff and of his governing council, the intention of the Ghanaians being from the outset to attach any Staff College for senior-management training to that institute.

These discussions provided a well-timed opportunity for Mr Mamphey to discuss with Martin-Bates the main things that would need to be thought about if the Ghanaians intended to have an Administrative Staff College. The aims of the college, for instance, might well be to bring together members of the public service, industry and commerce, the armed forces, banks and possibly trade unions, and to provide an education in management and administration. The size of a session might be about twenty-seven, the proportions of the three sectors on each session being approximately equal, the level of people being men and women who had 'substantial experience and clear ability and were likely to make further progress in their careers'. Given the representation of the three main sectors of the economy in each session, the precise details of the mixture on particular sessions could be flexible and it would be wise to start on a modest scale of operations (say one course a year) until the nature of the Ghanaian mixture became clearer and until it could be seen what the demands of the Ghanaian community on the college were really going to be. Consultation with the principal likely nominators on the main facets of the proposed college, including the broad nature of the work members might do on the course, the duration of courses, and the number to be held each year, would be imperative. On all these basic wisdoms Mr Mamphey and Martin-Bates seemed to be in general agreement.

Finally they discussed the constitution of the proposed college and particularly the relationships between it and the Institute of Public Administration. There was a strong case for these two institutions being placed alongside each other as was proposed. They would share many common facilities, for example. But in putting them next to each other there were some hazards. For instance, if the new college really was to cater for both government and business on the same course, then it must be seen to be a joint government/business venture and must be governed by a council or board which would have on it a strong representation from both government and business. It would be a real mistake to let the impression grow in the community that it was merely an extension of the Institute of Public Administration. The functions of the two bodies would be different. The educational methods would be different, and the relationship between the college and its nominating organisations would be of a special and distinctive kind. The college, for example, would have to work not only with government departments but also with industrial and commercial forms, and it would have to be free to develop the practices appropriate for a Staff College and not copy those of the institute unless they were entirely relevant. A great deal of care would be needed therefore in designing the ultimate government of both bodies.

These measures of mutual understanding terminated with a note on the kind of assistance that such a college might feel it needed from Henley in terms of visits by Ghanaians to see and participate in Henley operations and by any Henley staff the head of the Ghanaian College, when appointed, might like to have help him get his college started.

In the period between Martin-Bates's departure at the end of 1966, and 1968 when Mr E.A. Winful (who took over from Victor Mamphey as director) paid his first visit to Henley, a good deal seems to have happened. By 1968, for example, Archie Winful arrived as the director-elect of a college which, if not actually in being, seemed more firmly in contemplation. He and a few colleagues had visited the colleges in Pakistan and in India. He had now come to observe a whole three-month session in operation and was completely free to discuss with the members and staff anything he liked about the college. It was known that a building was to be constructed so the work was proceeding on a planned basis in Ghana.

Then, in the autumn of the following year (1969), Archie Winful came back to Henley to attend the Conference of Principals of Administrative Staff Colleges across the world, referred to in the previous chapter. He brought with him the news that the Ghana College of Advanced Management, conjoined with the Institute of Public Administration and later designated as the Ghana Institute of Management and Public Administration, had been brought into official being by decree of the National Liberation Council; he was now the appointed director. He had come making clear that he wanted to discuss with Martin-Bates and others on the Henley staff the nature of his first course, and he reckoned the college would open its doors early in 1970. He was in a position to ask formally if I would go back with him and help him start it. My mind had been prepared for the question – it did not come out of the blue. I was sixty-nine at the time. I was already finding that the writing of these accounts was pretty difficult and thought I might refresh my capacity to do it if I had another adventure. Most important of all, I liked Archie Winful. So my wife and I said we would go, but on one condition: that our stay in Ghana would be limited to six months.

By now, too, we had a better idea of the way the Ghanaians thought about their new Staff College as Martin-Bates had received a copy of a memorandum which had been circulated in Ghana to potential nominators. This described the kind of managers Ghana required in order to meet the changing needs of the day; laid great stress on the need for them to be self-reliant; proceeded to discuss the need for an institution to grapple urgently with the problem of their development and up-date their knowledge of management; discussed the limitations of in-service/in-company training schemes and made the case for an independent institution; and stressed the need for a dialogue between the major sectors of the economy for promoting the co-operative effort required in pursuit of national economic policies. Having described very briefly the Henley process and philosophy, it went on to set out the role which Ghana's College of Advanced Management was expected to fulfil.

As I entered the scene in the autumn of 1969, it was useful to see this reflection of Ghanaian thinking and see defined for the first time in writing the role that the Ghanaian College of Advanced Management was expected to play. This last was expressed in the following terms:

Ghana's College for Advanced Management is expected to fulfil a role similar to that played by other Staff Colleges abroad through its programmes of management development. While knowledge of techniques (the tools of management) is essential, the programme will not be confined to this, but will attempt to extend the mental horizon of the executive, stimulate thought on, and provide education in, the main issues and problems that arise in the management of single enterprises as well as the administration of the economic programmes of the country as a whole.

The College intends to bring together under the same roof private business executives and their counterparts from the public services.

The purpose behind this is threefold. In the first place, living, working and playing together will make it easier for course participants to understand one another better and, perhaps, provide opportunities for lasting friendships. Secondly, the dynamics of the social groupings involved will enable participants to appreciate each organisation's characteristic virtues and shortcomings, as exemplified in their representatives. Thirdly, the opportunities offered for new insights and fresh appraisals will help stimulate awareness and appreciation of the complementary roles which the various segments of the economy have to play towards the realisation of common national goals.

Thus equipped with a common frame of reference, the participants, having once learned to live and work together as a team, could provide an integrating force in the community. Such a force is evidently needed in developing countries, especially in those countries which have to contend with centrifugal tribal tendencies. Without such a unifying and stabilising element in the higher reaches of management, the forces of disunity could pose a real threat to national integrity and economic development.

The College has, consequently, the potential for building a bridge of understanding between private enterprise and government. This potential is already reflected in the constitution of the College's Court of Governors, whose representation spans the entire spectrum of economic and social life in Ghana.

The approach the College for Advanced Management intends to adopt is pragmatic and environment-orientated. Unlike the average run of training courses, which use the direct instructional method, the College's programme will be more in the nature of a structured and guided self-development effort. Whilst training at lower levels consists largely in importing job knowledge and knowledge of procedures, or the mechanics of administration, something less tangible but none the less real is required at higher levels. What is needed is the development of a mature outlook, a constructive approach, a broader perspective, and understanding of and the ability to use advanced management techniques in planning, organising, continually motivating others, designing controls for more effective delegation and objective appraisal of one's own performance and that of others.

The philosophy behind the College is based on three postulates: first, that planning for rapid economic development and social change requires good leadership; secondly, that the developing countries can, ultimately, raise their standards by their own sacrifices and efforts rather than by leaning too heavily on imported technological and managerial skills; and, thirdly, that investment in training to fit people for the responsibilities of influencing the planning and direction of a country's development yields handsome dividends.

The College for Advanced Management is thus meant to satisfy the current concern and the demand of many business houses for the upgrading of the managerial skills of their administrative personnel to fit them for higher responsibility.

Preparing in Henley

At the end of the Principal's Conference on 17 October 1969 Archie Winful stayed behind in Henley to talk about his first course. I had already retired and had not followed the whole development of the Ghanaian association, so I was not as familiar with the details of Archie Winful's thinking as I would normally have been. I recognised the familiar shape of its purpose but knew I could not give the Ghanaians the energy and enthusiasm that I had felt in the earlier colleges. I knew that Archie Winful had had some difficulty in recruiting members of the directing staff in Ghana but understood that he had succeeded in getting a fairly senior Ghanaian manager from Valco, Mr George Boateng, and an Indian, one Mr R.N. Jai, whose services he had obtained through the good offices of the Ford Foundation. Now it seemed that the college was to open on 1 March 1970. So, as I could not possibly get to Ghana until 1 February, I only had a month there before the course would begin.

In November 1969 I was laid low with a bout of bronchial pneumonia and was recovering when it became clear that a conference with Archie Winful was imperative as he wanted to get back to Ghana and I needed to bring myself up-to-date with his thinking. So he and I and Morris Brodie, then director of research at Henley, had a working tea at my house. At this I discovered three things: first, that while I knew Archie Winful had been thinking earlier of holding twelve-week courses in his college (as the other colleges had done when they started), just before he left Ghana for Henley his council had expressed the view that twelve weeks was too long. He had been thinking this over and had come to the conclusion that he would like to split his course into two parts. The first part, which would last for about three-and-a-half weeks would be followed immediately by a gap of two months, which in turn would be succeeded by the second part, which would last from six to eight weeks. He thought that a solution on these lines might meet the objections of his council. His reasons for splitting the course were:

> If, while a man was away at the college, his work was to be done in his absence by a more senior manager, it would be easier for the latter to carry the extra load for two shorter rather than one long period; and if a subordinate was to do the absentee's job while the latter was on the course it might well be easier for the subordinate to carry it if the incumbent was away for two short rather than one long period.
>
> The subordinate might learn a good deal more from the experience if the incumbent came back for a couple of months before leaving him to have another try.
>
> Archie Winful thought that the nominator, if he came to look at it like

this, might well see that the split course could be turned to considerable advantage in his plans for the development of his managers.

The individual member on the course might also see an advantage in the split course. He might like the idea of leaving a subordinate for a short period, returning for two months to see how he was getting on and then leaving him to it again, as preferable to being absent for a whole twelve weeks when, from his point of view, the risks might be greater.

And he might find it easier to leave home and go into residence at the college for two short periods than for a long one. Of course, Archie Winful thought of these two parts as being two parts of a whole. The earlier, shorter part would be preparatory for the second, longer part; it being crucial that everyone who attended for the first shorter part should return after two months to attend the second. He was quite emphatic on this last point.

I was surprised but thought I saw what he was after and agreed to help in the experiment.

The second surprise, which really did come as a bit of a shock, was that I was to design the first part of the course in Henley which soon after would be carried out by Ghanaians, about whom I knew next to nothing, in Ghana, which I had never seen. As a matter of fact, this was not quite as crazy as it first sounded. In this first part of the course Archie Winful not only wanted to arouse immediate interest in the members and through them in the community by presenting them with some new ideas which he thought they would recognise as stimulating and relevant, but also he had already worked out the ground he wanted to cover and arranged with Martin-Bates for the secondment of a member of Henley staff, Winston Rodgers, to Ghana for a short while to talk on statistical and operational analysis. More clearly he would deal with: (1) statistical analysis, in which fundamental statistical concepts essential to managers would be illustrated with examples from the Ghanaian economy, which would not only drive home the concepts but also familiarise members with some of the available Ghanaian statistics; (2) operations research analysis, in which some examples of the mathematical techniques used to measure work, speed up decisions, and eliminate guesswork would be explained and illustrated in government and business terms; the more sophisticated techniques that depend on computers would require only brief reference, as computers were far off in Ghana.

Archie Winful also knew that he wanted to include in this first part some instruction on the way that companies in the private sector analysed balance sheets and profit-and-loss accounts, and set about controlling costs; and he wanted to explain the facts about the Ghanaian economy, e.g., what Ghanaian economic growth depended on, how the economist looked at the problems of growth, how reliable his efforts were in trying to measure economic growth, and then go on to show with practical Ghanaian illustrations how to help the Ghanaian manager tackle some of the problems he encountered; the idea being that members would have some basic knowledge of the economic scene before they were asked later, in the second part of the course, to look at the problems of policy and its execution in some of the main fields of endeavour. For these last two areas of financial analysis and economic analysis, Archie Winful knew broadly what he wanted done, and believed he would have no difficulty at all in getting highly competent Ghanaian economists to cover this ground. My part would simply be confined to defining, with the help of the specialists we had on the staff at Henley, a little more precisely what these Ghanaian economists might be asked to talk about. Archie Winful attached great importance to this early analytical work but there was not much that could be done from here. In the course this field of study would be intermingled with other subjects but broadly speaking it would use up a little more than half of the first three-and-a-half weeks.

For the rest, Archie Winful was anxious to break into the study of organisation, which meant designing two or three subjects that members would do themselves in syndicates under their own management. The design here would not be an onerous job as we had a good deal of precedent for this kind of study and again he was clear that if we did want help from the Ghanaian community it would not be difficult to find it from the public or private sector. All these would not be wrapped into a programme or timetable, and everything would go out to him in draft and would be knocked about by him and his staff in Ghana. So quite a lot of the work would already have been done, and the idea eventually seemed really rather sensible. I set to with my friends in the college at home and in due course sent out letters to Archie Winful in Achimota with a draft of the programme and time allotments for each job that needed to be done, and suggestions as to the role of the various speakers who would have to be found in Ghana.

I also found myself involved in two other things which cut pretty deeply into my time. The first was to assist Archie Winful with the assembly of his college library, and the second was to assemble for him some equipment he thought he would need. Luckily space can hardly allow of any elaboration of the way we set about achieving these two further objectives. There was an agony and, believe me, no ecstasy in both but I took them as far as I could. We climbed on our aircraft and got to Ghana on schedule on the evening of 1 February 1970. On the way I remember wondering how, if you had a split course, you would create in the minds of the members during the first part a desire to return and resume work with their colleagues after two months back at home and work.

Preparing in Ghana

We had a month before the first session opened, a month that was devoted entirely to preparing for this immediate commitment. My impression of the situation on arrival was that Archie Winful was optimistic about nominations but had not yet started interviewing. Mr Winston Rodgers from the Administrative Staff College, Henley, was expected as planned and all he really needed was to be briefed on the kind of men he was likely to meet; Archie Winful and George Boateng, the newly recruited deputy director on his staff, had found speakers for the economic and financial series of talks though there were considerable details still to be tidied up. Jai, the project adviser provided by the Ford Foundation, had been there eighteen months; he understood the way the old institute, now School of Public Administration, worked; knew a great many people in Ghana, had played a strong hand in helping Archie Winful get the idea of the college accepted, and was the man to whom both George Boateng and Archie Winful turned for any advice and help needed in school and college matters. Jai had been on session 2 of the Administrative Staff College of India and had served later there on the staff, so he knew the Staff College process. He had a good deal of practical managerial experience behind him in the cement industry in India. I quickly found him to be a competent person, and a most considerate one. Jai, George Boateng and I worked together as a group, at which Jai usually took the chair, and the only difficulty we had in getting the first part of the course of studies ready for the men was that there were no typists. Believe it or not, Jai did all the typing while three raw recruits were gradually learning to type to the standard required. The presentation of the material which emerged from this process, while initially not immaculate, was in due course remarkably good.

Meanwhile in the field of nominations we wanted thirty men and we ran into two main problems in finding them. First, it was very difficult to get over the idea that when we asked a man to turn up for interview at the director's office at noon on Tuesday we expected him to do so. This was often not his idea at all. He did not get the message or could not quite make it, so we often never knew who we were going to meet or whether we were going to meet anybody at all. The second difficulty was that many of the candidates came with inadequate briefing on the reason for the interview – a few of them had not even the faintest idea why they had come for interview. The result was that we spent hours taking these men, in groups of five if we could get them, or one's, two's, etc., explaining what the college was about and trying to sell the idea that it would be to their advantage to come and attend the first course. Archie Winful did most of the talking, or the persuasive side of it anyway, and he was good at it. We could watch a candidate's mind change around gradually under his influence, and it was in this way that we seemed to get most of our members. It was a pretty hard slog in which it was not always easy to remember that the process of getting men spared from responsible jobs, explaining why an adult should 'go back to school', getting letters through the post dealt with quickly and fixing dates for interview is always new to everybody and in the developing countries is particularly difficult because the wheels of communication are not so well oiled. What we were doing, of course, was helping Ghana speed up the processes in its departments and companies and make them more aware of the fact of our existence.

This was a busy month, and we had no time to discuss the content of the second part of the course, which we had to leave to the two months between the parts of our split course. We were, however, very much concerned at this stage in creating a climate of opinion in the first part which would result in the men wanting to return for the second part. For this we relied on the quality of the speakers who would occupy roughly half of the men's time in the first part and on members finding satisfaction in managing their own affairs in groups we called syndicates, so that they would welcome the idea of returning to pursue this further in the second part. We had a subsidiary idea that we would find a subject that would form something of a bridge between the two parts. Members would begin it in the first three-and-a-half weeks, do some work on it during the two-month break and wind it up when they came back. I might say at once that this last idea was a failure. I chose the subject which was to act as this 'bridge' and I learned that much thought has to be given to its selection if it is to perform a function astride a two-month gap and that much care has to be taken in the way it is presented to members.

The first part of the course

Members came in on the evening of 1 March. Monday, 2 March, was devoted to an inauguration by the Prime Minister of Ghana, Dr K.A. Busia, and later to introductory talks by the director and staff. Work began on Tuesday, 3 March, and was opened by Mr Winston Rodgers.

Archie Winful attached great importance to Winston Rodgers's contribution to operational research and statistics. He regarded his society as being innumerate and was very anxious to wake them up to this fact. He wanted to show them some of the tools that were in the bag and for them to recognise the kind of Ghanaian problems that might be solved with their help; and to think what needed to be done to create interest in the tools and promote their use in Ghanaian management. He was not attempting to train the course members as specialists in these techniques. He was only trying to educate them as potential users. Winston Rodgers's performance was as good as it was in Henley, and there were a few Ghanaians who were familiar with the substance of some of the techniques he described, but the majority of members on that first course, I felt, found it pretty hard going.

The economists who came to explain the Ghanaian situation were first class. I doubt whether any group of Ghanaians could have a clearer, more down-to-earth description of the problems the country was facing. The series of talks – there were eight of them – took place after dinner and were in their content and in this case in their timing intended to contain an element of shock treatment – the notion Archie Winful had of waking his managers up to new and pressing matters. I understood this and felt he was probably right. But it took me no time at all to find out that members disliked the interference with their normal habits entailed in after-dinner work.

George Boateng had some success in securing the co-operation of five accountants in giving the series of financial talks, which exposed the session to the thinking of the private sector on the use and interpretation of financial statements, cost and financial control. I have never doubted the value in these early days of exposing civil servants to private-sector practice in this field, and Ghana was no exception. But in Ghana I had the same reservation as in the Philippines, namely that in a course where the public sector represented the majority of members, parallel consideration of financial control and its purpose in the public sector should be unfolded so that both sectors would get to know about each other's systems and the different circumstances in which they had to operate.

Towards the end of Winston Rodgers's talks we put the men into syndicates under their own chairmen to consider the relevance of operational research and statistics and to take three subjects, which we had included, to see how they took to the idea of working under their own management. One subject called for a survey of each member's organisation, a second for study of the factors affecting the growth of organisations, and a third we called Management Information. To an outsider the discussions in these early syndicates and conferences would have appeared pretty confusing. In syndicate, too many wanted to talk at the same time, and few found it easy to listen to anyone else's views; but this is not abnormal in the early days of a session in any of the colleges. What the college was trying to do, of course, was to get members to discover for themselves that there is a need for a measure of discipline in any group discussion. This always has to be discovered and it took a little longer in Ghana than in other places, but change had begun even in the first part of the course. I remember wondering at the time if this progress would be checked by the two-month break in the course.

Whether this was to prove at all serious we could not possibly know. But there were other things we could and, I thought, did find out in that first part. I was taking a syndicate in it and had begun to know my men a little, and I knew they were capable of becoming a team. They enjoyed meeting to compare ideas. Their knowledge of management might need a good deal of 'filling in' if discussions were to be effective in the second part. They did not seem to be able to generalise from the particular but they were willing to apply their minds to the work we put in front of them. My colleagues had been a bit afraid that the temptations of Accra would undermine the residential character of the college – everyone had a car and it was only a few miles away – but we had avoided the hazard of rule by edict and it had worked very well. They did not like some features in the arrangement of the working day and they disliked the after-dinner work. So we had a little to go on and a good deal to think about as we settled down to prepare for the second part of the course during the gap in between.

Preparing for the second part

The next two months, April and May, were given over entirely to the design and organisation of the second part of the course, which was due to open on 1 June and to run until the middle of July. The main headings of the course that was eventually unfolded to the men were as follows:

1. A quick review of the syndicate work done in the first part, and completion of the subject, Management Information.
2. A study of the 1969 Constitution of Ghana.
3. Personnel Policy and Practices
4. Internal Relations in Organisations
5. Delegation, Control and Accountability
6. Human Relations in Organisation
7. Industrial Relations
8. Decentralisation in Government
9. The Ghanaian Entrepreneur
10. Business Policy Exercise
11. Agricultural Development in Ghana
12. Population Policy
13. Biographies
14. Management and Leadership
15. The Role of the Directing Authority.

Except for (11) and (12), which were talk/discussions, the subjects were studied in syndicates, some of which were modified and all of which were supported by outside speakers, some heavily and some lightly. The membership was different in the modified syndicates.

As a general background a number of integrated talks were given on topics such as organisation, the process of management, basic human needs and motivation, the concept of authority and the social sciences generally, the grid and styles of management, many of which were dovetailed with a substantial list of films.

To hammer this list of subjects into a framework for presentation to members when they first arrived would have been my ambition and I daresay it was Jai's, too. I would have started this hammering, for example, by grouping the subjects perhaps on the following lines: (2) Constitution, (11) Agricultural Development, (12) Population Policy, and probably (9) The Ghanaian Entrepreneur. I would have called them 'supporting' subjects because they would not readily fit into my idea of a framework portraying the general management issues of the day but obviously had to be included in the course as they were vitally important. So often have I seen subjects placed in this category grow and develop until they occupy far too large a proportion of the course.

I would put (2) Constitution in the supporting category because I had no clear conception as to how it might develop. I would put (3) Personnel Policy, (4) Internal Relations in Organisation, (5) Delegation, Control and Accountability, (6) Human Relations in Organisation, into a group of their own entitled Internal Organisation and Administration. I would put (7) Industrial Relations, and (8) Decentralisation in Government, into a third category called External Relations. (10) The Business Policy exercise, should be part of a fourth category which would, I hope, become a synthesis of what had been studied earlier in the course, while (13) Biographies, (14) Management and Leadership, (15) The Role of the Directing Authority, would come naturally together in a group entitled something like The Exercise of Power and Responsibility.

I would feel that in this way I was laying the basis for a balanced and integrated course on which the Ghanaians could build if they wanted to.

Another ambition I would have liked to fulfil was to have ready for the men when they came back the two basic documents which the reader will have noticed from earlier pages were given to every session when they arrived at the other colleges. The first would be called something like 'Notes on the Course', which would be descriptive of the whole field of studies, brief but sufficient to enable any individual member at any time to 'take his bearings' if he wanted to see the interconnection between the various parts and take a measure of the path he was following. The second was a complete timetable from start to finish so that any member who wished to see when a subject would come up, when it would finish, how it related in time to another subject, or when the burden of his own responsibility was likely to be heavier, would be able to check the situation for himself. We did not attempt to produce either of these documents because it could not be done in the time.

As it was, we entered the second part of the course leaving too many subjects still to be completed and with too limited a margin to meet the unforeseen. But if we could not get perfection we did what we could to meet the needs that we knew would be felt. Briefly what we did was this. We told members what the *course* was about when they first came in. Then, as each subject came up, the DS in charge of it described orally to the whole group what the *subject* was about and what help they would be given by the college in doing it. Then, as further subjects gradually were completed and the facilities for each were arranged, we issued copies of the timetable for two weeks at a time, as the course proceeded. I spell this out because it is part of the price one pays for a rushed job as ours was, and at the same time it is an example of the kind of improvisation one has to make when one cannot get what one wants.

In the building-up of this second part of the course, Jai, George Boateng and I, joined later by Michael Bentil, another Ghanaian recruited as DS, worked as a team when we could and tried to keep each other in touch with our thinking. As far as I knew Archie Winful had the final say before any papers went to press. I do not think any speakers let us down. Of course, the documentation of the course was nothing like what it should have been and I would have liked to have had more of the subjects under our complete control when we started.

The second part of the course

After the break in the course two good members who might have contributed so much in the second half failed to return. Archie Winful fought to prevent this happening but was unsuccessful. The plain fact was that their nominators had not thought through the implications of the commitment they entered into when they were selected. This, I think, was one of the risks we took in splitting the course at a time when the college and the disciplines it would impose on planning were least understood by both nominators and college. So, in the second part of the course we had twenty-seven men, nine in each syndicate.

From our experience in the first part, we made some reforms in the day-to-day routine. We cut down the length of the formal syndicate periods from 1½ hours to 1¼ hours. There were very few after-dinner occasions. We put two short free weekends in at suitable intervals in the six weeks. On their return we made it clear to members that we expected five hours formal work every weekday and three-and-a-half on Saturday mornings, plus a daily quota of about three hours which would be spent in consultation with others, planning a subject as chairman or secretary, report writing as secretary, and reading. We arranged for twenty-four Ghanaians and eight expatriates from the community to come and contribute to the various subjects in the six-and-a-half weeks, and for Jai to contribute very substantially to the infilling of their knowledge of management which we felt would be necessary. We had added three outside visits. Our documentation was still pretty rudimentary. There were no problems in getting members to resume the course except that the idea we had of using our Management Information subject as a bridge between the first and second parts was proven to be a mistake.

There was not much wrong in the content of the second part of the course. The subjects outlined in the previous chapter were fair enough for the agenda of the remaining six-and-a-half weeks. So I shall confine myself to a few comments on substance, first on the content and subsequently on the method. If, in picking matters from which I believe there is something to learn, I appear to be critical, let me say now that I have no use for criticism for criticism's sake.

Content of the work

Archie Winful was very keen to include a subject on the Constitution of Ghana. It was a recent achievement, springing out of very recent Ghanaian history, and I think he felt everyone ought to understand what had been done to try and establish a national framework in which Ghana could look forward to greater stability in its affairs. I saw some advantage in getting members to study the papers, as the official constitution was not a very long document and I thought could be divided up reasonably by a chairman among the members of his syndicate. They would dig over this ground themselves and generate some understanding of the constitution in the process.

I regarded this as valuable but only as a prelude to a contribution by a speaker who had the knowledge and understanding, the courage and the lucidity, to describe its strengths and its limitations. There was such a man but, alas, he was out of the country. So the seeds in that somewhat arid constitutional soil were never brought to life.

The subjects Personnel Policy and Practices, and Industrial Relations were worth-while inasmuch as they succeeded in generating discussion on two subjects in which members seemed to be ill-informed; while to the DS they demonstrated what a lot of very hard work was required if members were to be given well-prepared documents to read, and how much care was necessary in selecting and briefing the speaker who we hoped would illuminate the scene.

The subject Decentralisation in Government was topical and real. By the time we came to consider it we hoped the relevant Bill would have been passed into an Act. As a first effort in looking at the way the Government set-up was organised and how it was proposed to alter it to meet changing conditions, it was very much in line with Archie Winful's ideas on the study of organisation. As a syndicate subject it was a pretty massive undertaking but as it took shape in the course I felt members were glad to have had this early look at what was to come. We got some very understanding assistance from senior people.

The Business Policy Exercise had good potential. It confronted members with the problem of what a public corporation should do when economic, financial and strong political considerations were in conflict. A major problem, which is common to so many developing countries, was that in its preparation it called for a quick response from the corporation concerned and a good deal of substantial collaboration between the college and the corporation, which is not easily generated in a short time. But the Business Policy Exercise worked reasonably well and held one very useful lesson for the DS: there was a clear requirement for the DS in charge to hold their own syndicates very firmly. The DS job is sometimes a rough one when standards are first being set.

The Biographies, which Archie Winful was keen to introduce, I took on rather reluctantly as one of my responsibilities because I knew how much they would depend for success on the assembly of very good documentation for each of the three characters who would be studied by separate syndicates. There was very little to be found in Accra. However, the Henley library surrendered some of its stock, and assisted us further by buying a few more volumes from Blackwells in Oxford, so we got enough to make it just possible – but it was not anything like it should have been. What surprised me about this exercise was the interest and the extraordinary amount of work my syndicate at least did on it, towards the end of the course when the work load was very heavy.

I cannot leave these comments on the content of the work without paying great tribute to the contribution which Jai made to the members of this first course on the subjects Internal Relations in Organisation; Delegation, Control and Accountability; Human Relations in Organisation; Management and Leadership; and The Role of the Directing

Authority. Jai was a born teacher and loved it. In the intimacy of a small room and with the help of various visual aids, he conducted a dozen talks which were well integrated with subjects on which the men were engaged at the time. He held the men absorbed and made me think that Jai fitted the Ghanaian manager's needs at the time remarkably closely. The questions was, Did it last?

The methods of work

There are a few comments to make on the methods of work. They are designed to illustrate the role of the chairman and of the DS on matters which may appear to be rather insignificant but which have a far-reaching effect on the conduct of the work. They were of particular significance in this second part of the course in Ghana. The chairmen as a whole were better than I expected they would be when I first saw them at the beginning of the course. As they settled down they improved, as chairmen always do, an improvement which springs primarily from the individual chairman's grasp of his role, which will differ a good deal in individuals but can be assisted greatly when the relationship between the syndicate DS and his chairman is close. This relationship in any syndicate subject is helped if, at the beginning of the subject, a DS personally briefs his chairman and if the latter has time to think over the briefing and prepare his plan before he faces the syndicate. They are then both in the syndicate room, with a knowledge of what is in each other's mind. But if the briefing of a subject is done by anyone other than the DS in charge of a syndicate, the personal element in the relationship is not the same. Because all DS had not had time to prepare themselves for briefing their own chairmen, the member of staff who had prepared the subject too often briefed all three chairmen; and since the whole programme was put together so hastily, there was little time between briefing and the moment when the chairman faced his syndicate for him to arrive with a reasonable plan to put before them. If one is dealing with adults, as we were, one must give them just enough time to prepare for the jobs assigned to them. To allow too little time gets a subject off to a bad start.

Then there was, at the end of any subject which concluded with a presentation, an opportunity for each syndicate to consider the reports of other syndicates and select from them the items for further discussion in plenary sessions. An agenda for this discussion was usually built up from the points that syndicates drew from each other's reports, and was put together by the staff. For the chairman and the members of his syndicate to pick out from a couple of other reports issues which would be worthy of discussion by the college as a whole is not as easy as it sounds. It requires a grasp of the subject and a sense of the issues that are likely to make for good discussion. Unless the DS in charge of a syndicate can help his chairman to develop the right kind of points in the early days of any course, members will not pick up the worth-while ideas and the agenda for the presentation will consist of only trivial matters, which will not satisfy anyone. On this first course there were far too many trivial matters on the agenda for the discussions at the end of presentations. The DS seemed unwilling to insist on anything better.

There was a tendency for chairmen, and indeed for visiting speakers, to talk for too long when they were speaking from the platform. The chairmen of syndicates were given a time limit and, because this was not enforced, tended to repeat too much of the detail in their reports instead of standing back from them and capturing the interest of their audience by recounting in some way or another the experience they had had in the subject. If visiting speakers were allowed to wander on beyond the forty-five or fifty minutes they had been asked to speak, they reduced the time members had to cross-question them on what they had said – the part of the occasion which is so often much more valuable to speaker and to members than the talk which preceded it. It is not easy to intervene and curb the enthusiasm of a chairman in full swing, still less to try and get a distinguished visitor to switch off and give the men a chance.

These are three examples which will indicate how much attention has to be given to detail if one wants to see the system work well.

Can one evaluate a first course?

Generalisations about the first course in Achimota – how it went, whether it was worth-while and so on – are of very limited value from a man who knew as little about Ghana as I did. Of course I would have liked to have helped start off an appraisal system by which, at the end of every course, the principal and staff would sit around a table while individual members were still fresh in their minds and try to assess for their own purposes each man's performance while at the college, against a standard which the principal would develop as he found out more clearly what he wanted to know. Such an appraisal system should emanate ideally from the principal himself but, wherever it comes from, in the climate of a first course it is not easy to introduce. We resorted therefore at the end of the second part of the course to the issue of a questionnaire, which gave each member an hour-and-a-half to say what he thought about the experience he had had. I have never been one who puts much faith into this sort of review. So many men I have found are not by then in a position to assess what has happened to them. However, just after the course finished, I went through the reports which each man wrote in response to this questionnaire and I summarise below the remarks which individuals made in response to the last question, which asked them to describe the general impact of the ten weeks on them personally.

> Comforting to know others face some of the problems that I do and to compare how we tackle them. Cannot go it alone, the collective approach is essential. One must be tolerant. It widened my horizons and deepened my understanding. I discovered my own shortcomings and learned how to overcome them. I feel I will have more confidence in tackling my boss. I got more understanding of the civil servant. I broadened my understanding of the private-sector approach to

management problems. I learned how much could be measured. I discovered the need to understand people better and how to handle them. I need to do much more for my people and help change their attitudes. I need to be more oriented toward the development of local talent and the use of local material. I observed a change in attitude in other people and thought the course so worthwhile. It wakened and sharpened my thinking. I learned the need to delegate. I learned to apply myself to the job. I was a little frustrated at having the problems of Ghana put in front of me but it is probably better to face them. Our bosses ought to come to Greenhill. There is no single solution to any problem. I got a higher sense of delegation and want to achieve results. It was an eye-opener for me to discover how much is expected of me. We Ghanaians must stand on our own feet. It was an opportunity to know myself better.

Whatever this may add up to in the reader's mind I will add my thoughts about this first session. The members went away able to discuss some of the issues of the day with much less emotion, with more tolerance and with more confidence in themselves and each other. I believe that this was the main achievement and that it was considerable. In this rather sketchy account of my shortest ever overseas assignment, in the emphasis I have given to the difficulties we had and the rush in which we did everything, I do not want to be misunderstood. One sees weaknesses and is concerned to point them out, not to knock anyone – as they say these days – but to do what I can to help others who may find themselves in a like predicament. What is not so easy to describe about that first course is the potential strength I felt it had. If its members could be helped even a little in a short time how much more could be done if the course and its methods were pursued patiently till it fitted the Ghanaian need more closely. I would not have missed the opportunity of sensing the potential strength of the Ghanaian manager.

So now the end of the day had come. Archie Winful wanted to maintain the split nature of his course with its first part of a month, then a gap of two months followed by the second part of six to eight weeks. The staff were all in need of a break and would not reassemble until 1 September. Jai would go home to India for a well-earned month's leave on 24 July, and George Boateng and Mike Bentil wanted to get off for a break as soon as they could. Winston Rodgers would be available again for the first part of the course and a Ghanaian was to go to Henley to understudy him. I was due to catch a homeward-bound ship at Takoradi on 12 August. So the whole team had only a few days before it broke up.

As far as the course of studies was concerned, we prepared an outline of the programme for the first month so that it could be discussed with Winston Rodgers by post and be ready for final settlement when the staff reassembled on 1 September. For the rest we confined ourselves to relieving the first part of some of its over-emphasis on analysis, and changing the order of a few subjects which we thought would be a move towards better integration.

The more pressing matter was the securing of nominations. Archie Winful was fairly confident he would get what he wanted from the public sector. We all knew that the really difficult problem would be getting men from the private sector. He and I had one interview with one of the big companies, which was not particularly encouraging. The other appointments he and I tried to organise did not materialise. Perhaps we should have used George Boateng with his intimate knowledge of the private sector but we never managed it. We saw about twenty men, mainly from the public sector, but the standard did not seem to be up to those who had come on the first course. So the prospects did not look too good when my time to go arrived. I had promised Archie Winful six months in Ghana and had thrown in for good measure the hectic months in Henley preparing for the early part of the course; I knew the time had come when I should leave all this to younger people. It was a distasteful decision to me who had not hesitated to extend my stay in Pakistan or in the Philippines for months and sometimes years. But I think Archie Winful understood that I had to leave him.

Mike Bentil kindly drove us all the way across from Accra to Takoradi and put us on our ship. A gracious gesture. We sailed that same evening and I wondered how long this Staff College type of operation would last in Ghana. More than anything it depended upon the right kind of member being forthcoming. Archie Winful seemed confident about it and would test his market. I had a feeling that if he wanted to prevent the college acquiring the reputation of a purely Government institution, he would have to try particularly to attract the private sector even if their men had not on the whole reached a point in their development when they could take advantage of the college. I wondered whether a course like the Australian intermediate course would be of any help to them.

7

REFLECTIONS

Some of the major matters which struck me as these years unfolded may or may not be apparent to the reader. The remarkable extent to which the Australians grasped the early Henley ideas and held on to the essentials that would make them work was one of the reasons that made it easier to make a successful start in Mount Eliza; the other reason was that the first Australian principal decided to take over most of the Henley course and its methods of the day and they did, in fact, fit the Australian scene. The first Pakistan principal had difficulty in reconciling the conflicting views of Henley and Syracuse on how best to serve Pakistani interests and get off to anything like a successful start when there were so many other new features in the situation and such an impossibly short span of time. Then there was the remarkable feat performed by the first administrator of the Philippine Executive Academy in getting off the ground at all with a part-time director of studies and a part-time staff in a community to which so many of the Henley ideas were new and at a standard which we all came to think was modest success.

I have had plenty of time to ponder whether it was really right to have tried to start in Pakistan in four months. I have come to the conclusion that it was the only course open to us. The idea, for instance, which has since seemed attractive to me was that we might have done better by the Pakistanis if I had revived with General Sheikh on 4 September 1960 an idea which had previously arisen. It was that the college could better start on a less ambitious scale with, say, a shorter course for a few specially selected senior civil servants. This would have enabled Henley and Syracuse to have talked it out together and with the Pakistanis, before embarking on a fully-fledged Pakistan Administrative Staff College. But the time for this had gone by; the whole scene was set for the full college – the building was in process of reconstruction; great sums of money were being allotted, consultants were emerging; Pakistani staff, in thought at any rate, were just arriving; everybody's minds were geared to the full-scale adventure, and we could not have called a halt. The only question was how long could we have and four months was at least a great improvement on the three weeks it might have been. But this train of thought has since made me wonder whether a small-scale operation might not have been a better way of starting in the Philippines and so challenges the wisdom of my going to Manila before I had really had time to digest the experience of Pakistan. However, begone with speculations on what might have been. Let me turn to the main issues which were at the heart of the Henley idea when they came to be tried out overseas in the full-scale colleges in Australia, Pakistan, the academy in Manila, and in Ghana. These were:

1. The level of members.
2. The mixtures.
3. The quality of the staff.
4. The role and quality of the consultants.
5. The suitability of the approach.

The level of members

In his original dictum, Sir Hector Hetherington suggested that the time it would most profit a man to get the type of experience we were offering in Henley was after about eight or ten or fifteen years experience. When it came to translating this idea into practice, Henley dropped the eight years and pushed the level a little higher using the bracket of ten to fifteen years as their target. It was possible to obtain and maintain sessions at this level in Britain and Australia, with an occasional minor lapse. In Pakistan and the Philippines it was more difficult — the level, which meant to me the level of knowledge and experience in management, was lower in 20 per cent and sometimes 30 per cent of members and the question then arose, What were the causes and what was the cure?

These were complicated questions which you could not solve by simply adding a few speakers to improve the thinking at a particular part of the course. They raise questions which are all interconnected, e.g, Is it that nominators have not got the kind of men you want? Is it that they do not want to send them? Is it the value of the whole operation which is being challenged? Is it the quality of the staff or consultants? Is it the vigour of your recruiting campaign? Is it just part of the battle of getting the college accepted, overcoming resistance? Rough questions demanding a sensitive finger on the pulse of syndicate, session, nominators and potential nominators.

The mixtures

The level of members and variety in the composition of sessions were complementary to each other in the early Henley concept. The one needed the other. The greater the variety the greater the built-in compulsion to compare, strike sparks, open minds and so forth. The higher the level and the greater the variety in composition, the stronger could be the Administrative Staff College. Neither level nor mix came of itself – they had to be fought for. In the battle for mixture a college's capacity to attract the composition it might like to have may be prescribed by the national circumstances. For example, in Pakistan the strength of the early sessions was diminished because the college could not at the time attract the number of representatives it would have liked from a very small private sector struggling to its feet; and it could not attract the number of specialists it would have liked from the public and private sector together as there were at the time so few specialists in existence in Pakistan. What this meant in practice in 1960-3 was that if the Pakistan College really thought its sessions would be strengthened by stronger private-sector representation it had to rouse and maintain the interest of the industrial and commercial companies. Otherwise a college will awake to find one day that it is too late – the private sector will not be easily persuaded to join a Government institution. The variety can, however, be strengthened by means other than securing a better private/public balance, or by increasing specialists: state, region, race, can be combined in the same men and would, for example, contribute over the years to the growth of stability.

The quality of the staff

Every college principal had to fight to get good men for his staff. This was understood in a college sponsored and financed by the private sector, which accepted responsibility for its well-being. In the colleges sponsored by the public sector, principals had a difficult time getting what they wanted. The point that was lost sight of was that it is a waste of time having a Staff College of the early Henley kind unless you make the sacrifice necessary to provide it with the quality of staff it needs and offer continuity of employment and, no less important, send to it members of high calibre and potential.

The role and quality of the consultants

In 1957 when I went to Australia I was seconded from Henley and became a temporary member of the Australian staff. This entailed a relationship with all the Australians in the college with which all of us on each side were familiar, and which did not, until I went to Pakistan in 1960 and the Philippines in 1963, acquire the more portentous-sounding title of consultant. As far as I know, this did not make the slightest difference in what I had to do. I was not an Australian, I was not a Pakistani, I was not a Filipino nor a Ghanaian. They were independent sovereign countries and these colleges were independent entities. I joined their staffs in turn on secondment from Henley and, when the chips were down, was only an adviser. If I suggested something should be done which the indigenous principal and staff thought was a nonsense, then it was a nonsense and I kept quiet. I wanted it to be their college and did not want to over-step the mark in setting it up or running it.

This sounds easy and most of the time was – but not always. True, advice can be accepted or rejected but the line between the two is not always clear. In the gestation period of a new project, one is often asked to do more than advise because there is not enough staff to begin with or because people are not used to working together and are not communicating normally. Or it may be that the adviser believes his advice has been accepted but it has not, because he has not yet understood the way his hosts like to do business or, again, in trying to restrict himself to advice it is hard to avoid playing a part in the making of policy. When pressing a view from experience elsewhere on a subject about which your host does not happen to know very much and you are not quite sure whether it 'fits' in his country, it may be all too easy to follow your own judgment. For his part he may find it pretty difficult to reject advice expressed with vigour and enthusiasm.

In theory, an adviser should know as much as he can about a country before he goes there. The best guidance I was given on how to do this was from Douglas Copland, who gave me the titles of a few books about the pioneering days in Australia which increased my enthusiasm and respect for Australia. I did not need this in regard to West Pakistan and made the mistake of failing to read anything about East Pakistan, about which I knew next to nothing. In the case of the Philippines I was given some modern research studies which purported to explain to me the culture and the manner in which the Filipinos lived. These were the sort of studies which meant nothing to me in advance. There, in a culture which was absolutely new to me, I had to learn first, and only when I had done that for three years did I begin to understand what the books meant.

One of my host principals, at a time when he must have thought I was over-stepping the mark, asked me to give him a note describing what I thought the role of a consultant to be. These few lines are drawn from that note which I understand put an end to his suspicions.

Every consultant has to have competence or all the behavioural instincts and skills will not see him through. I knew a good deal about my strengths and limitations before I went abroad for the college in 1957, a good deal more of the latter when I came back finally from Ghana in 1970 and still more of my limitations now that I come to the end of this account.

The suitability of the approach

Sometimes as I sat in syndicate or plenary session in these new colleges, especially those in the developing world, I used to wonder whether the treatment to which the men submitted themselves was really preparing them for higher responsibility in their own lands.

> If, for instance, the capacity for tolerance did not exist or was very dormant at the time, was it any good offering them a system which implicitly exposed them to the need for tolerance or did they find it too frustrating?
> If power was highly centralised in their society, was it a waste of time getting them to talk about delegating authority?
> If no senior man ever contemplated consulting anybody else before he decided on what ought to be done, was there any point in getting them to read western literature which seemed to suggest that we were living in an age when men were beginning to insist that they had some say at least in the things which affected them?
> If there were only a few specialists around and the time had not yet come when they were generally accepted in society as important, and it was unlikely that this situation would change for years, was it any good warning them of the inevitable if they were really determined on economic development?
> If the society was authoritarian, and had been for generations, would they profit from discussing other ways of running an organisation?
> If their ideas of loyalty, discipline and leadership were rooted in cultural tradition, did it help to ask them to contrast their views with mine simply for the sake of helping them to look critically at their society? Did these things really help or did they simply frustrate?

On the question of group work when one found oneself in a society where emotions seemed to run particularly high and to be roused very quickly, was it any good sitting round a table to find agreement among people when getting round that table seemed to be an ineffective way of doing business? Oh yes, of course some ancient specialisms existed and for centuries had applied science in their methods, for example, medicine and civil engineering, which were taken for granted; but was it too early to invite men to think of a new era when specialists would have at least an equal status with those who were still enjoying holding the reins of power? In short, was there any chance that we were making things difficult for members when they got back on the job rather than the opposite, to which we were dedicated?

I never had any doubt that in these sorts of things we were on the right track when we set out. I have heard western behavioural attitudes challenged, of course, as being quite irrelevant to an indigenous scene, abandoned by some and held too firmly by others as a session developed. The real strength of our position as foreigners in their midst, at least as far as the Henley approach to the education of maturing managers was concerned, was that we did not expect them, in my country or any other, to accept anything because the college, if it knew its stuff, had no dogma to teach.

8

CONCLUSIONS

═══════════

I close with a few words on the circumstances which enabled all these colleges to come into being as the independent entities that each of them wanted to be.

There were two fundamental principles which governed the relationship between Henley and the overseas colleges:

1. Henley had no desire to, and never did, impose its ideas on others. When its representatives went overseas to help, they went in response to unsolicited invitation.
2. Henley never financed any of the overseas colleges and so never created in the principals' minds any kind of obligation to accept anything which Henley or its representatives proposed or said unless they wished to do so.

The reason these two principles were so important was that together they represented the reality of the situation in which our co-operative work took place, and they were accepted by both sides with sincerity. It was this sincerity which enabled a relationship of trust to grow between us, on which everything depended.

Throughout these assignments I remained a member of the Henley staff. I could turn to Henley for help or advice when I felt the need of it. When I received it I knew I was perfectly free to accept or reject it, if I decided in my own mind to pass it on to the principal I was working for at the time, it was passed on because I believed it was right. I was never once instructed on what I should say or do.

My loyalty was to the principal of the overseas college in which I was serving. Nothing would have undermined this loyalty and so destroy my relationship with him if I had felt that I was not completely free to give him such advice as I thought fit. Never once did a doubt upon this arise in my mind.

I felt the need for support from home more in the Philippines than elsewhere. The reason for this, I am sure, was that no one from Henley had been to the Philippines and prepared the ground beforehand. In consequence I felt less secure. I think it was this that led me to initiate and sustain a correspondence with Martin-Bates, which he recognised for what it was and to which he never failed to respond. But let me be quite clear that what I passed on to Carlos Ramos was what I thought myself, even if Martin-Bates had helped me think my own view through.

In both Pakistan and the Philippines a third party had a very important role to play. The Ford Foundation in both countries was providing a significant part of the financial support for the new colleges and I was as much a consultant to their local representative as I was adviser to the principal of the college. It took me a little time to discover how strong a relationship a consultant could have with his local representative of the supporting foundation. I first imagined this to be a problem when I made rather a fetish of my loyalty to Khalid Malik in Pakistan. I was in some sort of trouble and felt unable inside myself to go and seek advice from the Ford Foundation until 'Mogy' Mogensen, a Dane and a member of the Ford Foundation's local staff said, 'Well, why don't you go and talk to Harry Case about it?' So I did, and I found in him a man whom I gradually got to know very well indeed and whom I counted as one of my closest friends. I discovered, of course, that his interest was exactly the same as Khalid Malik's and the same as mine. We all wanted the Pakistan College to be a success.

So from then on I never ceased to talk with Harry Case about anything, either in Pakistan, where he was the representative of the Ford Foundation for practically the whole of my time there, or later in the Philippines, to which it so happened he was transferred just about the same time as I arrived in Manila. One of my most treasured possessions is a letter he wrote me at a time when life was being particularly difficult. A very good Ford representative and a very good friend.

As I look back over the years, I think it was on these kinds of relationships that the base of each of the colleges was laid. Perhaps, too, this trust which was essential to their establishment is the real justification for the continuation of contact between college and college. We all know we are different from each other, independent of each other, pursuing our own individual paths. In the early days the principals used to meet. The generosity of the financing foundations enabled them to travel and to talk with each other. It is not for me to suggest what the present-day principals of these colleges might want to talk about. But we all know that a man who carries substantial responsibility usually welcomes the chance to talk face to face with someone on whose shoulders similar responsibilities lie, and also that there is a measure of routine in most jobs, and some men will welcome the chance of escape from it for a while, and others accept it and are probably in need of a shake-up.

Today, when so much change has taken place in all these colleges, when so much change is taking place in the world, can there be anything but good in the idea that a college seeks regeneration of its own spirit from that of another? This is surely a two-way benefit for all of them, however well established they may be.

PART II
The Scene Today

When my husband's manuscript was ready for publication in the spring of 1981, I sent a copy to Dr Harry L. Case, now retired in the United States. I did this because it was he who, in 1966, had encouraged C-J to write this book. He asked if there were any estimates of actual accomplishments in terms of better administration and any evaluations of the colleges' growth and development over the years. I thought about this and decided that the book would be more interesting if it were brought up-to-date. I wondered if each of the principals would write his own story about the growth and achievements. After contacting them, I set off in September 1981, first to Pakistan and then India, the Philippines, Australia, New Zealand, Bangladesh and Ghana. I was invited by the principals to stay in the different colleges and so met many staff and course members and old friends. It was good to be back in all these countries where C-J and I had lived and worked. He would have been delighted and interested to hear of their achievements and continuing development. The common thread that connects them all is very evident.

C-J worked in six of the eight institutions whose reports follow, written in most instances by their principals and in others by senior members of staff. They are all part of an international story in the education of senior managers.

UK – Henley	Mr Andrew Life
New Zealand – Wellington	Mr J.L. Robson
	Dr A.J. Barnard
Australia – Mt Eliza	Mr Keith W. Steel, AC, OBE
	Emeritus Professor W. Walker
India – Hyderabad	Mr N.P. Sen
	Mr M. Narasimham
Pakistan – Lahore	Mr Masrur Hasan Khan

The Philippines – Manila/Baguio	Dean Carlos P. Ramos
Ghana – Achimota	Mr R.K.O. Djang
Bangladesh – Dacca	Mr Abdur Rahim

The Administrative Staff Colleges represent a unique development in management education. They have spread across the world, starting in Henley in 1948, followed by those in New Zealand 1954, Australia, 1957, India 1957, Pakistan 1960, the Philippines 1963, Ghana 1970 and Bangladesh 1977. Norway, Denmark, the West Indies (later Jamaica), East Africa, Iran, Mexico, Nigeria, Zambia, Papua New Guinea, Indonesia, Argentina and Nepal have also drawn on the Henley experience.

Joan Cornwall-Jones

9

HENLEY'S CONTRIBUTION TO THE DEVELOPMENT OF EFFECTIVE MANAGERS: AN EVALUATION TODAY

E.A. LIFE

Any appreciation of the part played by an institution in the development of effective managers has to be viewed against a background of constant change reflecting the dynamics of the environment within which managers have to operate. Accordingly this note will briefly record the growth of Henley's contribution to management education and illustrate some of the means by which these have been evaluated, and subsequently modified, to meet the needs of its clients, as well as referring to recent innovations.

Initially, Henley, as C-J's story amply testifies, pioneered residential education for senior managers in Great Britain, building upon the parallel of the courses given to senior officers in the armed forces, and gaining support from industrial and commercial undertakings and local and central government. Henley was established in 1946; so, too, was the Advanced Management Programme at the Harvard Business School. Both were founded in the light of wartime experiences which senior managers had found useful, and both were perceived as potential sources of aid to the post-war reconstruction of society. Both required participant managers to be nominated and paid for by their employers, believing that this would encourage the careful selection of individuals, the assurance of high motivation and an atmosphere conducive to managerial growth.

Henley in particular saw itself being concerned with the transition of individuals from a specialist or functional role to a position involving the general management of a multiplicity of functions in either the private or the public sector of the economy. Since so much depends upon the mental and social capacities of the managers being developed, as well as their motivation, the college has always paid serious attention to these factors. The college requires all candidates from the United Kingdom for the General Management and Senior Courses to attend pre-course interviews, and the principal and his staff systematically review the performance levels of all members at the end of these courses to ensure that entry standards are being maintained.

Over the years the college and its past course members have recognised the mutual benefits to be derived from a continuing relationship. Following the success of its first course in 1948, the college inaugurated review courses held eighteen months after attendance at Henley. These enabled members of a particular course to return for a short period to confer on specified issues of topical importance, and to compare experiences after leaving the college. From 1958 onwards the college organised rather longer conferences for members in attendance ten years previously, and, in the 1960s, for those attending five years before. The members themselves created the Greenlands Association, a self-administering body of 'alumni' who meet from time to time on a regional basis.

By the mid-1950s, the success of the college with its General Management Course had attracted international attention, leading to the fruitful connections overseas described so graphically in the preceding pages by C-J. Within the college, research activities were originated which soon provided a range of publications in support of the course of studies or on matters of general interest in the field of management education. In the late 1960s, the college invited the Tavistock Institute of Human Relations to evaluate its General Management Course, seeking to discover through a form of action research whether some parts of the programme were more effective in terms of its goals than others, and whether individuals of various kinds from various environments responded differently to the programme.

The consultant researcher, Dr Robert Rapoport, helped to organise a postal survey of the views of Henley members attending the college between 1960 and 1966 and more than 70 per cent of them responded. Dr Rapoport's report subsequently laid the foundation for a number of changes in course content and operating policies, but at the time provided evidence that the original conception of the role of senior management underlying the design of the General Management Course remained valid.

At the time of the survey, a college brochure stated that: 'Our main object is to encourage personal development, and by this we mean a man or a woman's capacity to manage, not only in his present job but also in the kinds of tasks he may be faced with in the future.' As Brigadier Cornwall-Jones has continually emphasised in this book, the college saw work in syndicates as giving course members practice in skills appropriate to senior levels of management. Amongst other tasks, it believed, senior managers had to obtain information from colleagues of similar status but differing specialist backgrounds, to understand it, to assess its value and to use it in reaching decisions which others might have to be persuaded to support. Dr Rapoport's survey confirmed the correctness of these assumptions. Subsequent to leaving Henley, 70 per cent of the members surveyed reported greater responsibilities, roughly the same proportion participating in long-term planning. Sixty per cent increased their involvement with other managers from different specialisms and 47 per cent extended their dealings with people external to the enterprise, most of their problems being resolved by means of complex negotiations.

27 Ghana Institute of Management and Public Administration (GIMPA)

28 GIMPA—another view

29   New buildings, GIMPA

30 Chief Pastor Tetteh and Registrar E. V. Mante

31 Gathering at GIMPA. *Left to right*: (front row) Winston Rogers, R. N. Jai, Archie
Winful, George Boateng, C.-J.

32 C.-J. in action

33 Director R. K. O. Djang (right) with former Director, Dr Clarke, GIMPA

34 The Principals' Conference, 1969. *Left to right*: Maurice Brown (Australia), Carlos Ramos (Philippines), Archie Winful (Ghana), Dr F. Akbari (Iran), Sir Noel Hall (Henley) N. P. Sen (India), Khalid Power (Pakistan), J. P. Martin-Bates (Henley)

35   Henley. *Left to right*: Hugh Barrow, Dr A. H. Mehrassa (Staff observer from Iran),
George Evans-Vaughan, Aris Presanis, J. P. Martin-Bates (Principal), Tony Ormsby,
Maurice Brown (Principal, Australia), Paul Alston, John Adams, C.-J., Henry Taylor,
at the time of the Principals' Conference, October, 1969

36   100th Session Dinner, January 1980. The three Principals—Professor Tom
Kempner, Sir Noel Hall, Mr J. P. Martin-Bates

37   C.-J.

And not by eastern windows only,
When daylight comes, comes in the light;
In front the sun climbs slow, how slowly!
But westward look the land is bright!

'Say not the struggle nought availeth'
                        (Arthur Hugh Clough)

But how did members react to work in syndicates? The survey revealed that although only 10 per cent commented adversely upon syndicate work, some 42 per cent wanted less emphasis on it. At the same time a number of members criticised what they considered to be the undue formality and artificiality of the presentations of syndicate findings made at the end of the study of each subject, and many expressed a desire for more explicit personal appraisal and career guidance from the staff. Other members suggested 'more positive teaching, possibly on a tutorial basis, to meet particular needs . . . but not at the expense of the obvious benefits of the syndicate'. In fact, 30 per cent revealed support for more didactic teaching and pressed for talks on the potentialities of such aids to management as computers, statistical analysis, and the techniques of operational research.

Dr Rapoport's analysis of the data from the survey exposed the complexity of the process of managerial development. He demonstrated that members of the General Management Course who learned to deploy their capacities very much more effectively did so in accordance with one of three different patterns of development, depending upon their personalities, learning styles and working environment.

The application of Dr Rapoport's findings and the conclusions to be drawn from them inspired a number of changes in the General Management Course and in the role of staff. The number of presentations of syndicate findings to the rest of the course in plenary sessions was drastically reduced and staff were encouraged to end subjects with visits to syndicates in order to review their summaries at length in critical but constructive vein. This policy was in fact facilitated by the growing number of staff recruited by the college with lecturing skills in a variety of functional areas of management – a resource that hardly existed in Britain when the college was founded.

Another fertile line of collaborative research began in the late 1960s in support of a study of effective managerial groups by Dr Meredith Belbin of the Industrial Training Research Unit in Cambridge. This study led ultimately to a deeper understanding of the dynamics of syndicate work, and to the institutionalisation of the confidential use of psychological questionnaires. These provided members with information about their personalities which they could share voluntarily with staff in discussing their own personal development or the effectiveness of their syndicate, thereby satisfying more of the needs identified earlier by Dr Rapoport.

In the late 1970s and early 1980s, the roles and responsibilities of the staff were more openly differentiated. The old term 'directing staff' was dropped and for those responsible for a syndicate replaced by the description 'syndicate tutor'. Staff responsible for preparing subject papers and making the arrangements for a particular subject were designated 'subject tutors', but combined the two roles when necessary. Following the greater formalisation of their roles, syndicate tutors in the first week of each General Management Course were then required to discuss with each of their syndicate members their overt learning objectives and how these might best be met. Such discussions might cover the alternative uses by bankers and accountants of time programmed for lectures on basic accounting, in addition to advice upon the steadily increasing number of optional subjects introduced to meet individual needs. The college also allocated more time for tutors and their syndicates to review the effectiveness of the work completed by the group and the contributions of individual members, if they so wished.

So far in this note we have seen how Henley was founded to meet a perceived need for the development of senior managers in the public and private sectors of the British economy. Having evolved an institution and a method of development which nominators were ready to support financially, Henley then responded to what it regarded as the continuing needs of course members through review courses and conferences. The members in turn took the initiative in forming the Greenlands Association. Next came the requests from overseas for assistance with the establishment of Staff Colleges locally inspired – another widening of the Henley circle of influence, and another form of response to others' needs for which it had barely enough resources. At the same time the college started in a modest way to do research and to produce publications to underpin its constantly developing course of studies, which, incidentally, was systematically and critically reviewed at intervals throughout each session. In this critical spirit of review, the college used an impartial outside body to explore the reaction of members and nominators to the content and methods of study of the General Management Course in operation a decade-and-a-half after its original introduction.

The Tavistock Institute survey took place at a time when the success and uniqueness of the college in Britain had stimulated the establishment of competing institutions, much as the success of the Harvard Advanced Management Programme had led to its emulation by business schools in other American universities. In October 1963, a committee under the chairmanship of Lord Robbins investigating higher education in Britain had reported that there was 'scope in a number of centres for courses of management education for persons of mature years', remarking that 'The notable success since the war of the Administrative Staff College at Henley has shown that experiments here are likely to meet with a ready response'. The committee commented on the lack in Britain of any institutions comparable to the major business schools of the United States and recommended the building up of at least two major postgraduate schools, leading ultimately to the new business schools in London and Manchester, which launched their post-experience programmes in 1966.

The founders of Henley recognised that an independent institution would be freer to innovate than one set up in partnership with a university, which might trammel it with inappropriate policies, precedents and regulations concerning both financing and staffing criteria. We have already referred to examples of the speed and readiness with which Henley chose to respond to the needs of significant others in its environment, including those identified in the Rapoport report. The Tavistock survey in fact confirmed the existence of a widely held view amongst past members that the diffusion of new ideas within their enterprises might be facilitated if their immediate superiors were somehow made familiar with the concepts underlying the content of subjects in the General Management Course. Discussions with nominators resulted in the design of a new four-week programme (initially called the General Management Appreciation Course, later the Senior Course) to achieve that aim.

The success of this new venture soon led to ramifications. A major insurance company pressed for two similar courses to be run for more than a hundred of its own senior managers, and the college contrived to meet this request within the following two years. Conscious that some of its newer members possessed lecturing skills in areas of knowledge, such as statistics and quantitative techniques, in which past members felt themselves deficient, the college also started to offer short one-week programmes to satisfy this need. These in turn attracted the attention of a Government department which faced the task of transforming itself into a public authority, much concerned with commercial undertakings, and which aimed to develop in its managers an awareness of the knowledge and behaviour appropriate to its impending change in status.

Here, again, the college responded by initially adapting one of its existing courses, and then designing a series of new courses tailor-made to the specification of its client, which fostered a close relationship between the two institutions for more than a decade, and established shorter courses as an integral part of the Henley product range. The prospective income to be derived from these courses in fact encouraged the college to build additional accommodation for them with aid from the Institute of Directors, the recurring demand for a variety of educational experiences specifically designed to meet the management-training needs of clients leading in the 1970s to the formal setting up of the Henley Management Development and Advisory Service to meet this need.

The willingness of industry to subscribe funds for the creation of the two new British business schools in association with the universities of London and Manchester operated to the disadvantage of independent and apparently successful colleges like Henley. Firms found themselves committed to large sums for new ventures in university management education which left little over for the support of modest new developments in established institutions, although grants were sometimes forthcoming from other Government bodies and from sources like the Leverhulme Foundation. The rapid expansion in the number of universities in Britain during the 1960s and the generally larger scale of public investment in them thus prompted the college to explore the possibilities of associating with one on some basis of mutual interest. These explorations culminated in a productive arrangement with Brunel University, which had achieved its status by being elevated from a College of Advanced Technology, and which like Henley had evolved within a context of industrial and commercial practice. Furthermore its vice-chancellor, son and grandson of Nobel Prize winners, came to the post from a background of industrial research management.

The arrangement with Brunel in effect treated Henley as if it were in part the management studies department of the university (which did not have one). Brunel agreed to the introduction of a Master's degree in business administration, run on sandwich-course principles, housed at Henley and taught by college staff who had the status of approved teachers of the university. This soon attracted solid support from home and overseas. Henley staff in turn contributed lectures on management subjects as a service to full-time degree courses housed at Brunel and were responsible for conceiving and launching successfully a part-time MSc course in management, also held there, as well as operating a flourishing research department for those wishing to complete an MPhil. or PhD degree. For these particular activities the college received funds in the form of a blocked grant from the University Grants Committee to Brunel University, but earmarked for Henley.

Other courses at Henley continued to be funded from fee income, the college having to satisfy the needs of those who paid as well as those of the managers attending courses, insofar as participants were almost invariably nominated and paid for by employers. Consequently, the repeated willingness of employers to send managers to Henley may be construed as an indicator of satisfaction with what the college provides. In the early 1980s about 85 per cent of those attending the General Management and Senior Courses came from enterprises which had supported them previously, some for more than thirty years, and including a number located in Western Europe, the Middle East, the Far East and Africa. In company with its competitors in Britain, Henley in the early 1980s found it difficult to run its General Management Course at full capacity, because of the widespread and drastic cuts in training budgets, but the fact remains that in 1982 it was achieving an increased share of this very competitive market.

In 1981, Henley embarked upon an ambitious project to develop distance-learning programmes on management subjects for individuals and enterprises. These utilised texts and audio-visual cassettes to harness information technology and modern learning techniques to the needs of students studying at home or in the working environment. Here again was a readiness on the part of the college to take another initiative in the field of management as far-reaching as that which it pioneered in the 1940s.

This brief account describes the way in which the college, through a policy of diversification, has sought to meet the needs of a widening range of managers who have to cope with an increasingly complex and rapidly changing environment.

Andrew Life is a senior member of the directing staff.

10.1

NEW ZEALAND ADMINISTRATIVE STAFF COLLEGE: EARLY HISTORY

J. L. ROBSON

In 1944 I was appointed to the office of the Public Service Commission and became in 1946 the Superintendent of Staff Training, a position I held until 1951. In view of my official position I had access to documents coming from England dealing with the promotion of the Administrative Staff College at Henley. Not only was I interested from an official angle but I was also an active member of the New Zealand Institute of Public Administration. I have set out relevant developments within New Zealand as I remember them and in chronological order:

1. In 1949 I was chairman of a study group set up by the Wellington branch of IPA to consider the subject of education and training for administration, and in our report we discussed the English Administrative Staff College as one tenable approach. Their first course had been launched in 1948. For my part I was convinced that the idea behind such a course had definite potential for us, and I decided to take the initiative within IPA and strive to persuade our members to this point of view.

2. In May 1950 at the annual conference of the Council of the Institute of Public Administration, I submitted data I had gathered dealing with the establishment and progress of the Henley project. The pros and cons of the project were discussed by the conference and then the question was referred to the National Executive Committee for further action.

3. In the following month, June 1950, Professor R.S. Parker of Victoria University College addressed the New Zealand Institute of Industrial Management on the subject of the Henley development. He was aware of what was already happening within the Institute of Public Administration.

4. Steps were taken to inform the general membership of the IPA about the Henley project. Some detail was given in the IPA newsletter for June 1950 and then an informative article by the late H.A. Levestam was published in the newsletter for August 1950, which quoted a paper by Mr Noel F. Hall, 'Staff College in Training for Management', published by the British Institute of Management.

5.   The National Executive Committee, in reviewing the Henley scheme in the light of the earlier discussion in council, decided to appoint a sub-committee, of which I was to be the convener. Our task was to provide a further report on whether we should have a Staff College within New Zealand. In our subsequent report we sought approval for the proposal in principle and also for authority to discuss the proposal with interested persons in the realm of private enterprise.

6.   In May 1951, the council of IPA gave general endorsement to our proposals and authorised the National Executive Committee to proceed as early as practicable with arrangements for a course. Discussions subsequently took place with other interested organisations and a controlling committee was set up as follows:

IPA	D.F. Campbell
	J.L. Robson
	T.R. Smith
IIM	W.G. Rodger
	K. Schwarz
	A.H. Thomas
VUC	Professor R.S. Parker
Joint Secretaries	P. Eastwood
	H.G. Lang

I became the first chairman of this committee.

7.   In 1952, a course styled the Executive Management Course was launched, with Professor Parker as its first director. The methods used were similar to those used at Henley. However, the course was no more than a modest version of Henley, particularly as to duration.

8.   For us, incorporation did not have the significance it had for the Henley project. This came about because they sought financial aid from private enterprise, which in their turn claimed for deductions in their tax returns. We, for our part, relied upon fees to meet our running costs. However, we did go through the formality of incorporation in 1957.

9.   Noel Hall, the then principal of Henley, visited New Zealand in 1954 and we arranged for him to give a number of lectures. Our committee conferred with him on the question of the course programme. We found him to be a stimulating character.

J.L. Robson was chairman of the committee that set up the first Executive Management Course.

10.2

NEW ZEALAND
ADMINISTRATIVE STAFF
COLLEGE: A REVIEW

A. J. Barnard

The New Zealand Administrative Staff College ran its first course in 1952 and since then has run sixty-six residential courses for mid-career managers. At the present time it is running 5 four-week courses each year with forty students on each course.

The target group is made up of managers from the public and private sector who have reached that stage in their career where exposure to wider issues of management and administration is appropriate. The programme is particularly appropriate to those who currently have departmental or functional roles in an enterprise and who are being promoted to assume wider responsibilities. The target age group is 35-50 years old.

The programme is unique in New Zealand in that it has active support from the public and private sector. The course membership is traditionally split 60 per cent private enterprise, 40 per cent public sector, the latter consisting of civil servants, employees of state organisations such as post office and railways, members of the armed forces, police and fire service, and representatives from local government. It is a major college policy to maintain this wide representation on courses and it is generally accepted that there is great advantage in people from the private and public sectors being able to meet on neutral ground to discuss issues of mutual interest within the framework of a management programme.

The main basic assumption underlying curricula design is that each course member has significant job experience which he is prepared to share with his fellow course members. There is no required level of academic achievement necessary to attend the programme and in fact something less than half the course membership on a typical course will have had tertiary educational experience. Very few students will have studied business or public administration at university. It is vital therefore that the course programme is able to relate to the experience of the individual. It must either formalise experience or understanding already acquired or widen the horizons of it. Certainly new knowledge can be shared but again they must build on experience.

An associated criterion is that the programme must be seen to be related to conditions in the workplace. The problem of relating the course experience to one's own job, particularly when one returns to it, is a major issue. This is one of the major reasons the college uses practitioners rather than academics in its programmes. Tutors are drawn from the private and public sector to share their experience with course members for a part of the programme and the selection of these topic leaders is vital to the success of each programme, requiring not only knowledge or expertise in the subject but ability to communicate.

The course objective is to help members to become better managers for their involvement in their enterprise, a process of self-appraisal and development. The programme content is directed to this aim and each element of the programme is directed to the future rather than looking at the detail of the present.

One of the main areas of study comes within the general description of people at work. There are three areas of study in this section: firstly, organisation; secondly, human relations, where individual and group behaviour is looked at; and thirdly, industrial relations, where the formal outcome of human behavioural problems are dealt with.

The second area of study is concerned with planning and the future, where we identify two separate topics. The first of these is concerned with planning, where we study corporate medium-term and operational planning, and the second topic is called Challenge of the Future, where a significant study is undertaken concerning a part of New Zealand's future, either in land-use or technology or some similar area of investigation where planning and forecasting techniques and studies can be incorporated.

The other areas of study are concerned with financial management and marketing. These are to some extent stand-alone studies, however, having relevance to the programme.

The college is concerned with adult students and therefore it is appropriate that adult teaching methods should be used. The college is becoming increasingly interested in the process as well as the content of the learning programme. An early problem to deal with is the fact that most students have had little institutional learning experience since their schooldays and are mainly familiar with a didactic approach. The college programme is based on socratic teaching with increasing use of experiential programmes, workshop techniques and learning in groups smaller than the total course. There is a positive move towards reducing the amount of formal lecturing and the trend is towards a participative learning programme where topic leaders act in more of the role of a facilitator or catalyst. Two major problems with students is firstly an inability to listen and secondly in many cases little experience in intelligent reading. The course methodology has to take account of this and within the constraints of the time available to try to improve the communication skills of course members in these two areas.

Course evaluation remains a continuing problem as in all learning situations. Course assessments done by students during or at the conclusion of the course have limited use as they are generally highly subjective, and cannot measure the long-term impact that the course experience has on an individual. The main opportunity for measurement of the course's success lies in the hands of those enterprises which nominate students to the programme. In recent years the college has been more concerned with ensuring that the reasons and objectives as to why a particular student is sent on a programme are clearly understood by the student and by the nominating enterprise. If a nominator has clearly defined these reasons and what the enterprise is hoping to get out of the experience it is much easier after the programme has been completed to measure changed performance or attitudes in relation to these objectives.

In the past there has been a tendency for a residential programme of this sort to be used as a reward for good service or as a remedial programme. The course essentially is one of self-development and it is in this context that the nominating enterprise must judge the value and worth of the time and money spent in the experience.

Evaluation and review of each course is made by the college. It has the task of both anticipating the likely changes necessary in the programme to meet future managerial needs and at the same time taking account of the feedback from course members and reacting to the information received in this way.

Over the years the college has not changed greatly in its basic course programme but the methodology and emphasis has changed considerably and this has been due to the changing needs of management over the years. In particular the increasing pressures of social and environmental changes as they affect the manager's job have become increasingly important in the determination of course content.

I have been able to do a bit of research on the present positions of some of our members. 'Old boys' include the Controller and Auditor General, the Commissioner of Inland Revenue, the Secretary for Justice, the Commissioner of Police, the Director-General of the Post Office, Chairman of the State Services Commission, and a number of other Permanent Heads.

On the diplomatic side the present Deputy High Commissioner in London is a member, as is the New Zealand representative at the United Nations. In the private sector perhaps our two most notable members are the chairman of Fletcher Challenge Ltd, the largest New Zealand owned company, and the chairman of the Development Finance Corporation; overseas the managing director of the Fiji Sugar Corporation has been through our programme. An interesting situation in Malaysia is that the three top public servants in Malaysia have all been through the college programme.

Dr. A.J. Barnard is Principal of the New Zealand Administrative Staff College.

11.1

THE AUSTRALIAN ADMINISTRATIVE STAFF COLLEGE

W.G. WALKER

The Henley tradition is alive and well at Moondah today. Each of the principals since Professor Sir Douglas Copland – Sir Ragner Garrett, Mr Maurice Brown, Dr Ted Kelsall and myself – has in our way moved to retain that which C-J clearly regarded as best at Henley. Today, while there have been significant changes in course content, length and number of programs and many new initiatives both at home and abroad, the key 'Henley' elements of syndicate work, appropriate course-member mix, directing-staff diversity and constant course review are retained. So, too, are such characteristics as the use of speakers direct from the coal-face, visits to enterprises at work, encouragement of competitive sporting activities – and the Buttery.

It would be unnecessarily tedious to attempt to list all the developments at Moondah since 1966: it will suffice to mention some of the activities and innovations which, during 1980 and 1981, have preceded the celebration of the college's Silver Jubilee in 1982. These have included:

1. The reduction of the eight-week advanced course to a six-week Advanced Management Program.
2. The re-design of both the above program and of the old 'intermediate course', now the four-and-a-half week Management Development Program.
3. The introduction of eight programs per year, with an enrolment of sixty to sixty-six in each.
4. The development of a strong international thrust, typified by the holding in each year of a 'Moondah Abroad' Programme – 1980 in Fiji, 1981 in Brunei – and the offering of an ASEAN Management Development Program on behalf of the ASEAN-Australia Business Council in 1982.
5. The establishment of the position of director of Special Projects in

order to offer a much wider range of short and special programs than has hitherto been possible.

6. The founding of a twice-yearly action-oriented journal for executives, *The Practising Manager*.

7. The introduction of contract appointments for directing staff and the achievement of a more effective permanent-contract-visiting staff mix.

8. The carrying out of major improvements to physical plant, including the erection of a new kitchen-accommodation wing, the re-painting of Moondah in its original warm stone, the refurbishing of the Moondah entrance and the restoration of the Gatehouse to its original red brick.

9. The planning of the Jubilee Project, an extension to Moondah consisting of a major educational and conference centre which includes a new library, extensive syndicate-room and relaxation areas and forty study-bedrooms.

These developments, like those of previous decades, owe much to the enthusiasm and support of members of the college council, and especially of chairmen of council who, since Mr Essington Lewis, have been Sir Charles Booth, Sir Bede Callaghan, Mr Keith Steel (AC1), and Mr Charles Trethowan (AC25).

The word 'Moondah' means 'beyond the horizon'. For the college's jubilee year it has been loosely translated to mean 'Building for the Future'. I am sure that C-J would have been more than pleased with that.

Professor W.G. Walker is Chief Executive and Principal of the Australian Administrative Staff College.

11.2

THE AUSTRALIAN ADMINISTRATIVE STAFF COLLEGE: 20th ANNIVERSARY, 1977

K.W. Steel

The following extract is taken from a talk by Keith Steel, former Chairman of the Council, to the Rotary Club of Sydney, on the occasion of the 20th Anniversary of the Australian Administrative Staff College, September 1977.

About 5,000 men and women have now passed through the college's sixty Advanced Courses and its thirty-three Management Development Courses (as the Intermediate Course introduced in 1962 is now described) and at the very least, it is clear that it has not hindered them in their careers. Many of them today occupy high places in business, industry, government and trade unions. To name just a few, starting with my own comrades from session 1, like Sir John Overall, Don Craik (Commonwealth Auditor-General), Arthur Gardiner (Chairman, Victorian Public Service Board); or session 2, with Tal Duckmanton (now a member of the college council), AMP's Ray Craig, and Max Mainprize (General Manager, Colonial Mutual); Sir Jack Egerton and Ron Virgo (from session 7); Ron Elliott (Chief Executive Commonwealth Banking Corporation); Alan Reiher (Chief Commissioner, Public Transport, NSW); Joe Thompson (Vehicle Builders Union); Arvi Parbo (of Western Mining); Admiral Tony Synnott (Chief of Naval Staff); Don Little (Victorian Director General, Public Works); General Alan Stretton; Air Vice Marshal Lyn Compton (of Air Board). The list is endless, and the college counts itself proud to have enjoyed the talents of all those who have both contributed to and drawn from the wealth of experience that gathers in its syndicate rooms.

But I thought the nature of today's occasion warranted a rather more precise identification of the benefits the college has brought to its members. Accordingly, out of the seventy-one of my own staff who by now have been through the college we quizzed a random but very representative collection. Some attended fairly recently, others fifteen or more years ago. Each received a standard questionnaire with the aim of producing some kind of consistent evaluation of the courses. But their responses were far from standard, with many replies in considerable depth. I listed seven areas where some benefit could have been expected, and invited them to indicate how much help they had gained in each. The areas were:

training in principles and techniques of management
training in some technical field, such as accountancy
contact with the college staff
contact with visiting specialists
exposure to the views of their peers
opportunity to think in a semi-academic atmosphere
general mixing with the other members of the course

While management training scored highly – eight out of ten ranked it 'very helpful' and the rest 'helpful' – the most interesting feature was that the areas which scored a unanimous 'very helpful' were exposure to the views of their peers and general mixing with other members. To drive the message further home, when I asked which of the seven categories best expressed the greatest benefit they gained from their time at the college, seven out of ten plumped for exposure to the views of their peers. Now it could be said that such a result is not surprising from members of the insurance industry, which has the reputation of being fairly inbred and a bit insular; but talking around at college functions over the years has convinced me that the reaction is in fact a very general one.

Probing into this area still further, I advanced the suggestion that businessmen who attend courses gain from rubbing shoulders with people whose backgrounds differ from their own. The response confirmed this and indicated that the greatest gain had come from contact with public servants, followed fairly closely by trade unionists, while contact with female and overseas participants, though still of some value, had been less rewarding. Now this may merely reflect the fact that since female and overseas students were relatively few in number the impression they made had been swamped by the larger contingents from the public sector and the unions. Or it may in some way lend support to the claim that Australian men are not all that concerned about the views of the opposite sex or about other countries.

I am bound to say that use of the phrase 'rubbing shoulders' prompted the comment from one young man that the college environment was such that in his view to rub shoulders with a female participant would have been very beneficial. I might add that the sessions do include mid-term weekend breaks to enable participants to get home to their families for a few days.

Less modestly, I can report some satisfaction over the replies to a question which sought to compare the college management courses with those offered by other organisations. Of my ten respondents, eight had some knowledge of other courses and of these six said the college course was 'better' and two that it was 'different'. More significantly, all three of those who had actually attended other courses ranked the college course 'better'.

All ten felt at the end of their courses that their participation had been worth-while, and all ten still feel the same today. Eight of them believe that their contact with the college led to a long-term change in their attitudes to work or to other people. One man from a company associated with mine – not one of my respondents – in a very frank report back to his chief indicated his intention in future to show more concern for his staff and to involve them more in understanding why and how his company does things.

One of my respondents reported at some length his increased respect for the Australian Public Service, whose representatives he found to be dedicated, enthusiastic, knowledgeable and good communicators, a respect well earned by most public service participants. He was also struck by the obvious sincerity of the trade unionists on the course, whose views were invaluable in discussions on industrial relations.

Back in 1971 Dr Sherman Adams of the Fidelity Bank in Philadelphia spoke to a meeting of businessmen like this one. He noted that in the early 1950s four Junior Fellows at Harvard University had produced a study entitled 'The American Business Creed'. Then he went on to say: 'Re-reading this book today, one is impressed by how obsolete much of this material seems. The ideology of businessmen has changed radically within the space of two short decades.' In 1977 the change has become even more radical. The first challenge that any educational institution has to face is the necessity to keep the content of its courses up to date and to prepare its students to cope with further change. The college has met this challenge. It is placing heavy emphasis on the importance of change and will continue to do so.

But perhaps most important of all is the fact that the ethos of the college is becoming more and more relevant in these days when ideologies and causes are tending to divide deeply and even polarise the community. There just is not time today to probe into the factors that have produced this situation, but I firmly believe that one important way of easing tensions and promoting harmony is the improvement of genuine communication and co-operation between those who are the nation's opinion-leaders. By its nature and its structure the Australian Administrative Staff College is almost uniquely well-equipped to perform this function.

12.1

THE ADMINISTRATIVE STAFF COLLEGE OF INDIA

N. P. SEN

India's policy-makers showed quick and commendable awareness of managerial, scientific, and technical competence for a strong training infrastructure as essential for development as well as self-reliance. There was early recognition of the special features required of institutions established for this purpose which distinguish them from the more academic mould of universities with which India was already reasonably endowed. Wisely it was decided to review carefully various models in different countries and this encouraged the conclusion that the British method at the Administrative Staff College at Henley had much to commend it. The Henley pattern of self-learning through cross-fertilisation by peer groups strongly attracted the founding fathers of the Administrative Staff College of India.

Prominent among those who deserve credit for these wise decisions are the late Shri T.T. Krishnamachari, Minister for Industry and later for Finance, and the late Sir Jehangir Ghandhy an eminent business administrator. The late Dr John Matthai, India's first Finance Minister and a noted economist was the first chairman of the Court of Governors and the late General Shrinagesh the first principal. Owing to ill-health, Dr Matthai had to resign the chairmanship within two years but the college was very fortunate in his successor, the late Dr C.D. Deshmukh, successor to Dr Matthai as Finance Minister; in a tenure over almost fifteen years, Dr Deshmukh contributed greatly to the stability and growth of the college. He was succeeded by Dr Dharma Vira, a former Cabinet Secretary and Governor of West Bengal, who continues as chairman with great success. When General Shrinagesh was appointed Governor of Assam he was succeeded by the late Mr R.L. Gupta, an experienced civil servant who had been Secretary to the Government of India in a number of ministries; in his tenure of almost ten years, the college established a sound reputation throughout the country. I succeeded Mr Gupta; after ten rewarding years I joined the Commonwealth Secretariat and was succeeded by Mr D'Souza, Secretary to the Ministry of Works and Housing and a senior civil servant. Continuity of chairmen and the principals has ensured the college a level of stability, with changes at reasonable intervals ensuring that fresh approaches and ideas continue.

Henley extended strong support to the college in its early years. The Indian College is indebted to Principal Noel Hall on many counts, the most important one being the services of his colleague, John Adams. In those early years John Adams was a source of strength to General Shrinagesh. I myself recall with great pleasure John Adams's renewed association with the college in introducing the first Review Course, and subsequently as well. General Shrinagesh often told me of how much he benefited as much from the philosophy as from the syndicate method which Henley made uniquely her own. Much of this he brought back to the college in India, not as a straight 'transplant' but appropriately modified with the help of John Adams to suit India's need and climate. Mr Gupta, who succeeded General Shrinagesh, also spent time at Henley and I myself had attended the Senior Course several years before I took over as principal. Closer links between Staff Colleges would be mutually beneficial and should be promoted.

After the first seven years the Indian College developed a very diversified programme of shorter courses in specific areas of management and administration and expanded its activities to meet needs of those both junior and senior to participants of the Senior Course it had developed on the Henley pattern. This was followed up by close review of the methodologies, a mix of methods including the case-study method to supplement syndicate work. The college has been an important pioneer in developing case studies and case-study skills in the country.

By 1968 the college had moved into the field of consultancy and applied research, where its services were used by governments as much as by industry. The Consulting and Applied Research Division (CARD) had made considerable contributions to the development of consultancy as a means of improving effective management and administration in India. The training programmes have also benefited by the infusion of a greater measure of practical experience but it must be confessed that the link between training and consultancy has yet to develop as closely as had been expected and there may have been advantages in consultancy activities being an integral part of training rather than a discrete activity. Certainly, this deserves further study.

Traditionally, the importance of management has not received proper recognition in as wide a field of national endeavours as it should. This applies particularly to fields such as education, public health, science and technology and other fields important to national development and which subsume very substantial measures of a country's resources. The college in India moved into these activities from the early 1970s and its work in research, training and consultancy has made commendable contributions to improved performance. This is an aspect on which I think Staff Colleges, particularly those in developing countries, should focus attention. In the latter half of the 1970s the college in India worked on developing skill and understanding as well as the necessary physical infrastructure in the field of computerisation.

Rapid growth and diversification can lead to problems, such as in staffing, in dilution of objectives and effort. Nevertheless a national institution in a developing country, particularly one which receives considerable moral as well as material support, cannot escape obligations to meet pressing national needs. In the balance the college in India has gained confidence, a sense of achievement and a reputation from its response to national needs. This again presents an opportunity for staff colleagues to share their experience to their mutual benefit.

The Indian College attached great importance to financial self-sufficiency. Even in a normal period this presents difficulties: these are accentuated when national needs require unusually rapid growth and diversification. The right balance between financial viability and long-term investment in professional 'capital' is not easy to attain. This is a problem Staff Colleges should share.

In the last two-and-a-half decades many thousands of senior managers and administrators from very diverse walks of life have passed through the portals of Bella Vista and the college is reasonably justified in taking pride in the contributions it has made to the development of one of the world's largest countries.

N.P. Sen was Principal of the Administrative Staff College of India, 1968-78.

12.2

THE ADMINISTRATIVE STAFF COLLEGE OF INDIA: A PERSPECTIVE

M. Narasimham

The previous piece by Mr Sen has shown the way the college has evolved in keeping with the changing requirements in the country. The process of evolution is a continuing one. While the general management development courses of eight weeks duration continue to be offered, the college has, increasingly, turned its attention to offering specialist and short-term courses tailored to specific requirements. We thus have a continuing series of programmes on hospital management, management of education, environmental management, technology and R & D and command area development. New courses are being added, and some old ones are being dropped. This, indeed, is the essence of change. Even among the generalist courses, there are some which are geared to the needs of specific sectors. We now have courses for government administrators; some other programmes are meant for those involved in economic planning, and the emphasis here is increasingly on policy issues rather than on the mechanics of administration. Specialist courses in management are in the offing to cater to the requirements of the large and growing cadre of public-sector corporate executives. A short-term programme on tax policy and administration is under contemplation in collaboration with the concerned department of the Government of India. The college has also had a long and rewarding relationship with the Economic Development Institute of the World Bank. An interesting extension of this is that we are planning to hold in the spring of 1984, a regional course, in collaboration with the Institute, on national economic management for the countries of South Asia.

Looking to the future, the college will aim at a closer integration of its various services and facilities. This has reference to its consulting and computer divisions. The attempt is being made to use the rich material based on real-life experience gained from our consultancy work in the form of inputs into management education.

The Computer Centre is being reorganised primarily with a view to providing in-house facilities, and as an essential aid to management education. We now plan to have modules on computer-aided decision-making and problem-solving as essential ingredients of general management education. We are also contemplating the possibility of having fully-fledged computer-aided management courses.

Applied research is another area the college is increasingly giving attention to, not only for its own sake but again as a useful aid in management education.

Management education and consultancy have become highly competitive areas in the country. The college has the advantage of having been a pioneer, and of having specialised in post-experience management training and in bringing together executives from the Government, the public sector of industry and corporate business. The prospect is thus for the college concentrating on its main objective of providing post-experience management education and improving the quality of this service better to meet the evolving requirements of the Indian economy. In the twenty-five years of its existence well over 20,000 corporate executives have passed through its portals and many of the top executives in India's corporate sector and the Government have been alumni of the college. The college has, if one were to make an immodest claim, largely fulfilled the expectations of its founding fathers. It has done so by a process of adaptation and change and by widening its horizons to areas that were inconceivable at the time of its inception. The Administrative Staff College of India of today is quite a different institution from that of 1958. I dare say a similar comment would be made by someone looking at the college at the end of its second quarter century.

M. Narasimham is Principal of the Administrative Staff College of India.

13

PAKISTAN ADMINISTRATIVE STAFF COLLEGE

Masrur Hasan Khan

From the very beginning the college has kept in step with the successive Five-Year Plans in meeting the respective requirements for improving and strengthening the public-administration machinery to meet the development goals. For supporting the aims and objectives of the first three plans (1955-60; 1960-5; 1965-70), the main emphasis of the college was on equipping the senior civil servants with the capability to plan wisely and execute efficiently the development programmes for enabling the newly born state of Pakistan to achieve a fast rate of growth. While this objective was achieved fairly satisfactorily by the end of the third plan, economic inequalities and social disparities had started becoming inconveniently noticeable by the time the fourth Five-Year Plan (1970-5) was conceived. The secession of East Pakistan, the energy crisis, the socialistic philosophies of the regime in power, and large-scale nationalisation, were the highlights of this plan period. Equitable and orderly growth, social justice, Pakistan ideology, the relevance of Pakistan ideology to the socialistic philosophy of the party in power, efficient management of the nationalised sector and public enterprises, and re-organisation in services and Governmental structure, therefore, became the main topics of study and discussions in the college as of direct relevance to the development process of Pakistan during that period.

By the middle of 1977, the nation had decided to look for a new leadership wedded to the purity of the ideology which brought Pakistan into being. The present regime took over in July 1977 and declared Islam as the source of all public policies. Our college courses were accordingly restructured in accordance with the imperatives of Islam. We have undertaken massive efforts in rediscovering and redefining the precepts and concepts of Islam in areas like public administration, economic development, financial and economic management, and dynamics of administrative leadership. Our effort to develop documentation and resource persons in these fields has already started bearing fruit. Side by side we continue to cover the subject areas relevant to development administration as in our previous courses. The comparative study helps our participants to understand the respective approaches and provides options for adoption and adaptation.

Apart from the two Advanced Courses a year – each of three months duration, we also run shorter courses of five weeks or less in specified functional areas. These are compressed courses for senior administrators who can find time only for shorter courses for familiarising themselves with the latest knowledge, techniques and skills in any particular function relevant to their responsibilities. Some such courses are (1) Investment Analysis, Decision Making and Implementation, in collaboration with the Economic Development Institute of the World Bank; (2) Management Systems and Methods Course, in collaboration with the Royal Institute of Public Administration, London; (3) Public Enterprise Course in collaboration with United Nations Asian & Pacific Development Centre, Kuala Lumpur; and (4) Computer Orientation Course, in collaboration with private firms of systems analysts.

Side by side we have also been organising courses for a deeper understanding of the administrative and economic systems of other countries, to give senior administrators comparative experience of other countries. We have held seven China courses and eleven RCD (Regional Co-operation for Development – an organisation consisting of Pakistan, Iran and Turkey). For the last-mentioned two courses a particular subject of study is selected in each case. A field research study tour is arranged of the countries concerned, and based on the information and facts collected, a final report is prepared, mainly for training purposes.

We also hold a review session every year with the participants who have attended our courses previously. These are intended as a feedback from the participants on the relevance of the courses attended by them to their job requirements. Also, such reviews provide valuable guidance for re-structuring the course for the future.

Our methodology of training has not changed much over the period. We still work on a syndicate system. Individual research papers are still prepared but these are now in the form of case studies by individual participants based on some important decisions (or lack of them) pertaining to their departments and relating to some critical aspects of management. We still undertake field research study tours, after which the participants prepare and present their reports on some specified problems of planning and development of the area visited.

Since July 1980, successful participation in our advanced courses in management and development has been made a pre-condition to further promotion to the highest levels in Government or public enterprise. The evaluation of each participant by this college is an integral part of his/her annual performance-evaluation dossier.

Our participants are mostly from Government and state enterprises. The private sector received a setback during the nationalisation of the 1970s. It is being revived and it is hoped that this sector will again start taking advantage of our courses. We also have participants from Asian and

African countries, particularly in our advanced courses.

Our research side has been quite active and to date seventy-three research studies have been prepared, basically as a training support. Some sixteen of these have been published but the demand has been so pressing that some of these are out of print. Our last major research study was at the request of United Nations Asian and Pacific Development Centre, Kuala Lumpur, on 'Training and Education for public enterprise managers' and has been very well commented upon by the concerned organisations. In line with our objective of professionalising public administration, we have held to date forty-one short seminars on important economic, administrative and financial issues with very encouraging participation and deliberations. The last two seminars were on Public Enterprise Management and Resource Mobilization and their proceedings are available as published documents.

We publish a bi-annual journal, *Public Administration,* which is widely subscribed both within the country and abroad. In addition, we publish a quarterly newsletter giving the details of our activities in each quarter for the benefit of our ex-members and for those who are interested in our functioning.

We have an association of ex-members called Pakistan Administrative Staff College Association (PASCA), located in the various provincial headquarters and at the Federal Capital, Islamabad. Our alumni at these places hold social get-togethers and also invite, periodically, scholars and senior administrators to speak on important national issues. All PASCA members are entitled to stay at concessionary rates in the college hostel whenever they visit Lahore.

Our senior faculty has never exceeded seven in number. From the mid-1960s we have been wholly staffed by Pakistani experts and scholars. Some of them have come from universities; others are on deputation for a specified period of time from Government and other organisations. Most of our senior faculty have high academic qualifications from within the country and abroad. We now have posts of Director Course of Studies, Director Research, and Members Directing Staff in the subject areas of financial management, economic development, social policies, public administration and business administration – the last one was added in 1979-80 to meet the requirements of the growing state-enterprise sector in the field of corporate finance, and planning and implementation of projects.

The college completed twenty-one years of its life on 2 November 1981 and has now entered the 22nd year. At the rate of two advanced courses of three months each, it has held forty-three such courses to date. In addition it has held about seventy short and other courses. Some 780 participants in advanced courses and 1,544 in other courses have passed through its portals. Its alumni occupy some of the highest positions in Government, state enterprises and the private sector. The aim of the college has always been to develop a class of professional administrators for playing their role as catalysts of change. The college has attempted to achieve this objective through training, research and publications. In all humility it can now claim to have played a pioneering role in creating a growing cadre of senior administrators and executives with the appropriate professional attitude and expertise.

And yet while the first principal, Mr A.K. Malik, and C-J would have looked back with satisfaction over what has been achieved in these twenty-one years, we in the Pakistan Administrative Staff College feel that it is only a beginning. Our ultimate aim is to create an enduring interest in the study and practice of development administration as a science and art so that generation after generation of professionals in this discipline learn to plan the nation's destiny with wisdom and translate its goals in such a manner that the fruits of development reach every hearth and home of our land.

Masrur Hasan Khan is Principal of Pakistan Administrative Staff College.

14

PHILIPPINE EXECUTIVE ACADEMY, UNIVERSITY OF THE PHILIPPINES

Carlos P. Ramos

As the decade of the 1950s was coming to a close there was need for leadership training as an important part of the national effort for development. The Philippines then, located in the heart of Asia, had just come out of a period of reconstruction as a result of the last war, achieving independence from the United States of America.

The country had some options through sources of technical assistance as to the kind of institutionalised training to adopt. Amongst models of executive training, for example, were the training programs of the American Civil Service, the Harvard Business School, and several other noted ones mainly within the programs of universities abroad.

I was then director of the newly established Institute of Public Administration, an academic institution within the state university, the University of the Philippines, offering degree courses in public administration. I had visited some of the excellent institutions. In 1959, through the help of a member of the Australian Public Service Board who was then a visitor in the country, I joined the fourth session of the Australian Administrative Staff College under the Colombo Plan. I was glad to have had the opportunity to go through that course. It was there in Australia that I learned at first hand what was meant by a 'staff college'; its distinctive features and attributes in comparison with others, the structure of the program, the special methodology employed and, above all, what one might call its integrative discipline. And it was there also that I learned that this training system had roots from a mother institution called the Administrative Staff College at Henley-on-Thames in the United Kingdom. I was rather convinced then that if adopted the Staff College idea would easily lend itself to the Philippine setting.

Returning to Manila, I decided to pursue the possibility further. The training work we had already been doing, mostly training of trainers (Training Officers Course), and several training courses for supervisors, were all integrated into a new program to include a new major effort: an executive training course for senior officials of the country. By action of the university's board of regents in 1962 the Philippine Executive Academy was established as an applied wing of the Institute of Public Administration. The Congress of the Philippines in 1963 then adopted legislation providing special fund support to the Philippine Executive Academy.

A generous grant from the Ford Foundation, for which we are most grateful, made it possible to utilise needed resources for staff development, the services of valued experts from England, Australia, the USA, even from as far as Norway, and for the development of indigenous teaching and training materials through research.

It was then that we made contact with a senior member of the directing staff of Henley who was on consultancy in Pakistan. He was Brigadier A.T. Cornwall-Jones. To C-J, as we were wont to call him, I can attribute the main source of guidance and persistence that enabled us to construct the PEA's course of studies and bring the program of the academy into being. It was both a joy and a creative experience to have had C-J and his charming and devoted wife, Joan, work with us.

C-J, I believe, has accurately chronicled the details of this creative period of institution building, which ended in 1966. This report deals more about what has happened afterwards.

I should note initially that since C-J left, we have been running the operations of the PEA ourselves. Except for one other expert, who had come briefly just after C-J, the directing staff and the rest of the PEA complement were entirely in Filipino hands.

On the substantive side, as might be expected, our main effort through the years that spanned a decade and a half has been to constantly adapt to the local environment and its needs and to keep pace with the rapid, and at times drastic, changes in the economic, technological and political fields.

The Philippines is, of course, one of the developing countries of the Third World. By definition, it is a poor country, with the greater mass of its rapidly growing population in the rural areas, generally under depressed conditions. On the other hand, our academy participants both in government and business come from the modern sector. As urban administrators, invariably of the elite class, they have been by their life styles isolated culturally and emotionally from the conditions of under-development. The major effort on our part thus has been to carry out a course of studies that is more and more development oriented. After all, the main thrust of the Government for the past two decades has been development.

The whole of Part I of the course of studies has been devoted to the Philippine environment in preparation for a major two-week field exercise in the rural villages. In this exercise the senior executives live with the peasant farmers, mostly in depressed areas of the country. Their task is to transmit technology, in particular management technology, to the village leaders in the simplest terms possible and in the native dialect. The end in view was helping the village people plan and organise practical income-generating projects that would be acceptable and ready for implementation upon the termination of the exercise. The exercise is conducted under a brief designed to reflect the concepts and methodologies of integrated rural development and is a major modification of the early briefs on manufacturing enterprises.

The need to keep pace with the changing environment constitutes another aspect of the course of studies. Policy shifts, technology change, crisis management, trade and investments, market and contingency strategies, as well as corporate management, run through the entire course. Through notes on briefs, DS's guidance and workshop design, the course has become increasingly centred upon the management of change.

Another innovation we have adopted concerns the 'panels', which is the term we use for the 'syndicate' ('syndicate' here is a bad word). We believe we have considerably strengthened panels through sensitivity training. The availability of skilled professionals especially trained for the purpose has enabled us to have all panel members go through a T-group experience during the first $25\frac{1}{2}$ hours of the session. Through this device participants are drawn to each other and personality barriers lowered right at the inception of the course. This is at the level of the individuals. The ensuing panel meetings have in effect themselves become sensitivity sessions on a group level.

The Philippine Executive Academy continues to hold its sessions at the Pines Hotel in the City of Baguio in the Mountain Province. The session returns to the lowlands for the village exercise, which incidentally now has been expanded to include urban development primarily due to the interconnection of rural and urban development through migration and the poverty issues. Pressure from nominating agencies from government and business has obliged us to reduce the main course for senior executives from twelve to eight weeks.

The $4\frac{1}{2}$ hectares of land owned by the Philippine Executive Academy at a high plateau in Baguio regrettably remains vacant. Members of the directing staff and faculty consider it too much of a sacrifice to uproot their families in Manila to take up permanent residence there. Most of their wives are professionals working in Manila where the children also school. In addition, PEA conducts annually several other training programs in Manila and it would be almost impossible, not to say prohibitive, for the staff and faculty to commute over some 250 kilometres to Manila and return in order to service the different programmes of the academy. Participants are generally happy about present arrangements. Planning, research and operations are still centred at PEA headquarters in Manila.

Through the years, the participants that have gone through PEA's main senior executive course number close to a thousand. A great many have since assumed top positions in government and business. Such posts include the heads and deans of universities, heads and managers of manufacturing and insurance companies, directors of government bureaux, heads of industrial estates, government commissions and government corporations. Also, former participants are now found amongst the ambassadorial level of the Foreign Ministry and the top echelons of the military.

Senior men and women from overseas have come to join the sessions of the academy, nominated by their respective governments or business enterprises. Many are also sponsored by the United Nations Development Program (UNDP) and the United States AID program. Participants have come from the developing countries of Afghanistan, Hong Kong, Indonesia, Iran, Kenya, Korea, Malaysia, Micronesia, Nepal, Papua New Guinea, Singapore, Taipei and Thailand. At one time or another we also had participants from Australia, Japan and the United States.

From the beginning, sectoral participation has been on the basis of a tripartite mix with participants from government, public enterprise and the private sector generally of the following proportion:

Government	39%
Public enterprise	24%
Private sector	37%

The other programs of the PEA on contract basis include seminars for legislators in residence on policy studies and parliamentary procedure, to which participants come on a voluntary basis and nominated by the Speaker of the *Batasan Pambansa* (Parliament). Another concerns a training program for senior officials of the Tanod Bayan (Government's Ombudsman organization) on management information systems and a similar one for Medicare including its installation within the Medicare system. Others include a seminar project for the National Power Corporation on management analysis, a program for public corporations on fiscal and financial management, and another in partnership with the PEA's alumni association (APEX) for time management. With the exception of the first two projects cited above, participation has been mainly from middle and upper-middle management.

In partnership with international organisations the PEA plays a significant role as a regional training institution in Asia. With the collaboration of the Eastern Regional Organisation for Public Administration (EROPA) and at various times, with the Economic Commission for Asia and the Pacific (ECAP), UNDP, and the German Foundation for International Development, the academy has annually held, for six consecutive times, a three-week seminar for Asian commercial attachés and economic counsellors posted in Asia, Europe and the United States. Together with the Asian and Pacific Centre for Development (Kuala Lumpur), it conducted a three-week seminar on the management of public enterprises in Asia and the Pacific. Under contract with UNICEF the PEA conducted, in Bangkok, a Regional Seminar on Programme Management for the UNICEF staff in the East Asia and Pakistan region.

It is inevitable that an institution like the PEA would have an influence on sister institutions. Within the public administration complex, for instance, the panel (syndicate) method has become a familiar method employed in the conduct of seminars and training programs. The Chief of Staff of the Philippine Armed Forces Command and General Staff College was a participant of the academy and so was its academic director, who came especially to experience the academy's field exercise for possible inclusion into their own courses. Various members of the directing staff are engaged as consultants to other training and development institutions such as the Civil Service, the reorganisation commission, National Defense College, Manila Metropolitan Commission and others.

In conclusion, I wish to state that whatever it was able to accomplish through these years, the PEA is very much indebted to C-J, who left with the academy an indelible imprint of his ideas and sense of precision. Furthermore, it was both a pleasant, as it was indeed, a fruitful experience for the Philippine Executive Academy to have had the opportunity to be associated with one nurtured by the Administrative Staff College at Henley. The academy is a Staff College in a country that is not a member of the British Commonwealth. None the less, I believe we are a member of a small family of distinguished Staff Colleges in the world today, a distinction about which we feel no small amount of pride.

Carlos P. Ramos is Administrator of the Philippine Executive Academy.

15

GHANA INSTITUTE OF MANAGEMENT AND PUBLIC ADMINISTRATION, 1961-82

R.K.O. DJANG

The Ghana Institute of Management and Public Administration (GIMPA) lies some eight miles north of the capital city, Accra. The institute is housed in spacious new buildings on 150 acres of high ground at Greenhill, off the Achimota-Legon University road, within a stone's throw of the University of Ghana. The institute can be classified as a post-entry training centre for senior public servants; post-experience senior management development centre; research and consultancy centre in management and public administration.

The institute was originally established as an Institute of Public Administration (IPA) under the joint sponsorship of the Government of Ghana and the United Nations Special Fund, on 30 June 1961, as a body corporate with academic, financial and administrative autonomy. It remained under this joint sponsorship until 30 June 1966 when it came under the sole sponsorship of the Government of Ghana.

On 12 August 1969, however, the institute was redesignated the Ghana Institute of Management and Public Administration and enlarged to incorporate two constituent wings, namely:

1. School of Public Administration (the school), i.e. the former Institute of Public Administration.
2. College for Advanced Management (the college, which was charged with responsibility for organising Staff College type courses).

In 1974, the research activities in the institute were expanded and constituted into a third wing designated Research and Consultancy, responsible for conducting institutional research into immediate as well as long-term administrative and management problems in Ghana and for providing management-consultancy services to outside bodies. Further developments in the administrative restructuring of the institute in 1980 regrouped all faculty activities with respect to training under one divisional head and all research activities under another divisional head. Consultancy services and library services which are common services to both training and research are grouped under the administration headed by the director of the institute.

Management training and development programmes of GIMPA (1970-1982)

The Institute entered the 1970 decade concentrating its management-development and education efforts on three regular courses.

1. Diploma Course in Public Administration – a nine-month post-graduate diploma course begun under the original IPA in 1961/2, for graduate new-entrants earmarked for the administrative class and analogous grades in the Civil Service.

2. Certificate Course in Public Administration – a three-month certificate course also begun under the original IPA in 1961/3 as an introductory management course for specialist officers in the purely professional/technical services who may be required relatively early in their career in the public service to assume managerial responsibilities alongside their normal professional duties.

3. Senior Management Development Course – a ten-week course, begun under the College of Advanced Management in 1970 for administrators and managers holding positions of some authority in the public services and the private sector who are expected to qualify for still greater responsibility.

Further growth and development in the economy in the mid-1970s in both the public and private sectors, necessitated the planning and establishment of a number of general and sector-specific courses at the institute, to meet certain critical manpower needs. By the end of the academic year ending 30 June 1982, the institute had added the following regular courses to its annual fixtures.

1. Personnel Management Course – a three-week course begun in 1974 as an offshoot of the Senior Management Development Course, to provide executives in both private and public enterprises having a functional responsibility for personnel administration with a clearer understanding of their role in solving the human problems of management;

2. Agricultural Administration Course – a nine-month diploma course begun in 1975 for senior technical officers of the Ministry of Agriculture engaged in agricultural extension work in the field;

3. Health Administration and Management Course – a two-month regional (international) course begun in 1975 for qualified senior health personnel in positions of authority in the medical and health services in Ghana, Nigeria, Sierra Leone, Liberia and the Gambia, and organised by

GIMPA in association with the Ghana Ministry of Health and co-sponsored by the West African Health Society and the Commonwealth Secretariat through the Commonwealth Fund for Technical Co-operation (CFTC);

4. *Project Planning and Management Course* – a twelve-week course begun in 1976 to provide middle-level professional and technical officers in the public service with a sound working knowledge of relevant methodologies and approaches to the planning and management of development projects.

5. *Budgeting and Financial Management Course* – a twelve-week course begun late in 1976 to upgrade the financial management and budgetary skills of public servants having responsibility for the preparation and administration of departmental estimates.

The senior management development course

The first Senior Management Development Course at GIMPA, designed early in 1970 and given in two parts – the first (introductory) part of $3\frac{1}{2}$ and a second part of $6\frac{1}{2}$ weeks with a break of eight weeks in between – proved to be quite successful. Participants numbering twenty-nine were drawn from government (fourteen from the Civil Service), eight from public enterprise, and seven from purely private enterprise. Twenty-seven participants completed the course as two members (one each from public enterprise and private enterprise) failed to come back for the second part. About one-quarter of the participant group was drawn from the private sector: this was thought to be a good augury as it made the course truly reflective of national concern for effective management.

Four courses of the same design as the first were given in the next two years (1971-2) with almost the same number of participants and the same distribution pattern between the public and the private sectors.

Two interesting elements that were introduced into the composition of the second and subsequent courses were representation from the armed forces and female participation. Participation was further extended when the first self-employed Ghanaian business executive applied to attend the sixth course in 1974. And in the same year, the GIMPA course admitted its first overseas candidate from the State National Trading Corporation of the Gambia. Subsequently eight other overseas candidates have attended the GIMPA courses: four civil servants from Swaziland in 1977, two from Sierra Leone in 1978 (one from a national trading organisation and the other a lady from a private company), and two economists working in the Ministry of Planning in the Republic of Zaire in 1978. The design of the Senior Management Development Course was reviewed and modified at the end of the fifth course in 1972. Since 1973, the course, which is now given in one stretch lasting eight weeks, has embodied six main areas of study as follows:

1. An understanding of the environment – economic, social and political factors in which managers and administrators have to work and produce results.

2. A study of the internal management of an enterprise, with specific emphasis on organisation structure and internal relationships in an organisation (both formal and informal); the nature of authority and problems of delegation; the control function in management; together with an understanding of the human factors in administration that pervade an organisation and influence management decisions and actions.

3. A study of human resources in management, aimed at understanding human behaviour at work and managerial attitudes, policies and practices that take account of people's behaviour. This part of the study includes personnel administration and industrial relations.

4. A study of the process of management and of decision-making, including an appreciation of quantitative methods – i.e. statistical analysis and operations research, and the use of financial and cost analysis for planning, controlling and evaluating programmes and performance.

5. An understanding of what constitutes effective leadership in management, and helping members to examine critically their own styles of leadership and the possible ways in which they can be more effective. This also involves a look at the findings of behavioural scientists, in so far as they help understand factors that motivate them to work well and gain satisfaction.

6. A business-policy exercise which enables the participants to examine the management of an on-going enterprise with respect to its organisational structure, human-resources development, corporate growth and financial management. As the exercise comes on at the tail end of the course, it enables the participants to bring to bear on the management exercise their total knowledge and experience gained so far on the course.

Methodology

The following teaching and training methods and techniques have been used on the Senior Management Development Courses:

(a) a study of all subject texts and reading material circulated to participants;
(b) lectures and talks by members of the faculty and guest speakers;
(c) group discussion (in syndicates) under the guidance of a member of directing staff who acts as moderator;
(d) case studies and exercises;
(e) report writing and syndicates, presentations, panel discussions and conferences;
(f) tutorials and special assistance by directing staff to individual participants;
(g) management films and other audio-visual presentations;
(h) visits to organisations as an integral part of a business-policy exercise.

Deployment of GIMPA alumni

The alumni from GIMPA's regular courses over the twenty-year span (1961/2-1981/2) now number some 2,770. A majority of the present crop of top public servants in Ghana have attended one GIMPA programme or another in their progression up their respective (public-service) career ladders. Former participants of GIMPA's programmes of training can be found in many responsible positions in the country. In particular, alumni from its seventeen senior management development courses organised so far number more than four hundred and are found to be holding very top positions in government, in industry, in banking, and in finance. The head of the Central Bank in Ghana attended the first course twelve years ago and the head of the Civil Service of Ghana attended the second course.

A Greenhill Alumni Association, which has been dormant for some time, is to be reactivated to serve as a focal point for periodic re-appraisal of management practices in the country. The association may also offer the faculty of GIMPA a worth-while feedback from the practical realities of the work situation.

Tailor-made courses and special-purpose courses/seminars, etc.

From time to time, the institute organises special courses tailored to meet the needs of particular organisations and functional groups, or to develop expertise in acknowledged problem areas. In the recent past, the institute has organised courses in this series for senior police officers, for senior military officers, for senior managers in two separate commercial banking institutions, namely the Standard Bank Ghana Ltd, and the Bank for Housing and Construction, as well as for the State Hotels Corporation and the Ghana Broadcasting Corporation. Seminars/conferences/workshops organised in the past two years include three seminars for Ministers of State, for Permanent Secretaries and for professional heads of Government departments.

Research and consultancy assignments

Major research projects undertaken by the institute during the past six years include: (1) Research into the structure and procedures of the Ghana Civil Service (an assignment undertaken at the instance of a Government Commission on Civil Service Reform); (2) Research on the institutionalisation of career policies and guidance in Africa (a task undertaken in collaboration with the Centre for African Research and Development (CAFRAD) based in Tangier, Morocco as part of a continent-wide research project).

Consultancy assignments in the form of the management audit of a number of public boards and corporations were undertaken at the request of the Government of Ghana on the following state enterprises:

> Ghana Cargo Handling Company
> Glass Manufacturing Co. Ltd (GIHOC)
> Food Distribution Corporation
> State Farms Corporation
> Ghana Publishing Corporation

Library and documentation services

The history of the GIMPA library dates from July 1961 when part of the collection of publications belonging to the erstwhile Administrative Academy was transferred to the Institute of Public Administration to form the nucleus of this library. This consisted of 129 books and 102 journals and other pamphlets. In November of the same year, another set of sixty volumes of Government publications, mainly annual departmental reports, were collected from the then Ministry of Construction and Communication to augment the stock. In June 1962 a Canadian UN expert, Mr Jean de Chantal, arrived to take control as the first librarian of the Institute.

Since then, growth has been quite rapid. About 2,400 volumes are accessioned every year. The institute's library has established for itself the reputation of being the best equipped special library in its field in the country. The stock is now 20,000 volumes, excluding unbound volumes of periodicals. The library also subscribes to about 500 periodicals and official publications in the fields of management, public administration and related disciplines. The particular strength of the library lies in materials on management practices in government and industry, public finance, law, economic and development planning, personnel administration, and related materials drawn from both French- and English-speaking African States.

National Documentation Centre of Management

The main function of the documentation centre is to stock materials which would essentially support reference and research needs of the institute. The collection is made up of government publications, namely, Acts and Statutes, gazettes, departmental annual reports and proceedings of Commission/Committee of Enquiry, speeches of heads of state, commissioners (ministers) and other important public officials, case studies, course notes and archival records/documents of the institute, e.g. registry files, minutes books, etc. Newspaper clippings, and documents of international organisations such as the United Nations, the Economic Commission for Africa, the Organisation for African Unity, etc., are also available. The centre also has a strong collection of Gold Coast and Ghana official documents and is particularly proud of the fact that it possesses a rare collection of the *Gold Coast Gazetteer* dating back to 1895.

Relations with other bodies

As an institution operating at the postgraduate and post-experience level, the institute works as far as possible in close co-operation with other institutions of higher learning in Ghana. In particular, by reason of proximity, and by courtesy the institute shares certain common facilities with the University of Ghana at Legon and generally maintains good inter-institutional relations with that body. Several GIMPA faculty members are part-time lecturers in several departments and schools of the University of Ghana. University of Ghana lecturers are also regular guest lecturers on the GIMPA programmes.

The institute co-operates and maintains healthy relations with the public service, especially with the Office of the Head of the Civil Service in Ghana and the Public Services Commission of Ghana without compromising its administrative autonomy. The institute is a corporate member of the Ghana Institute of Management (GIM), a non-profit national management association.

The institute co-operates with and enjoys the support of Administrative Staff Colleges within and outside the Commonwealth. Faculty members of the institute, both past and present, have attended orientation programmes at, and/or visited, the staff colleges in Henley, in Britain, in Hyderabad, India, in Lahore, Pakistan, in Manila, Philippines, in Mount Eliza in Australia and in Badagry, Nigeria. Visiting directing staff from Henley and Lahore staff colleges, acting as consultants, assisted GIMPA from 1969 to 1972 in establishing its Staff College wing.

The institute is not only a corporate member but also the Ghanaian National Section of the International Institute of Administrative Sciences, Brussels. It generally keeps in touch with other schools and institutes of public administration throughout the world, in the pursuit of common objectives.

The institute also represents the Government of Ghana as a member of the Centre for African Research and Development (CAFRAD) based in Tangiers Morocco, and is a member of the African Association for Public Administration and Management (AAPAM).

R.K.O. Djang is Acting Director of Ghana Institute of Management and Public Administration.

16

BANGLADESH ADMINISTRATIVE STAFF COLLEGE

ABDUR RAHIM

The need for a sound system of in-service training institutions in Bangladesh was felt keenly ever since the emergence of Bangladesh. Before liberation, there was a training institute called the Gazetted Officers' Training Academy for training the new recruits to the then provincial civil services. In Bangladesh the Civil Officers Training Academy was assigned the responsibility for training the new recruits to her civil services. The National Institute of Public Administration in Dacca had been training mid-level officers and executives since 1961. But in the arrangement of in-service training, there was a big gap in Bangladesh. There was no training institute for senior administrators and senior executives until 1977. Since 1975 thought had been given to the need for establishing an Administrative Staff College. It was, however, in the middle of 1976 that concrete ideas emerged in a paper containing the plan for establishment of an Administrative Staff College, given by the late Dr Khalilur Rahman, a member of the Senior Education Service and ex-senior member of directing staff of Pakistan Administrative College in Lahore. In preparing the paper, Dr Khalilur Rahman was assisted by Dr Ali Ahmed, another member of the Senior Education Service and ex-senior member of directing staff of Pakistan Administrative Staff College. In February 1977 it was decided by the Government to establish the Bangladesh Administrative Staff College and positive steps were taken to set it up quickly.

To begin with, a senior member of the Civil Service (Administration) was appointed as the project director early in the second week of February, 1977. At this stage, it may be noted, the Bangladesh Government did not require the assistance of any foreign expert. Dr Khalilur Rahman acted as the adviser for formulating and implementing the project. By a resolution of the Government, dated 2 March 1977, a board of governors was constituted, with a member of the Council of Advisers to the President as chairman. The President of Bangladesh was pleased to be the patron-in-chief of the college. The Members of Parliament Hostel at Sher-e-Bangla

Nagar was selected for housing the college temporarily, pending construction of its own building with necessary facilities in an appropriate site to be selected in due course.

To start with, Mr A.S. Noor Mohammad, a senior member of Civil Service (Administration) was appointed as the principal. Dr Khalilur Rahman became the vice-principal, with Dr Ali Ahmed as one of the two member directing staff and Mr S. Mahtab (a senior member of the postal service who had training at the Administrative Staff Colleges at Lahore and Henley) as the other. It is with this brief preparation within a very limited time schedule that the Bangladesh Administrative Staff College had its opening ceremony on 5 June 1977 as the apex institution in the system of in-service training in the country. Twenty senior administrators participated in the course that was inaugurated on that day.

The two-storied MP's Hostel buildings at Sher-e-Bangla Nagar where the Administrative Staff College started functioning were fairly suitable for their purpose. But the college had to be shifted to a few hired houses at Dhanmondi Residential Area in 1979 when the MP's Hostel buildings were to be vacated for the MP's. The college functioned until 28 February 1982 at the hired houses.

The college was shifted to the present location on 1 March 1982. The present building, which is quite magnificent and suitable for the Staff College, is at Sher-e-Bangla Nagar, Dacca. It has a spacious lecture hall, good office accommodation and a commodious library. In addition, there is good open space with beautiful gardens which add to the beauty and comfort in the campus. But there is no residential accommodation for the trainee officers. They have to live in hired houses which, for obvious reasons, were not expected to provide all the facilities of fully-fledged residential accommodation. The members of the faculty and other officers of the college also have no accommodation within the college campus. It may be mentioned that the present building also is not the permanent accommodation for the college.

It has been decided that the permanent site of the college will be at Savar about twenty miles away from the metropolitan city of Dacca. In fact, a Public Administration Training Complex in one campus is going to grow where the Bangladesh Administrative Staff College would be co-located along with certain other administrative training institutions like the National Institute of Public Administration and the Civil Officers Training Academy, for reasons of economy and common facilities. Though a little away from the metropolitan city proper, the site has all the advantages of the city. It is well connected by metalled roads in all directions. It is on the Asian Highway and is hardly thirty minutes drive from the city. The permanent site, when completed around 1985, is expected to provide the college with all the necessary facilities.

The Bangladesh Administrative Staff College has multiple aims. Briefly speaking, the college is designed to widen the experiences of those who already occupy senior positions in the Government, in public corporations and in the private sector of commerce and industry and who are likely to be called upon to discharge greater responsibility. The college provides an opportunity for such administrators and executives to obtain a better understanding of the new and vigorous environment in which they work, to study the administrative problems involved in the national development programmes to which Bangladesh is committed and to develop their awareness of the complexity of development administration and the importance in this whole process of personal initiative and enterprise.

The principal objective of training in the Administrative Staff College is to improve the capacity of the participants and make them sensitive to the goals of achieving higher productivity and maximum possible social welfare through better and more effective methods of organisation and management.

Administratively the Bangladesh Administrative Staff College is an attached office of the Establishment Division of the Government of Bangladesh. The principal is an executive academic head of the college. In administrative matters he is assisted by the registrar. The registrar, in turn, is assisted by an accounts officer, a comptroller and ministerial staffs. The academic staff comprise one vice-principal with six members of the directing staff to assist him. The faculty is assisted in the discharge of its duties by a secretary (course of studies), two research officers and one publication and public relations officer. The library is managed by one librarian with the help of one assistant librarian and other subordinate staff.

Bangladesh aspires to become a welfare state. As a result, the activities of the Government have increased beyond the usual routine and in fact there have been very serious stresses and strains on our senior administrators and the senior executives in performing their new roles and responsibilities. Keeping this situation in view, we have designed a course which is expected to help the senior administrators and senior executives to face more boldly their responsibilities and solve efficiently the new problems. Generally the course covers the following aspects of public administration:

Part I   Lecture-discussion: principles and theories of development administration and development economics constitute the main subjects of these lecture-discussions.

Part II   This part includes four main constituent areas of public administration. It is here, if anywhere, that BASC is a little different from other Administrative Staff Colleges, e.g. Henley and Australia, where the number of participants from the private sector is significant and hence the course is designed with special reference to industrial management.

             II(a)   Organisational part of administration.
             II(b)   Personnel administration and human relations.
             II(c)   Financial administration.
             II(d)   Development planning.

Part III   Seminar paper – there is a list of topics on development administration and development economics. Every participant has to write a paper of 10-15 typed pages on any one of them under the guidance of a member of the directing staff.

Part IV   Field research. This takes place in the middle of the course.

Part V   This is designed to deal with the administration of development programmes in some crucial sectors such as agriculture, education, family planning and population control, local government, public enterprise, rural development, etc., in Bangladesh. The syndicate method is used also in discussing the problems related to these subjects.

Part VI   The senior administrator, his role and responsibilities. This is the last subject of the course. It is taken up as a separate syndicate exercise. It provides the climax to the whole course and an opportunity to sum up what the training programme as a whole may mean to the participants.

Part VII   Short visit to a foreign country, if possible. Visits to other developing countries help senior administrators and senior executives to carry out a comparative study of the development projects and their implementation.

The main training course is of three months (which is known as the long course). This course is held twice a year. Additionally, the college offers short training courses of one to two weeks duration. Two Regional Training Courses (Asian and Pacific) on Training of Trainers in Management, one of two weeks and the other of six weeks, jointly sponsored by IRDP and USAID, Dacca and conducted by Practical Concepts Incorporated (PCI), Washington, USA, in co-operation with the BASC, were organised at the college during July-August 1978.

A seminar on 'Personnel Management in Public Administration' was organised by the college in January 1979. The German Foundation for International Development participated in this seminar through resource persons. Senior administrators in the Government, corporation chairmen, managing directors of private companies and university professors, also participated in the seminar.

The college also organised a one-month course in 1982 on Development Policy and Investment Decisions, in collaboration with the Economic Development Institute of the World Bank, and twenty-seven senior administrators and senior executives from Government autonomous and semi-autonomous organisations participated in the course.

The BASC adopts different methods of training. There are first of all lecture-discussions: the conventional method and one of delivering formal lectures to the trainees. This aims at imparting knowledge on a particular topic. The speakers, who are supposed to be resource persons, are generally from the college faculty. Guest speakers are university professors, senior administrators from the ministries, and senior executives from public and private enterprise.

The second and most distinctive method adopted is the use of syndicates. The member of directing staff in charge of the subject usually sits in the syndicate room almost as an observer and a passive partner. He does not control the discussions, but will contribute if the syndicate happens to be going off the rails and, at times, also will stimulate the discussion by injecting fresh material and by raising pertinent questions.

The discussion of a syndicate subject culminates in a report prepared by the secretary of the syndicate in consultation with its chairman. The reports of the syndicate are exchanged and questions are raised by each syndicate on other's reports. The syndicate reports are then presented in a formal meeting of all the syndicates. This is usually known as the presentation.

The third method is the writing of seminar papers. In spite of the suitability and the special value of the syndicate technique for senior men, the end product, i.e., the report, remains at the level of the lowest common denominator. This is due both to the facts of group psychology and the limited time within which the syndicates must finish their work. The college, therefore, looks for some technique which provides individual members with scope for significant personal study. The answer is found in the seminar.

The fourth method of training is field research. The member of directing staff, before the commencement of the session, selects a topic in consultation with other members of the faculty and prepares a brief on it for the field research. Participants are divided into two groups. Both groups study the same topic separately in two districts of Bangladesh on the basis of the guidelines given in the brief. Actual stay in the field lasts for about ten days including the time taken in journeys to and from the college. On return to the college, each group prepares the final report. These reports are then discussed like syndicate reports at a joint session scheduled in the timetable.

The college also adopts other methods of training such as case studies, role-playing and sensitivity programmes.

The members of the directing staff formulate and organise the course of studies. They hold the responsibility for the detailed preparation of the course of studies, but they do not play the role of teachers: they work as guides, friends, and helpers to the participants.

At the end of each session the college evaluates the performances of the participants. Based on this, reports are sent to the Government and the employers of the participants. The college also evaluates the course of studies after each session for necessary change and improvement on the basis of the suggestions put forward by the trainees. The college also holds a follow-up review session once a year. The main objectives of these sessions are: (a) to provide to the former participants an opportunity to get together and exchange freely and frankly their administrative experiences since attending the training course at the Bangladesh Administrative Staff College, with special reference to the application of new concepts and principles; (b) to provide the college with an opportunity:

(i) to evaluate the impact of the training on the participants and the administration;

(ii) to understand the obstacles and difficulties faced by the participants in the practical field in implementing the ideas and principles, and the techniques and skills acquired from the course;

(iii) to identify, in the light of the participants' experiences in the field, the strengths and weaknesses of the course of studies and the methods and techniques used, so as to introduce necessary changes for improvement.

The college has an excellent library, is planning to publish the third issue of its *Administrative Journal* in 1982, and a college society for past members is under way.

The college has already taken steps to become a member of different relevant international and regional associations and organisations of public administration. The college maintains close links with the different training institutions and organisations in the country and also with the universities and other relevant national organisations.

The training courses are offered to senior administrators and executives of the Government, autonomous, semi-autonomous and other organisations in the country. Private enterprise may also depute its senior executives and managers for training at the college. There are provisions for short training courses for (i) Secretaries and Additional Secretaries of the Government, (ii) chairmen and managing directors of corporations and autonomous bodies and other executives and officers of similar rank and status, and (iii) Joint Secretaries, Deputy Secretaries, Deputy Commissioners and other officers holding similar rank and responsibilities.

The basic condition for admission to the course is not merely academic qualifications but practical and prolonged experience of administration in any large organisation. Candidates should normally be between the ages of 35 and 50; but special consideration may be given to candidates outside these age limits if their experience and level of responsibility are adequate. In accepting nominations, the college pays due regard to securing in a session as broad a diversity of knowledge and experience as can be made available from different sectors, organisations and regions. Nominees are, therefore, required to furnish full particulars in the nomination forms supplied from the college.

Foreign nationals working in Bangladesh may be eligible for training at the college provided that (i) they are permanent employees in any agency in this country, (ii) they are likely to continue in their services here for a reasonable period of time and that, (iii) the Government of Bangladesh gives necessary clearance for their admission. Applications of overseas candidates, if any, may be welcome depending on necessary agreement between the Government of the overseas country concerned and the Government of Bangladesh.

The college insists that all trainees (called members/participants) of the long course will live on the premises of the college where furnished rooms will be provided for them but not for their families. No exception can be made in this regard, not even if a member's home may be at a stone's throw from the college premises. This is an essential condition.

The college is still in its infancy. Many of the arrangements within the college are in the shape of experiments. Hence it is too early to make any systematic evaluation of the college. Nevertheless, it can have a great future provided, of course, that the problems vitally connected with its working can be solved with success.

Abdur Rahim is Principal of the Bangladesh Administrative Staff College.

APPENDIX

LIST OF COLLEGES IN WHICH THE AUTHOR WORKED

The Administrative Staff College, Henley-on-Thames, UK

1950-7   member of the directing staff, with one year as director of studies

1958-60   registrar and secretary of the Greenlands Association

During periods of absence abroad, remained a member of the directing staff at Henley

The Australian Administrative Staff College, Moondah, Mount Eliza, Victoria

1957-8   director of studies and member of the directing staff

Pakistan Administrative Staff College, Lahore

1960-3   Consultant, filling the post of director of studies for three sessions and member of the directing staff for five

The Philippine Executive Academy at Manila and Baguio

1963-6   Consultant

The Administrative Staff College of India, Hyderabad, Andhra Pradesh

1968   January to March Observer only

Ghana Institute of Management and Public Administration College of Advanced Management, Achimota, Accra

1970   Consultant for six months

INDEX